Postcard History Series

Hanover

POSTCARD HISTORY SERIES

Hanover

Hanover Area Historical Society

ARCADIA
PUBLISHING

ISBN 978-0-7385-3899-0

Published by Arcadia Publishing
Charleston, South Carolina

Printed in the United States of America

Library of Congress Catalog Card Number: 2005927991

For all general information contact Arcadia Publishing at:
Telephone 843-853-2070
Fax 843-853-0044
E-mail sales@arcadiapublishing.com
For customer service and orders:
Toll-Free 1-888-313-2665

Visit us on the Internet at www.arcadiapublishing.com

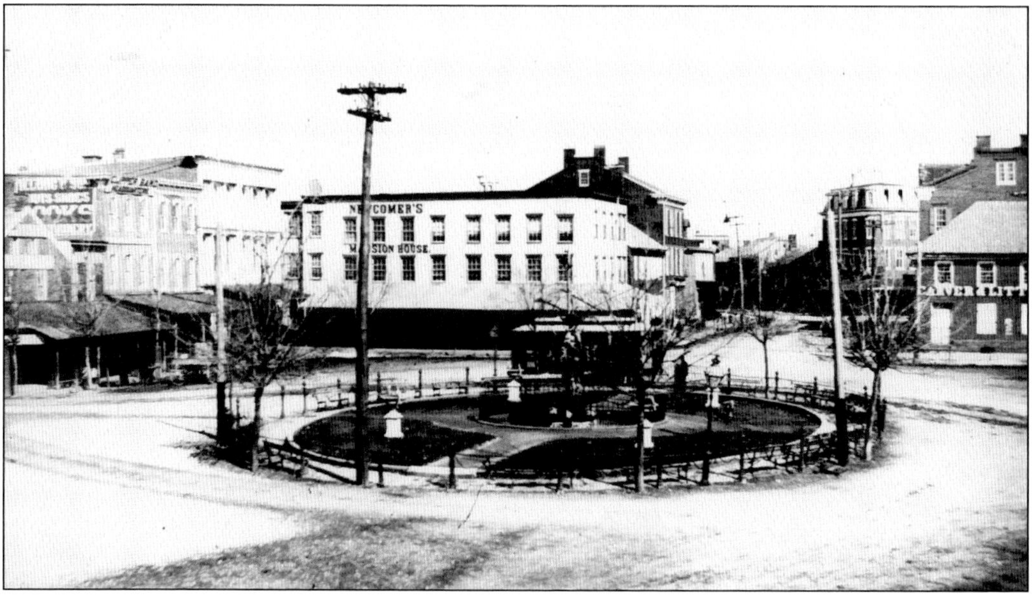

This *c.* 1895 view of Center Square looks from Frederick Street toward Broadway. The Mansion House Hotel, in the center, was owned by David Newcomer from 1889 to 1897. The N. B. Carver and John W. Little dry goods store can be seen on the right.

CONTENTS

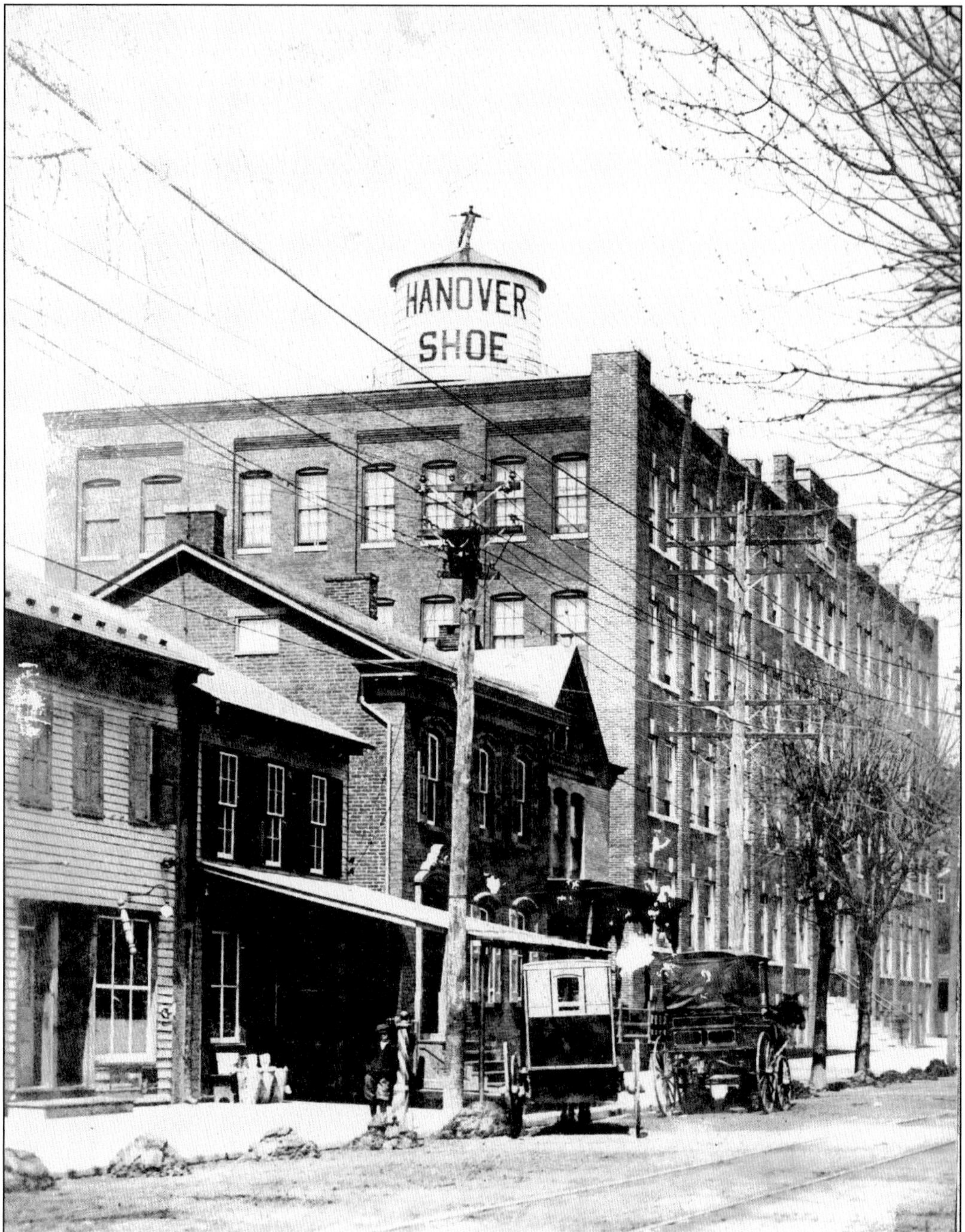

Seen here is the Hanover Shoe water tower at the shoe factory located at 220–232 Carlisle Street. The man standing on one leg on the tower was Paul E. Sprenkle, a local sign painter who had just finished lettering the tower. Prior to World War I, Sprenkle was a painter and stripper at the Hopkin's Wagon Factory at Maple Avenue and the Western Maryland Railroad. After serving in the war, he studied painting at the University of Sorbonne in Paris. The barbershop of Oscar J. Reese at 212 ½ Carlisle Street is on the left, followed by the Herman Teaman grocery store at 214 Carlisle Street.

INTRODUCTION

Hanover, Pennsylvania, from its early days as a colonial town to the present day, has always been industrious. Hanover was laid out by Richard McAllister in 1763. Unlike many prosperous communities of the 18th, 19th, and 20th centuries, it did not have easy access to navigable waterways to distribute its products. The Susquehanna River, and thereby access to the Chesapeake Bay and the north, was nearly 30 miles to the east. The ports of Baltimore and Philadelphia were 50 and 100 miles distant, respectively. Benefiting from the town's location at an important intersection for travelers and settlers moving west during the colonial period, early craftsmen prospered in the small town. Important clockmakers, gunsmiths, silversmiths, coppersmiths, cabinetmakers, and even a niche of coffee mill manufacturers thrived, and their products today are highly regarded.

Freight and passenger trains arrived in the second half of the 19th century and eventually service was provided from both the Pennsylvania and Western Maryland Railroads. Trolley service to nearby communities was also established. The prominent mid- to late-19th-century industries of farm machinery and carriage manufacturing would be replaced by a number of cigar and shoe factories, most notably Hanover Shoe, toward the end of the 19th century, and these would in turn all but disappear in the 1900s. Today furniture manufacturing, vegetable and snack food processors, power steering, wire cloth, and specialized packaging are some of the industries that bring worldwide recognition to the small town. This collection of postcards documents the business, social, religious, educational, and other aspects of this prosperous community.

The Hanover Area Historical Society is extremely grateful to Austin Ruth and Bill Marquet for making available their extensive collections of Hanover area postcards, without which we could not have produced these volumes. We believe that we have chosen the best of the postcards, which represent far less than half of their collections.

We are already planning a second volume, which will include nearly 50 postcards reflecting community entertainment, including local bands and orchestras, the Hanover Fair, and local parks. We anticipate also publishing numerous postcards depicting the 1915 tornado and the centennial celebration that took place only weeks later and included six parades. Another significant event, the 1932 Washington bicentennial celebration, will also be included. Many of these postcards are one of a kind, not to be seen anywhere else. Please look for volume two in the coming months.

-Hanover Area Historical Society photography committee

One

Center Square and Monuments

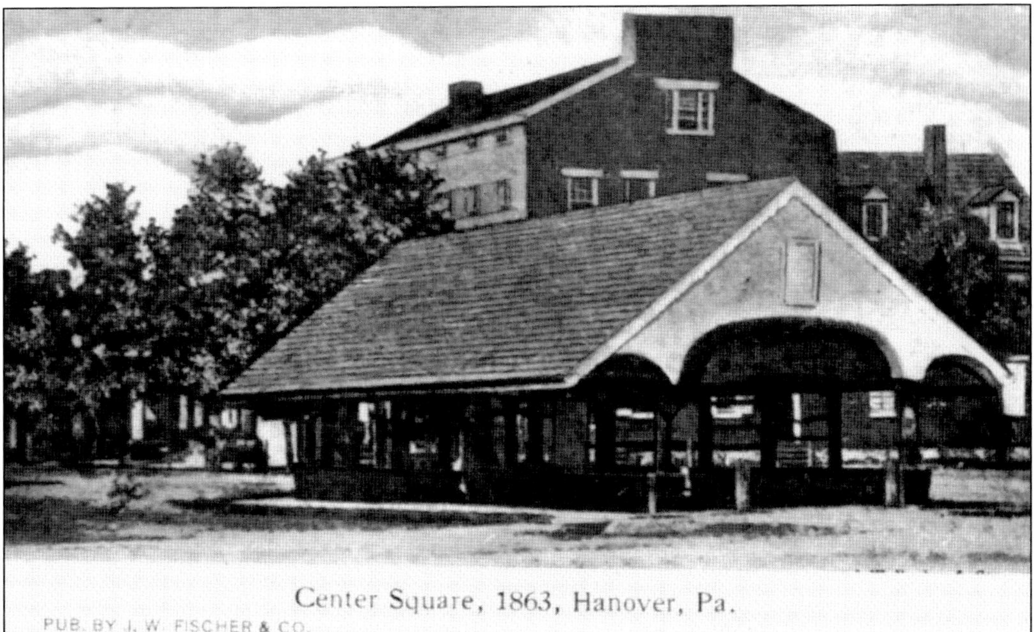

This image of Center Square in 1863 reveals the markethouse in the center with the Central Hotel in the background. It was published by J. W. Fischer & Company of Hanover.

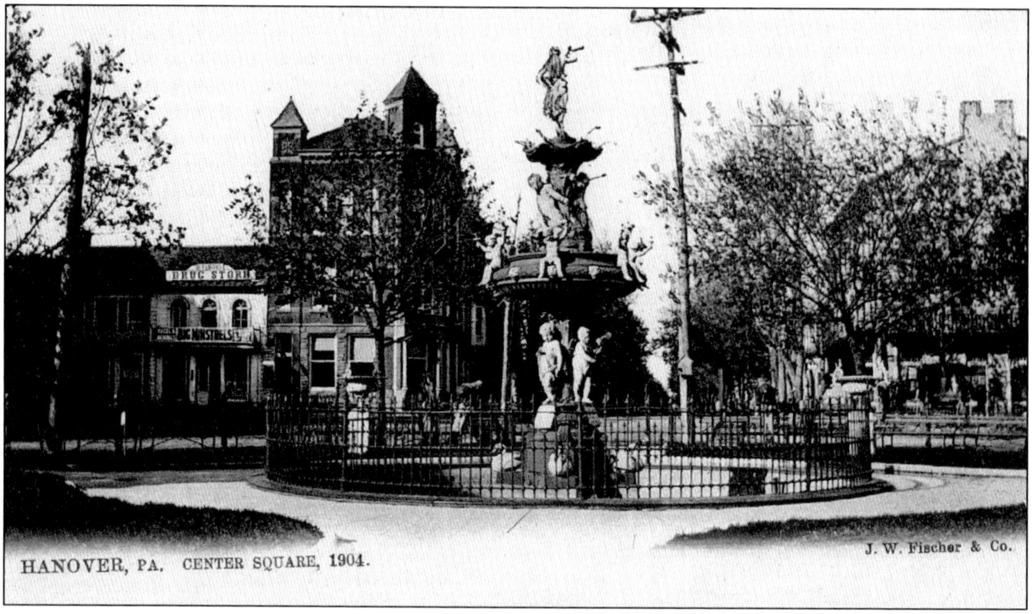

This image of Center Square looking west as it appeared in 1904 was published by Raphael Tuck & Sons', "art publishers to their majesties the king and queen," and was printed in Germany for J. W. Fischer and Company. The tall building to the left of the fountain is the People's Bank, and it is only one-third of its finished size. The Central Hotel is to the right of the fountain.

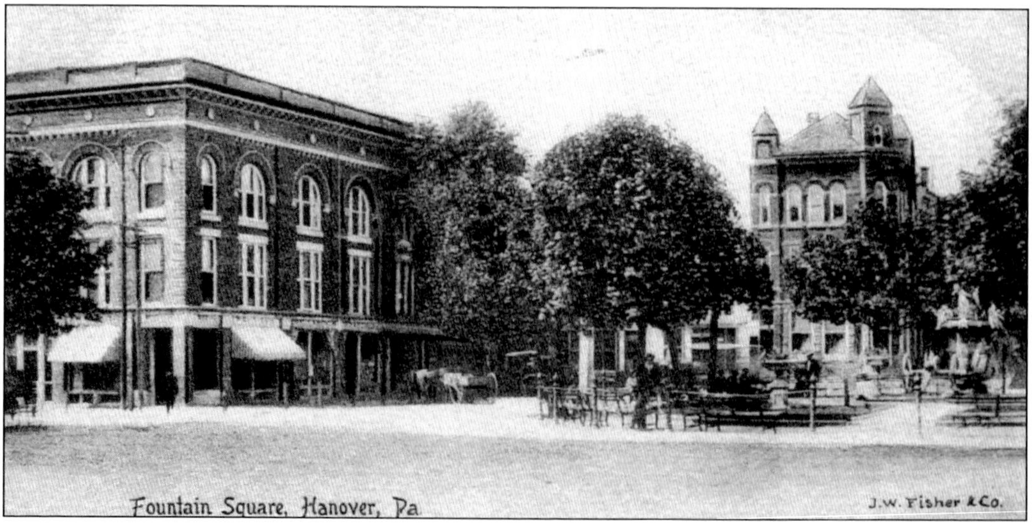

This postcard of the square was mailed October 12, 1906. From left to right are the Gitt building, the People's Bank, and the fountain.

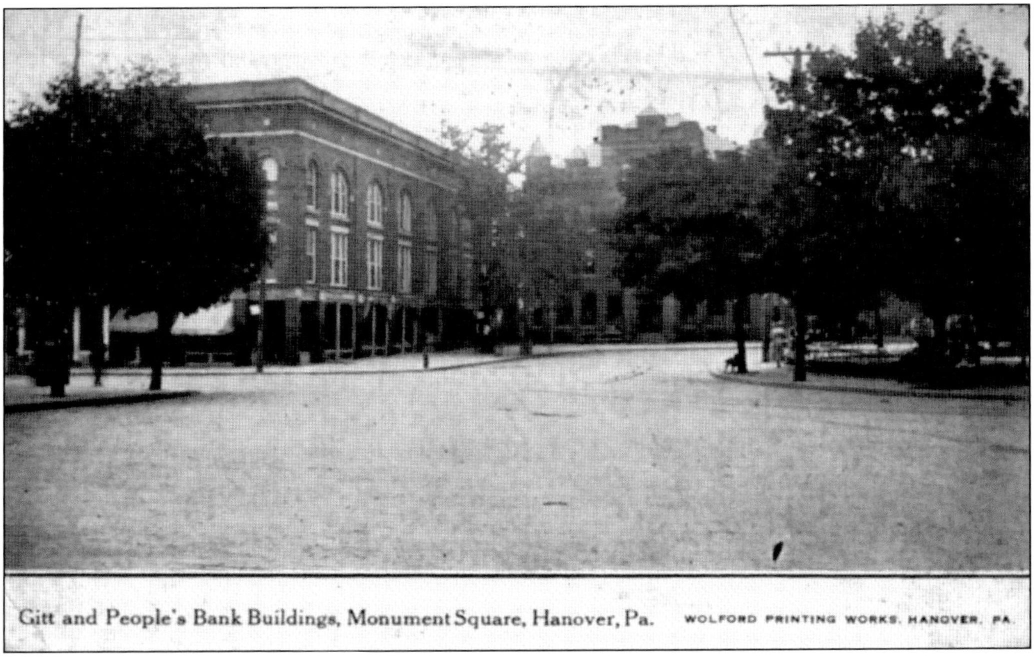

The Gitt and People's Bank building on Center Square was printed by Wolford Printing Works of Hanover. "Iron Mike," a cast iron Labrador, was standing at the left edge of the oval. The card was mailed September 15, 1915.

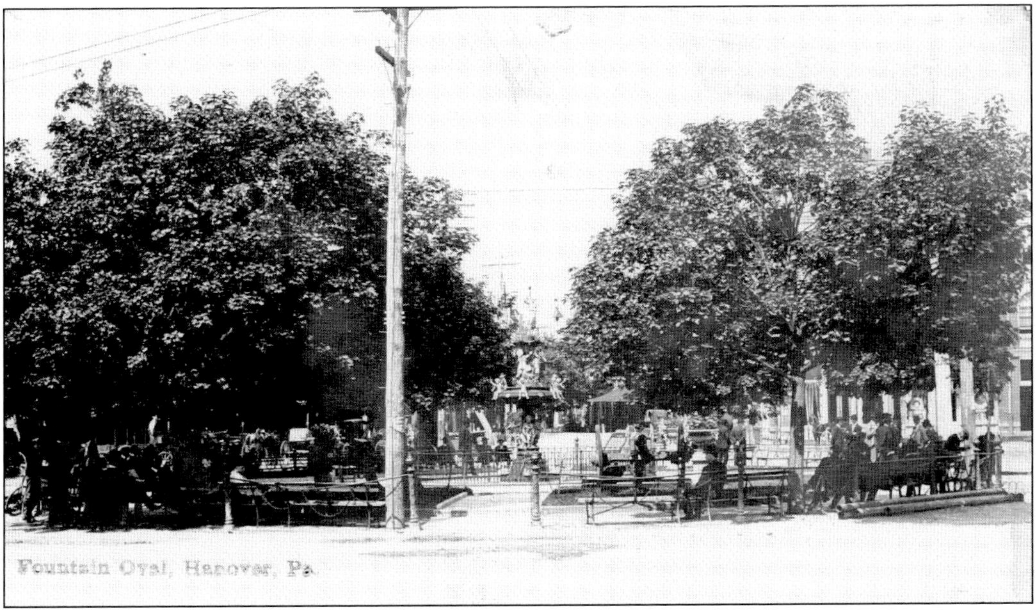

The fountain was photographed by Swords Brothers, Hanover photographers, prior to 1904.

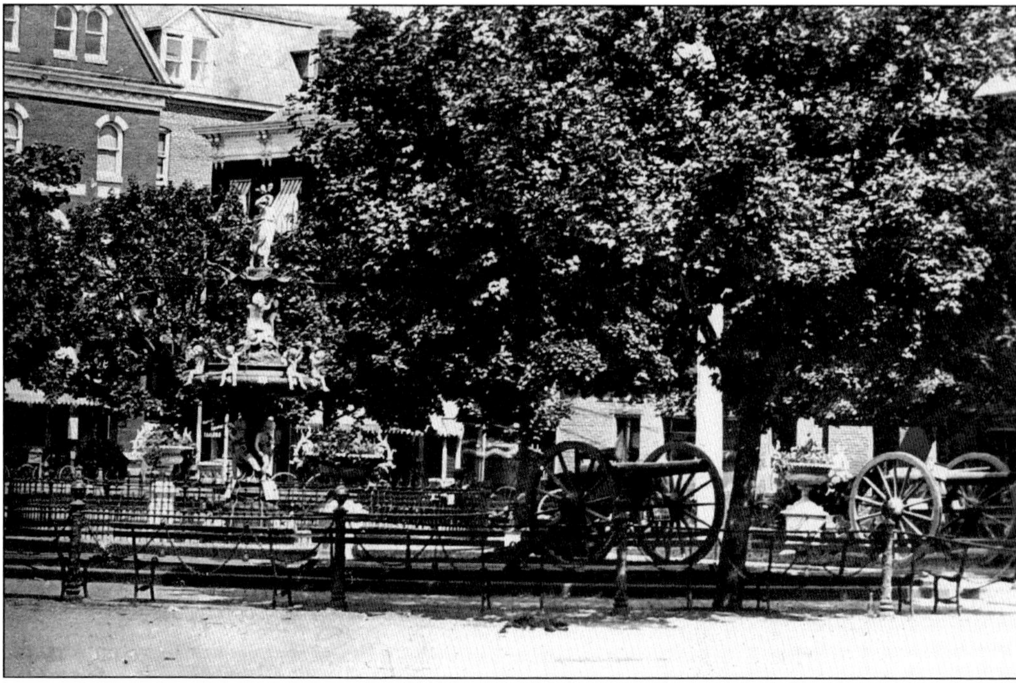

This is another image of the fountain as photographed by Swords Brothers. The back of the card was for address only.

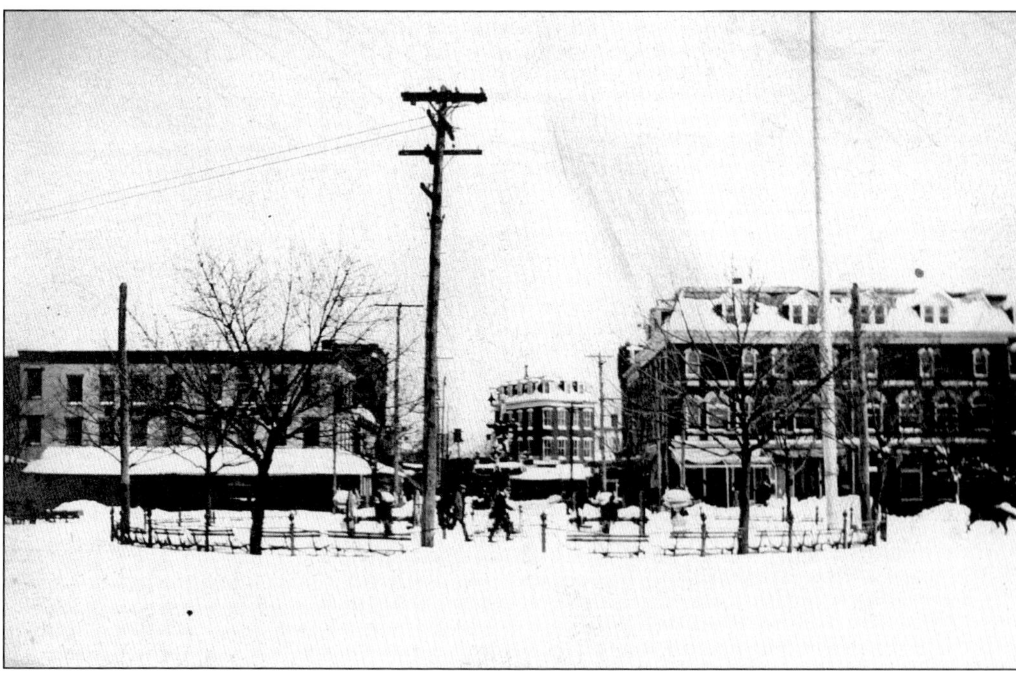

This image of the Center Square before 1904, with the fountain still in the oval, shows the Mansion House Hotel on the left, the Sprenkle building in the center, and Hanover Hotel on the right. It was taken by Swords Brothers.

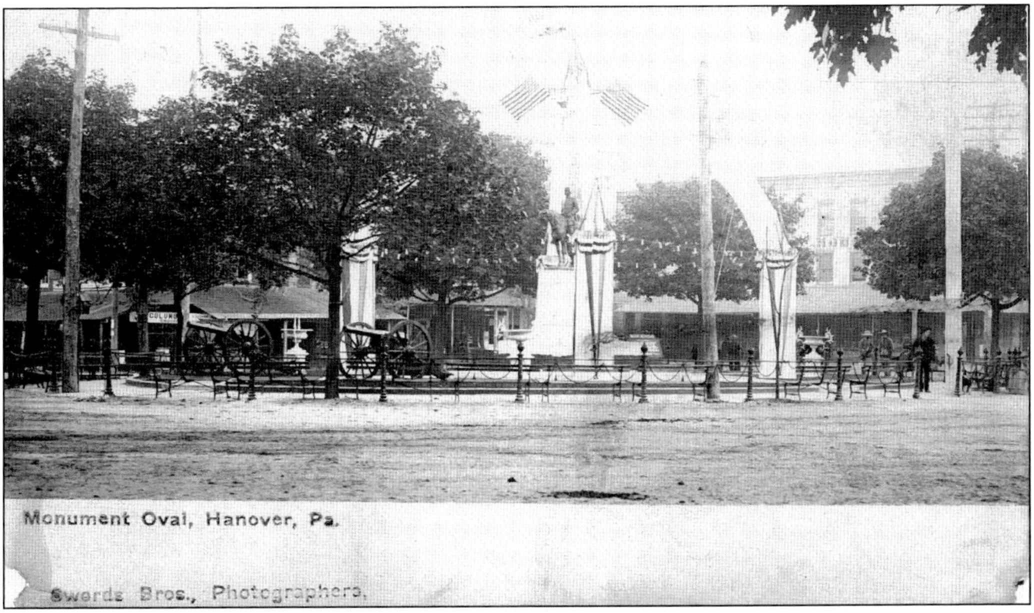

In this Swords Brothers photograph, the monument oval is decorated for the 1904 dedication of the Picket Civil War Monument.

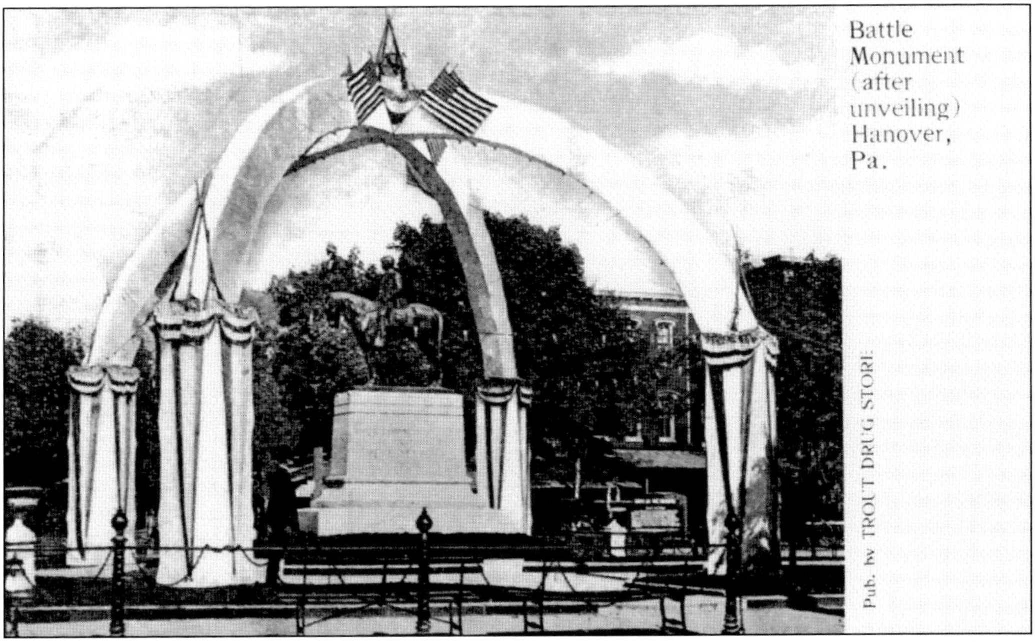

The Battle Monument, seen here as it appeared after its unveiling, was erected in 1904 to honor the men of Hanover who served during the Civil War and to commemorate the Battle of Hanover. The card was published by Trout Drug Store of Hanover.

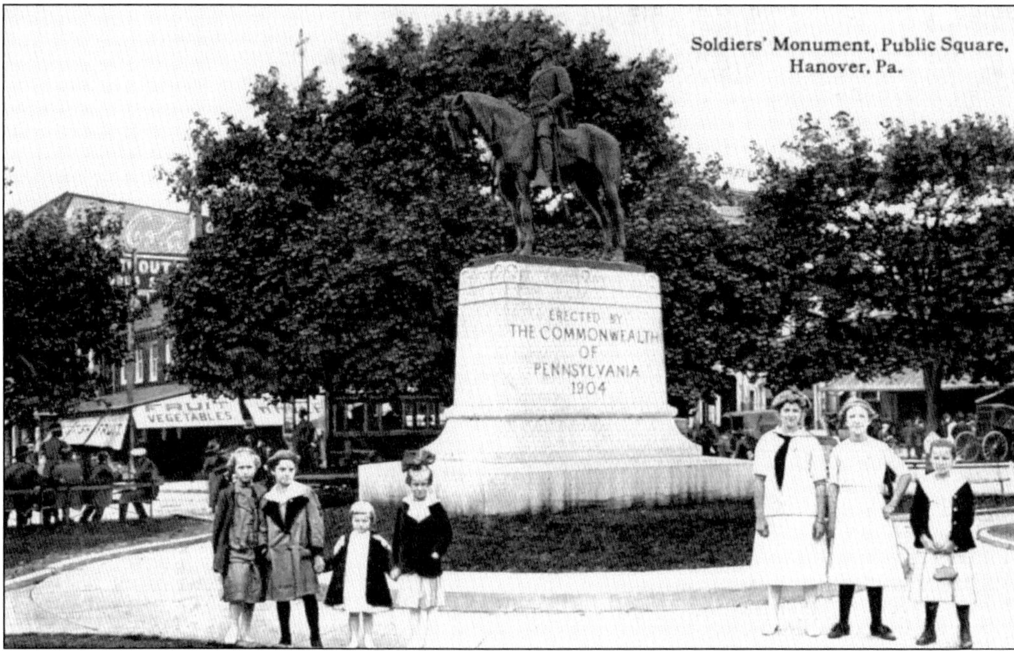

This image of the Soldiers' Monument on the public square was printed by C. T. Photochrome for the "Fair and Square" Bargain House of York, Pennsylvania. This is one of very few Hanover cards to use posed people.

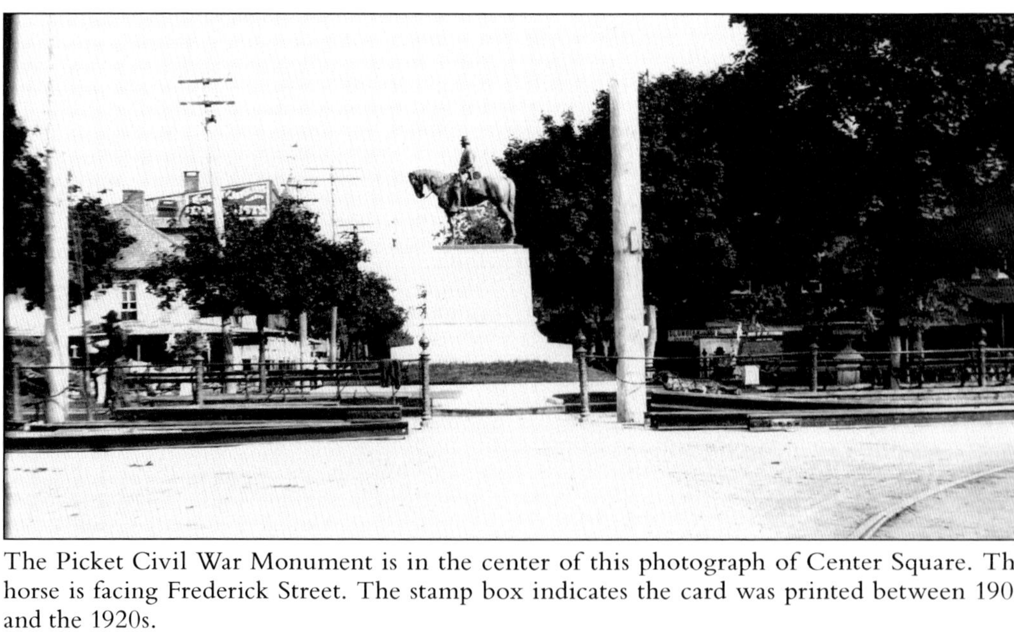
The Picket Civil War Monument is in the center of this photograph of Center Square. The horse is facing Frederick Street. The stamp box indicates the card was printed between 1904 and the 1920s.

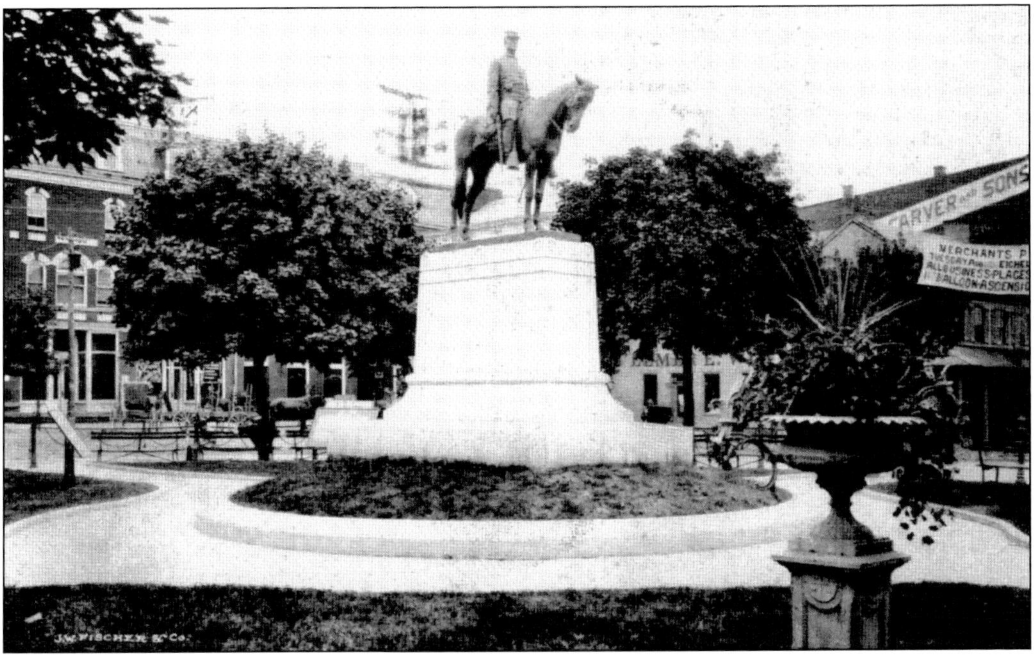

The Battle Monument on Center Square is seen here facing Frederick Street. This image was published by J. W. Fischer. The banner over Baltimore Street proclaims the Merchants' Picnic to be held at Eichelberger Park. The card was postmarked May 8, 1909.

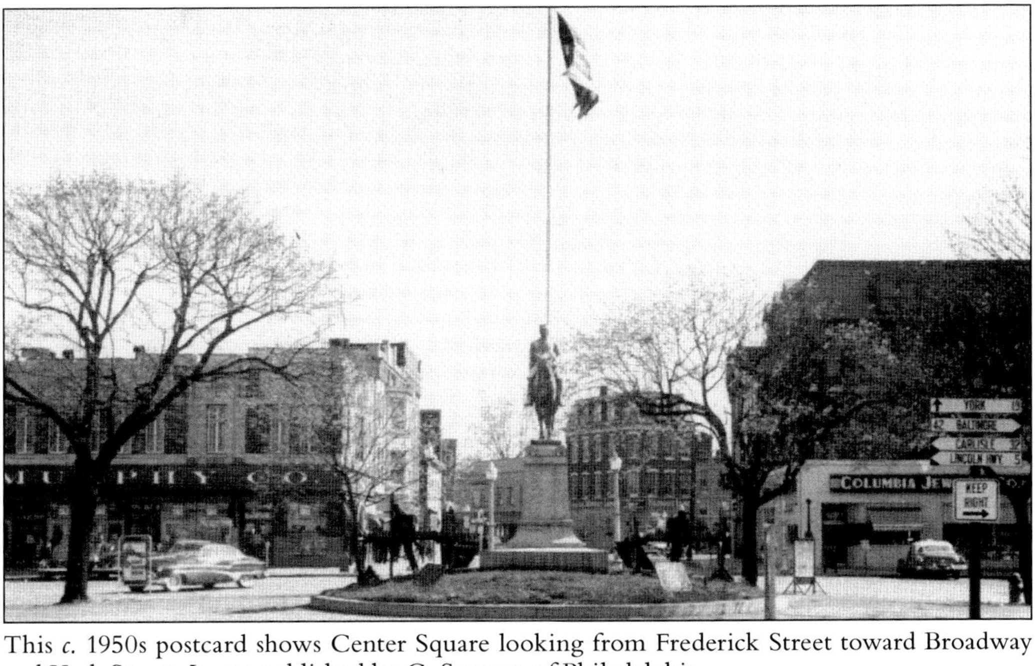

This *c.* 1950s postcard shows Center Square looking from Frederick Street toward Broadway and York Street. It was published by C. Seeman of Philadelphia.

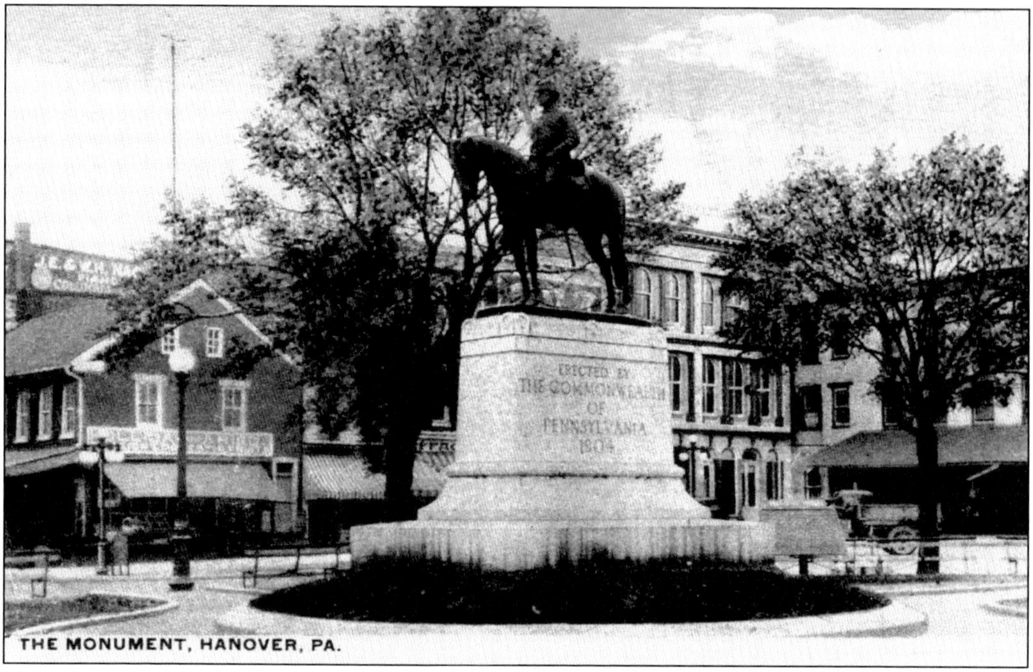

This photograph, taken in the 1920s, shows the Picket Civil War Monument, which was erected in 1904. The Holiday and Arigo Green Grocery is on the left. This card was published by David Kaufman of Baltimore.

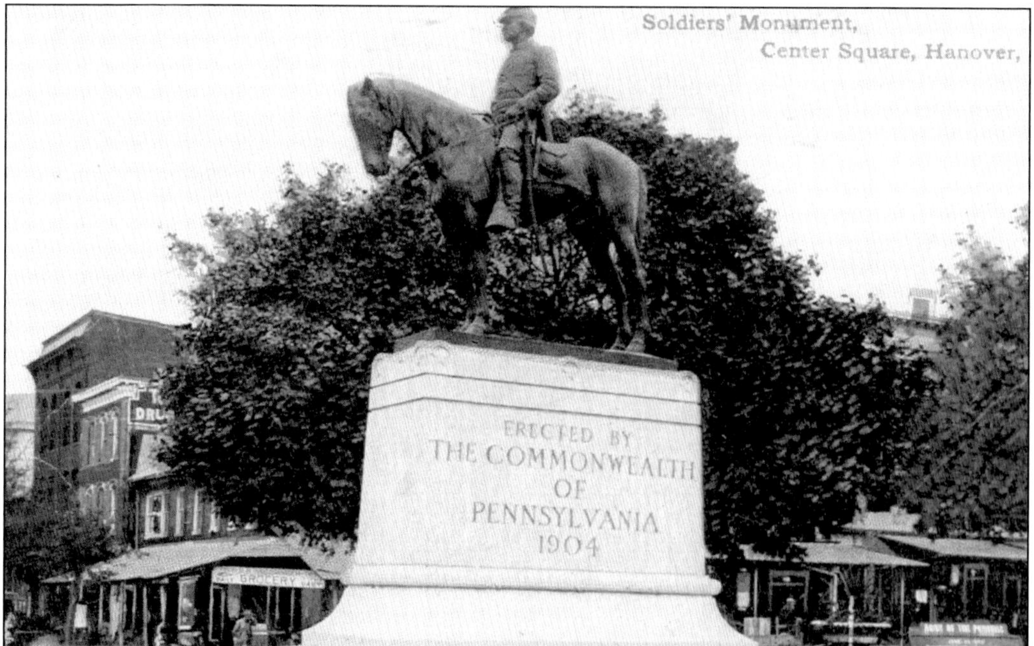

This postcard depicting the Battle Monument was printed by Leighton and Valentine Company of New York City and was mailed in Hanover on October 24, 1917.

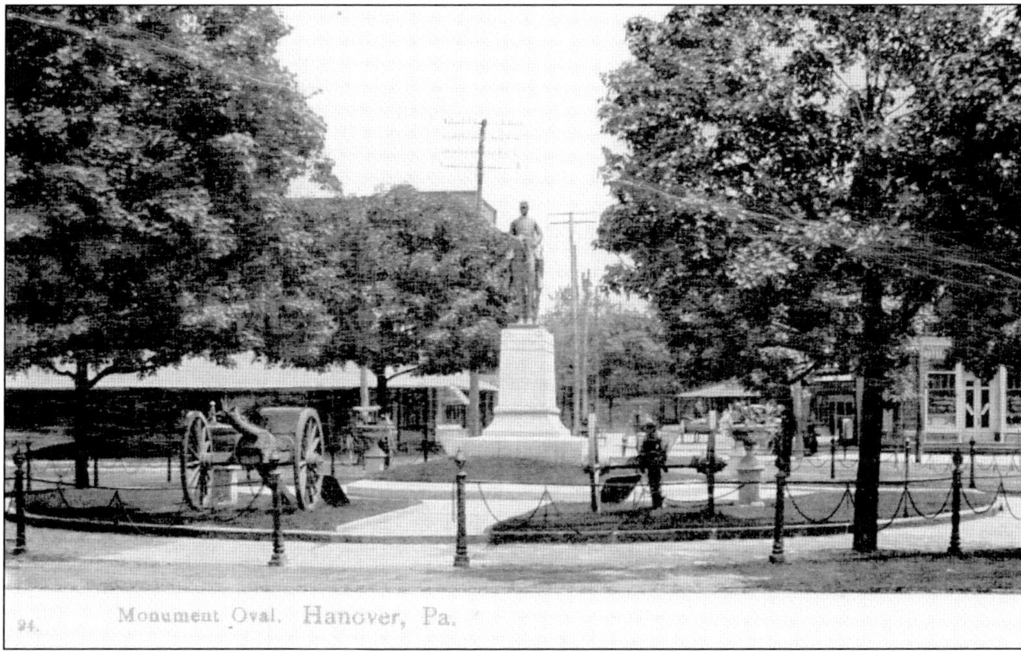

In this view by C. E. Wheelock of Peoria, Illinois, the monument oval is seen looking from Frederick Street toward Broadway. The Mansion House Hotel is on the left and the Battle Monument is in the center.

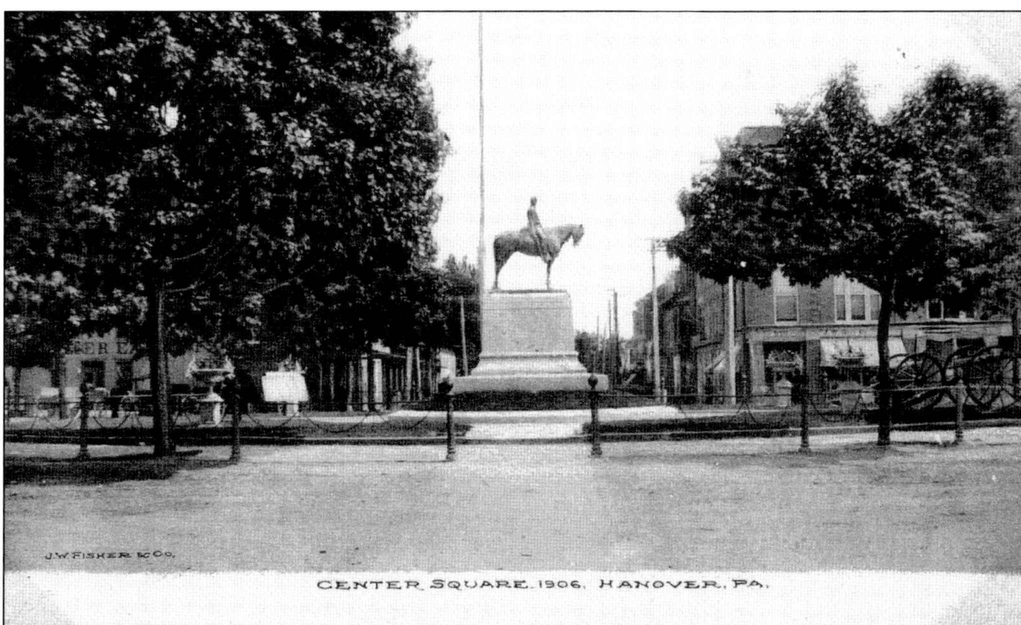

This scene shows the view from Carlisle Street toward Baltimore Street through Center Square. The monument was placed in the oval in 1904. The J. W. Gitt Department Store is on the southwest corner of Baltimore Street and the Elmer E. Wentz dry goods store is on the left. This J. W. Fischer card was mailed July 30, 1906, from Hanover to Dillsburg, Pennsylvania.

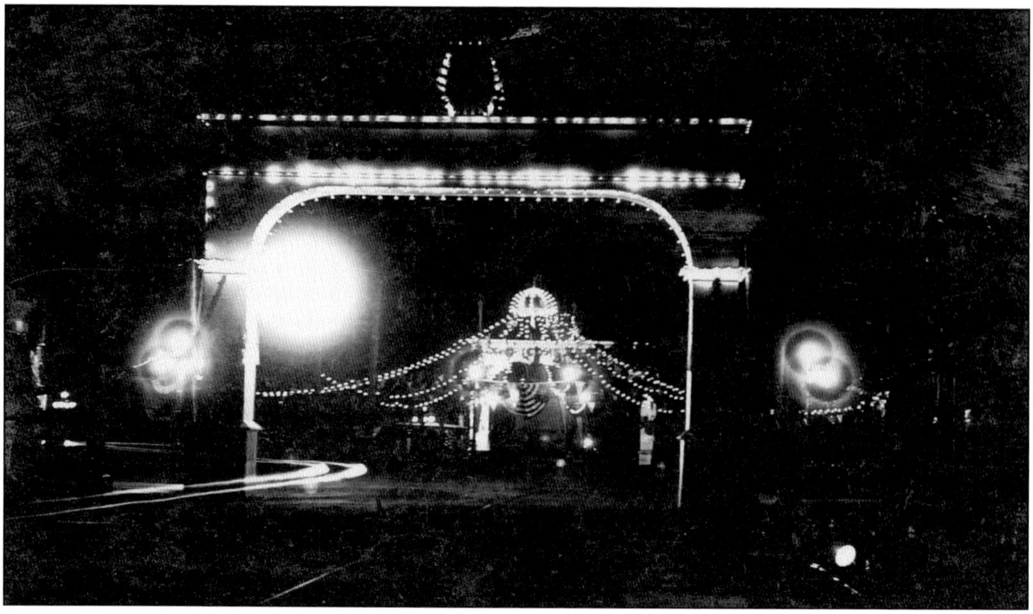

A nighttime photograph depicts the 1915 centennial celebration decorations on Center Square.

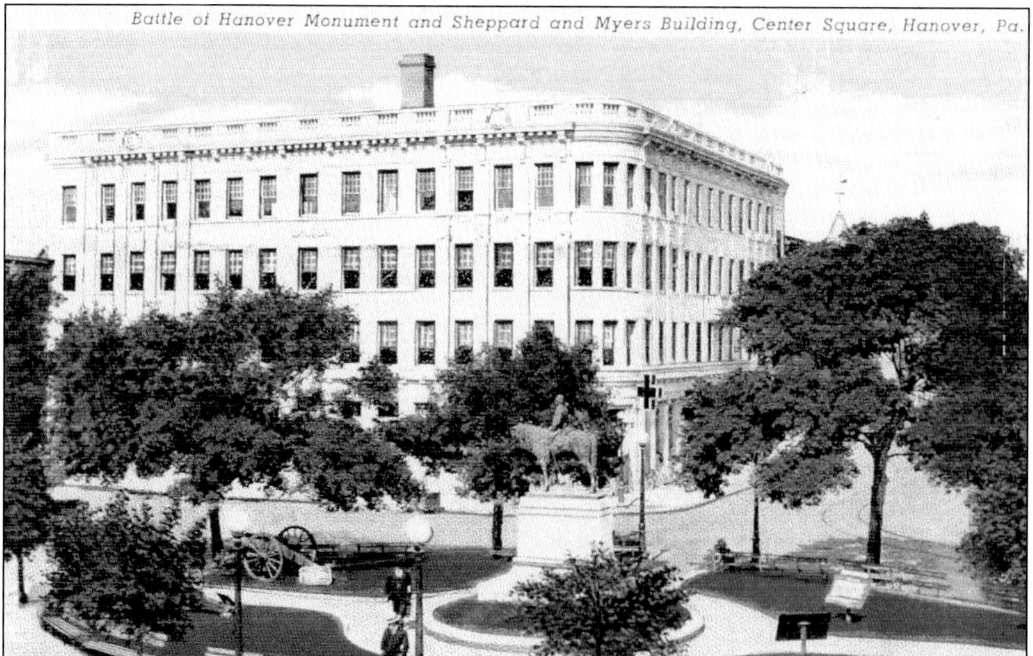

The Battle Monument and the Sheppard and Myers building are on Center Square. This card was published by C. T. American Art, Chicago, for J. P. Walmer of Harrisburg.

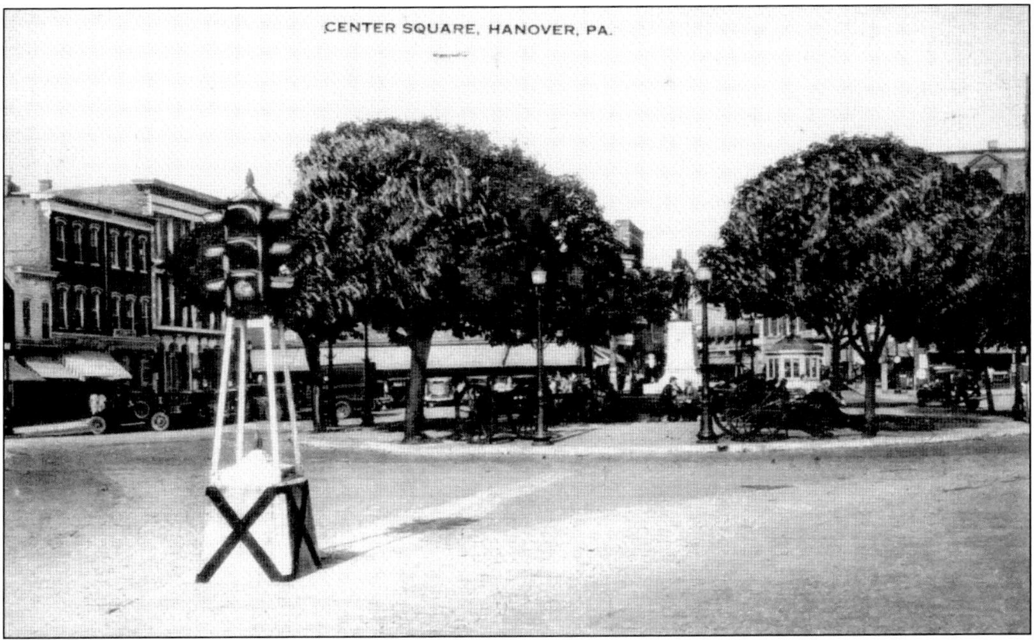

A 1930s view of Center Square looks from Frederick Street toward York Street and Broadway. Note the traffic light in the foreground and police gazebo on the far side of the oval. This postcard was published by Artvue Post Card Company of New York City.

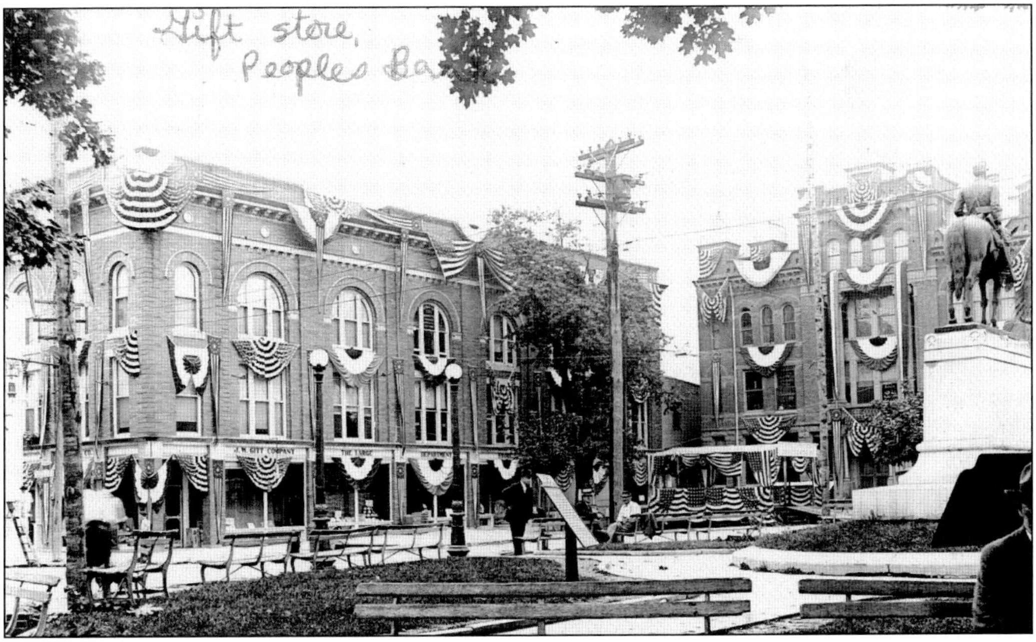

A previous owner of this postcard wrote "gift store." This may be, but the correct name was the J. W. Gitt Department Store. It was also known as the "large department store" and, before that, the "big store."

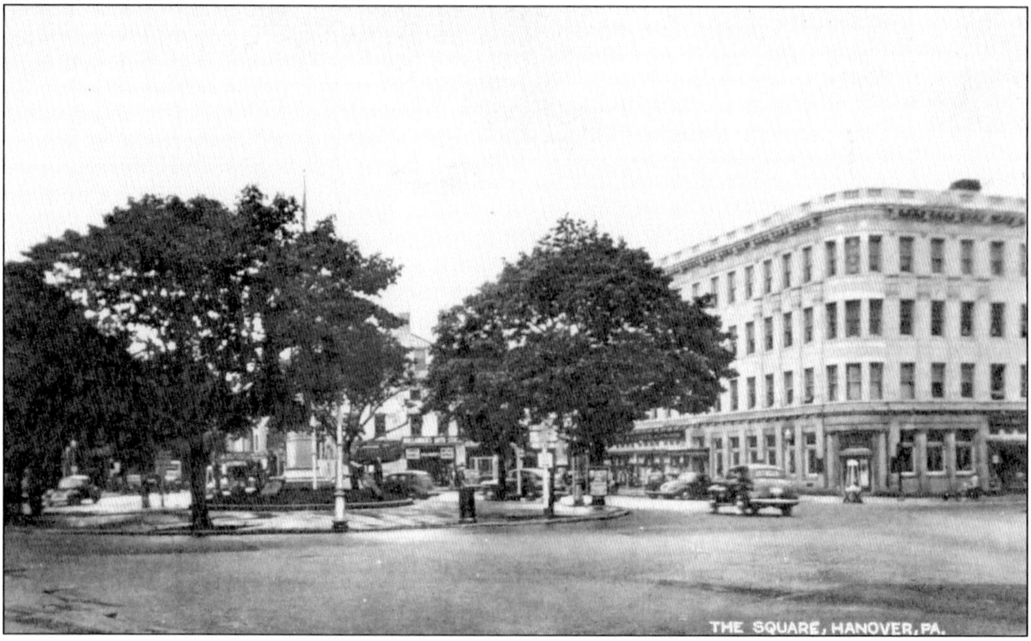

This 1930s card is by the Tecraft Company of Tenafly, New Jersey. The Sheppard and Myers building, in the northwest quadrant of Center Square, is on the right and the Central Hotel is behind the trees.

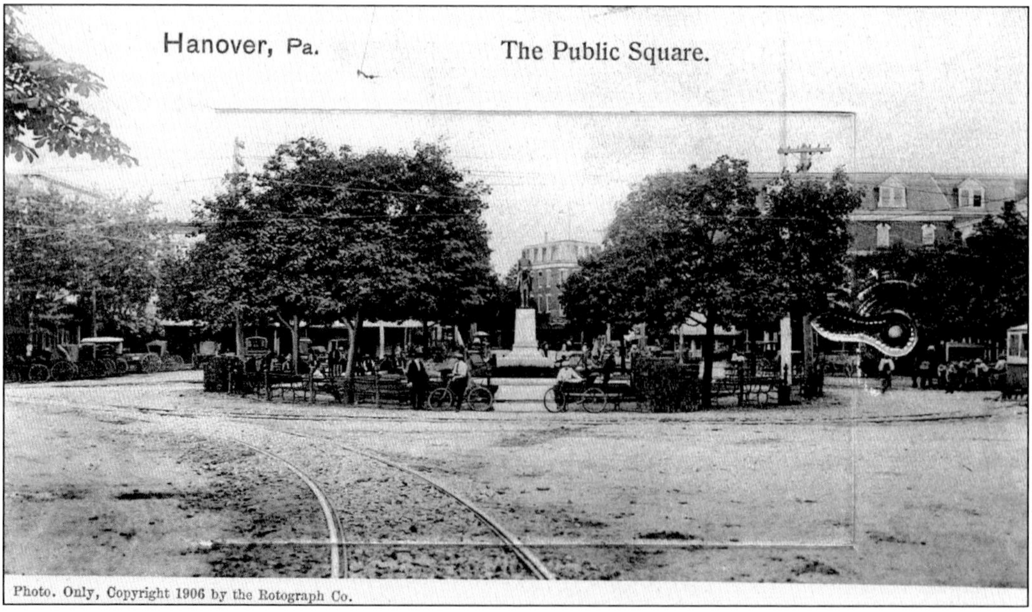

This postcard of the public square was published by the Rotograph Company of New York City. The card is hinged and when opened exposes 12 miniature accordion-pleated photographs of Hanover. The card is backed by hardboard. Note the brass latch tab to the right of center.

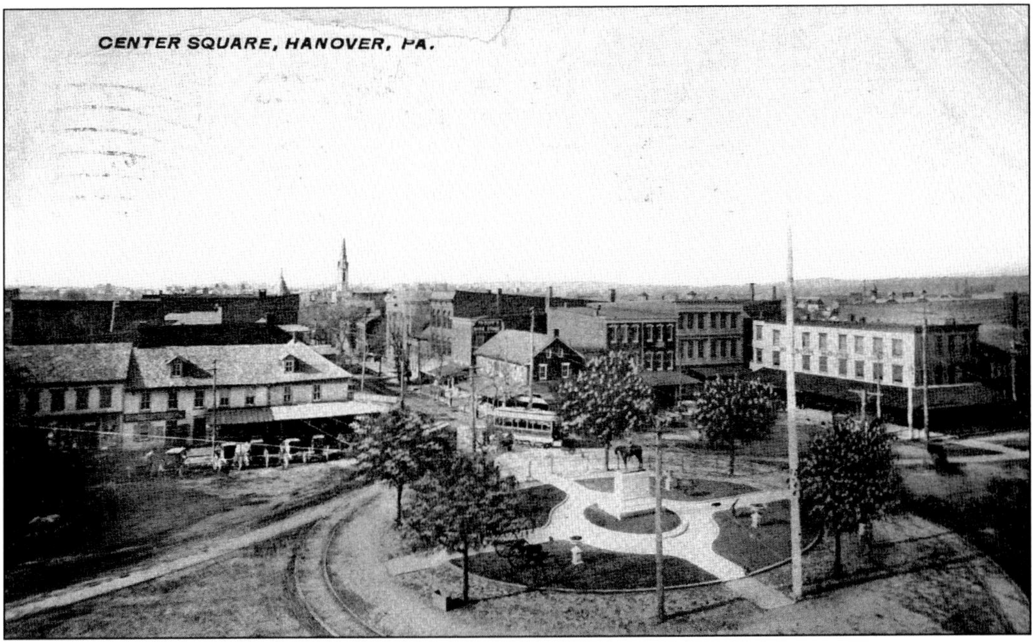

The tracks of the Hanover Street railway circle Center Square, with one of the closed cars exiting onto Carlisle Street. This photograph was taken from the top floor of the People's Bank building looking north. In the oval can be seen a huge flag pole, four flower urns, one of two Civil War cannons, and the Picket Civil War Monument. The light building in the right center is the Mansion House Hotel. The tall building on the right side of Carlisle Street is the Hanover Saving Fund Society bank, which was constructed in 1906–1907. The large building in the left center with the two dormer windows was the store of A. H. Melhorn, purveyor of general merchandise and liquors. This Swords Brothers postcard is postmarked September 13, 1914.

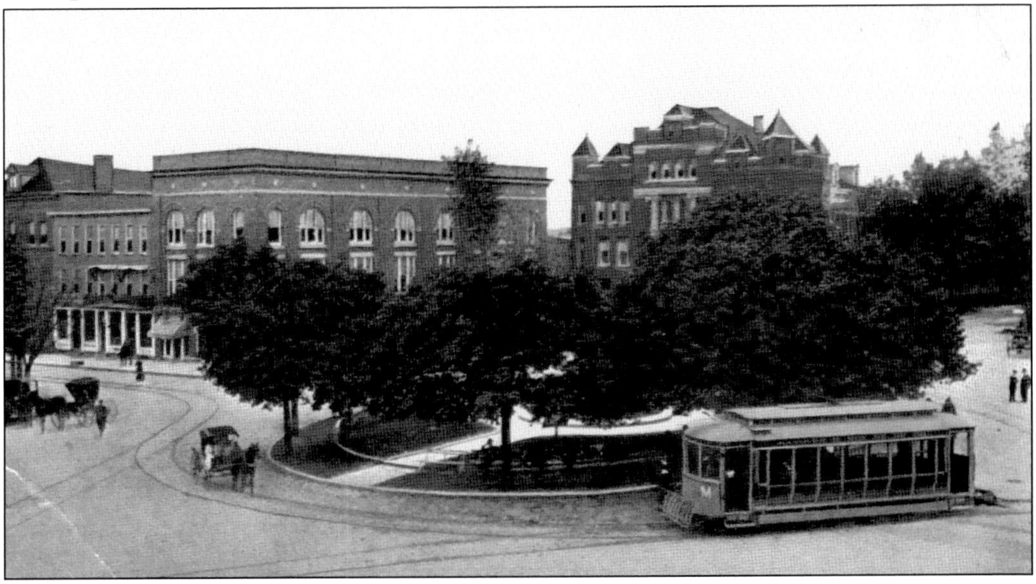

The building to the right is the People's Bank, and the building to the left is the J. W. Gitt Department Store. This public square scene was published by the "Fair and Square" Bargain House of York.

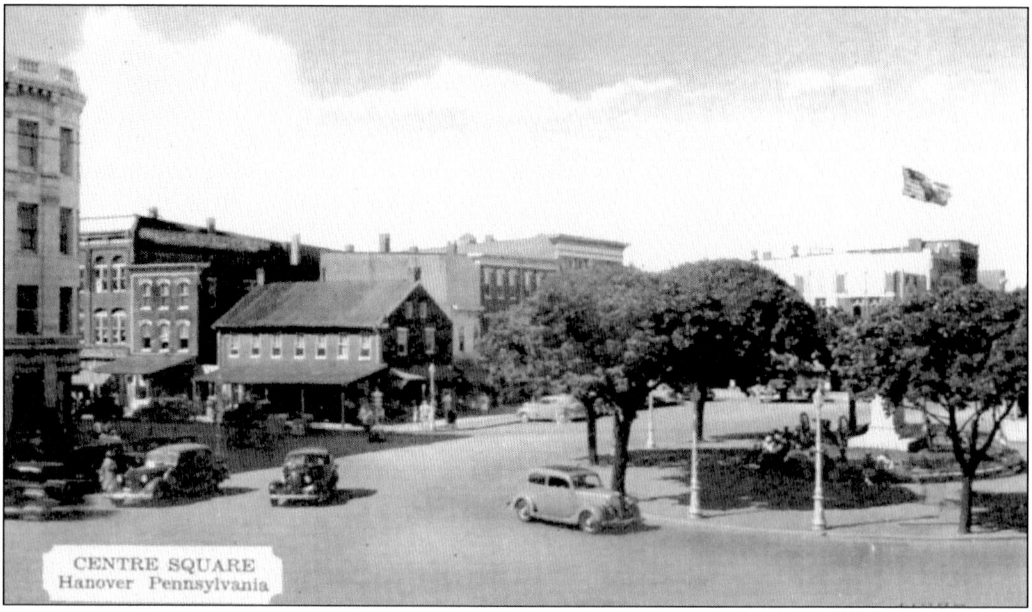

This image of Center Square in the late 1930s shows Carlisle Street, with the fruit market owned by J. Norman Stauffer and Paul B. Forry on the northeast corner of the square.

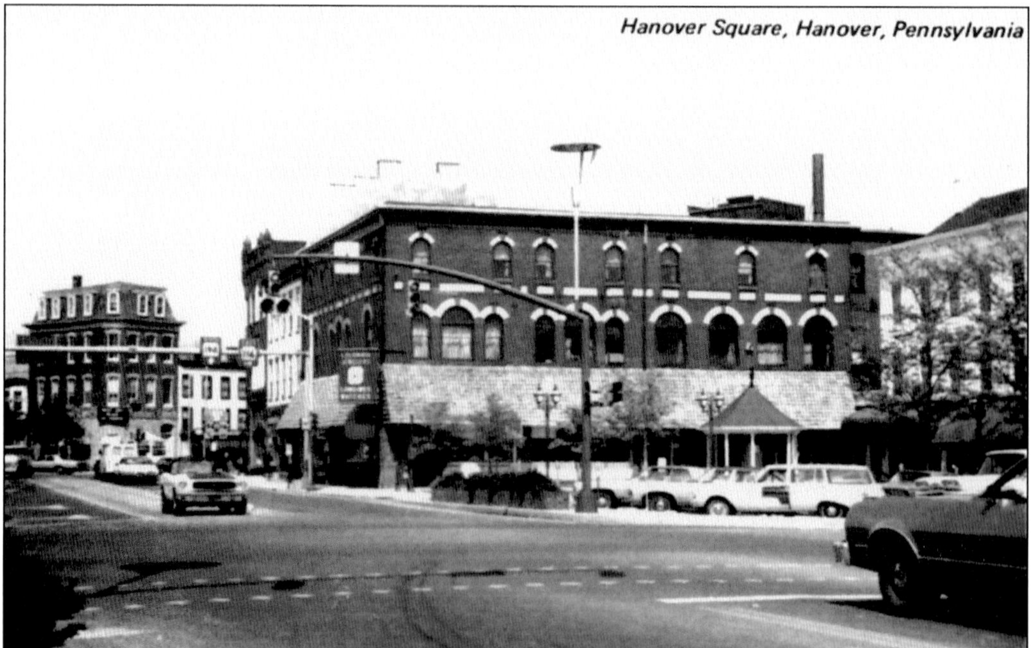

This 1970s scene of the square looks east. The top floor of the Hanover Hotel, in the center of the photograph, has been removed as the result of a fire.

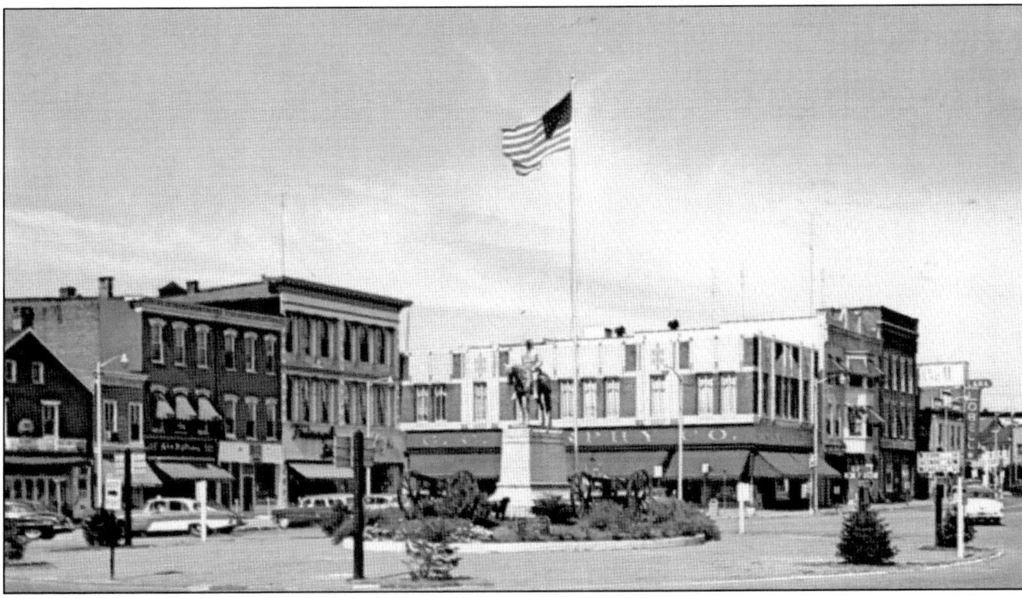

This photograph from the late 1940s or early 1950s shows the northeast quadrant of Center Square and the Battle Monument.

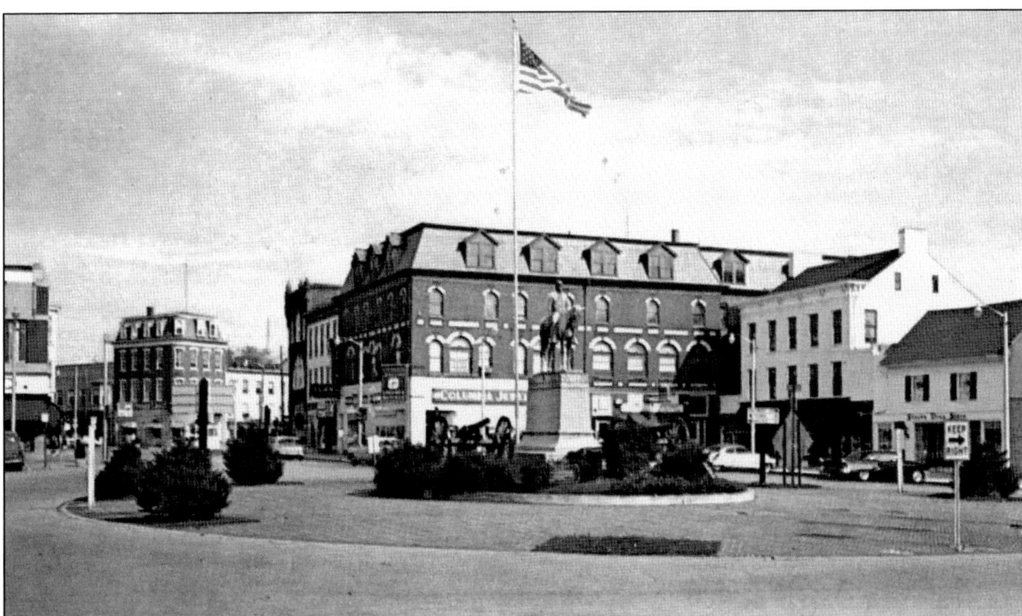

"Greetings from Hanover, PA" shows the southeast quadrant of Center Square before the oval was removed and features the Picket Civil War Monument.

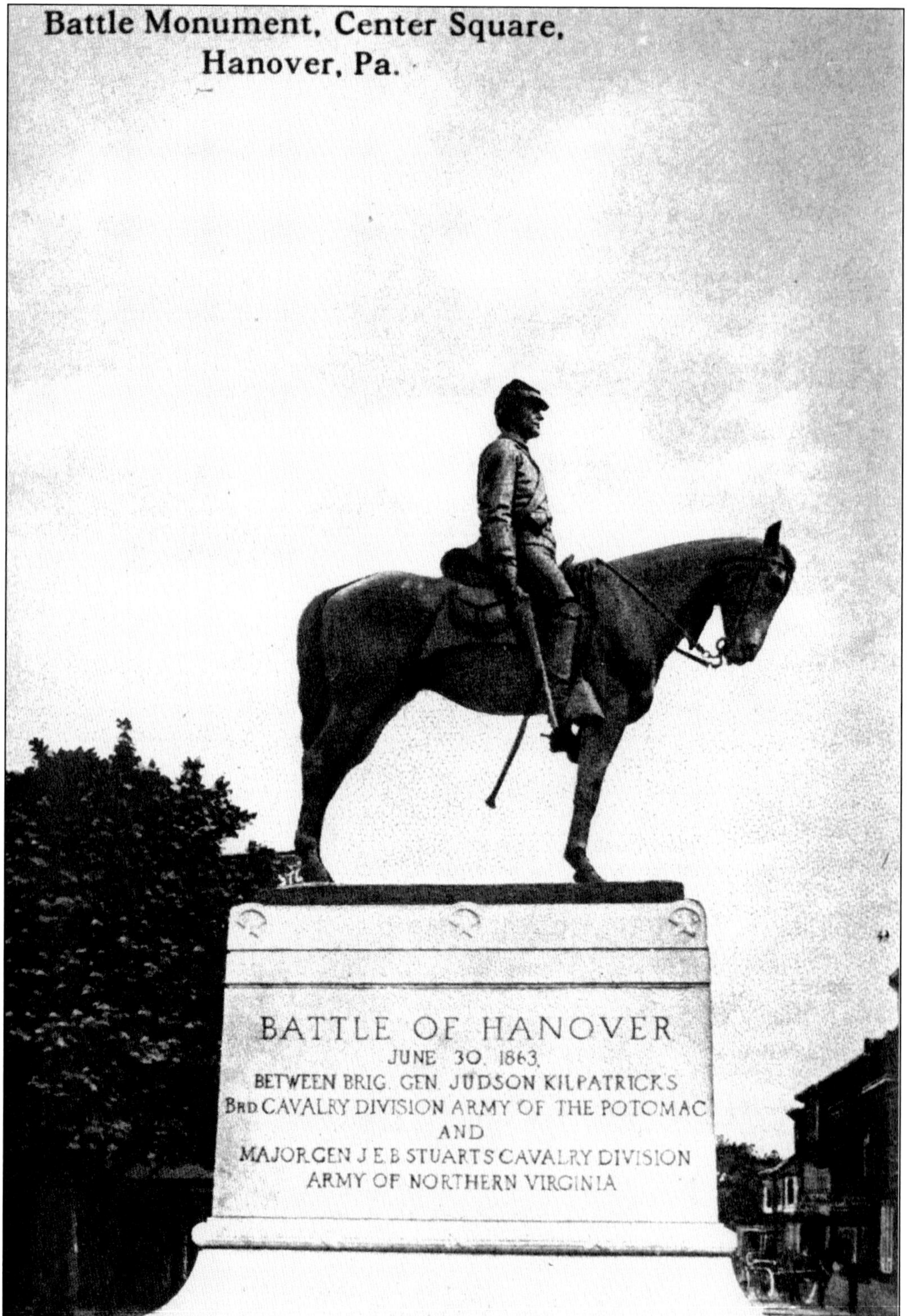

This postcard offers another view of the Battle Monument in Center Square.

Two

STREET SCENES

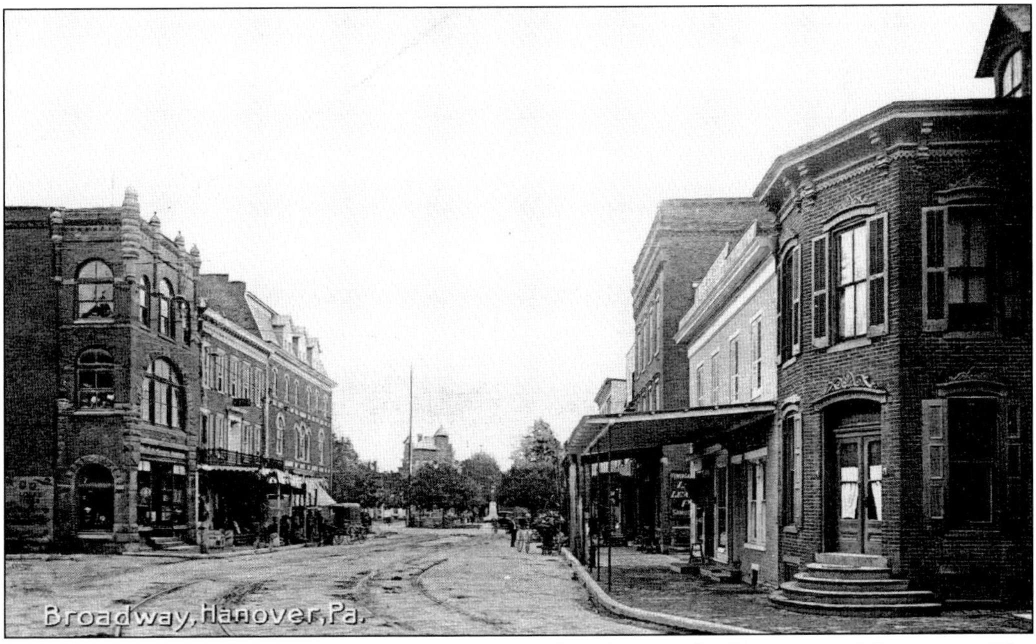

This view from Broadway shows the intersection of York Street looking toward the square. The first building on the left is Tanger's Hardware, and the original portion of the People's Bank is in the center background.

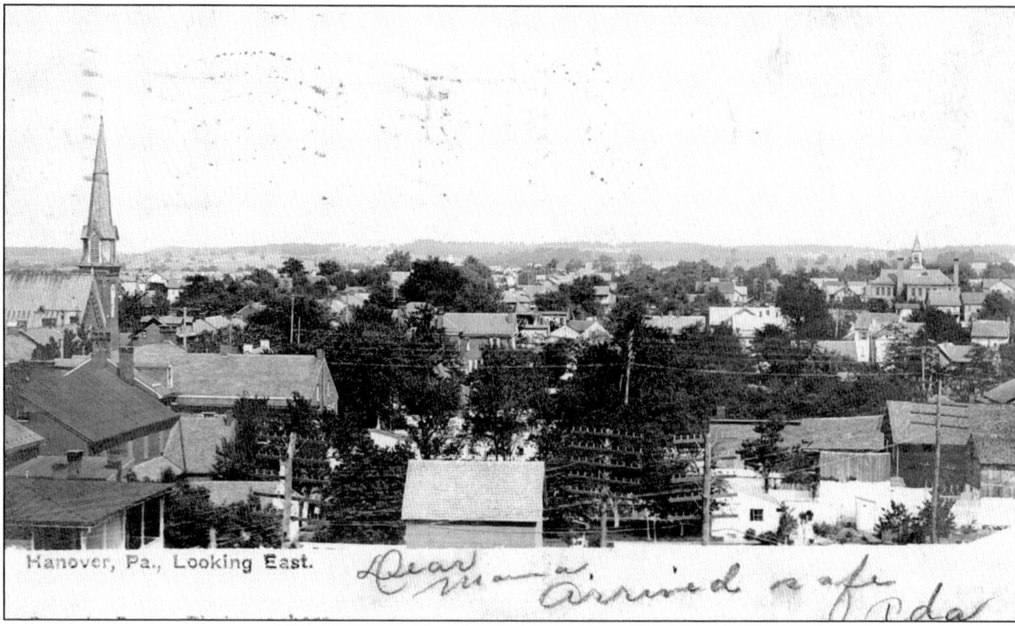

This view from the east shows High Street School in the background on the right. The photograph is by Swords Brothers, photographers of Hanover, and the card was mailed October 16, 1905.

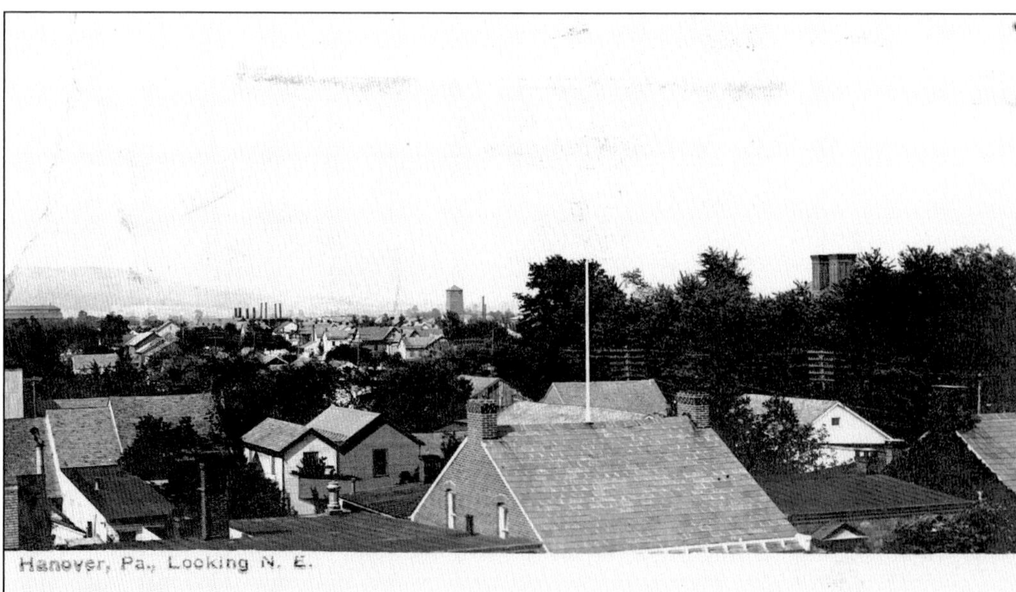

The building on the horizon on the far left is probably the O'Neill Silk Company. The photograph was taken by Swords Brothers The stamp box indicates the card was made between 1904 and the 1920s.

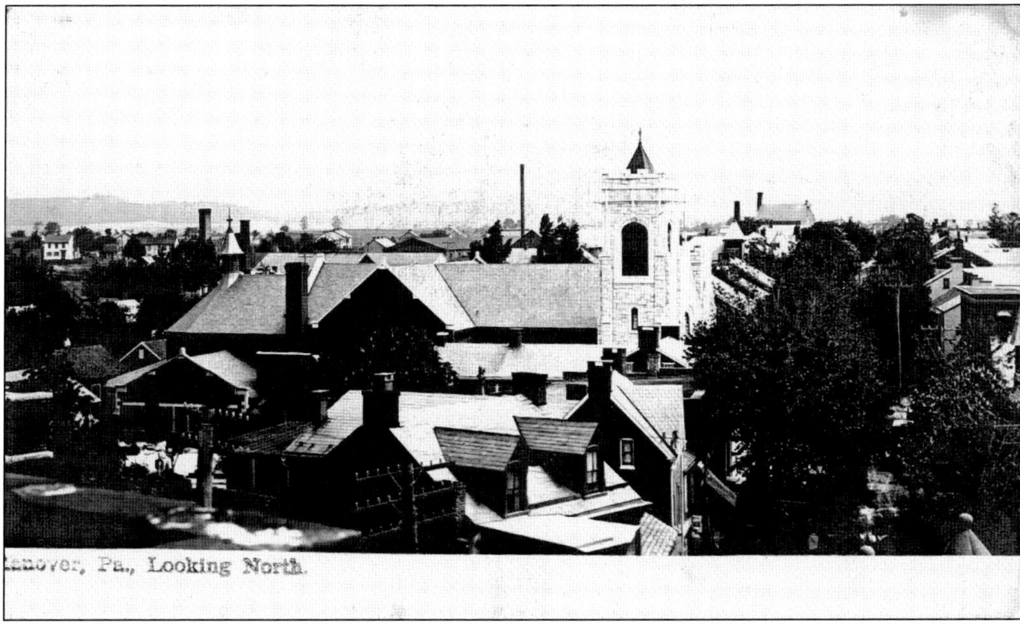

This photograph of Hanover, looking north, shows the Emmanuel Reformed Church steeple in the center and the peaks of the Pigeon Hills in the background.

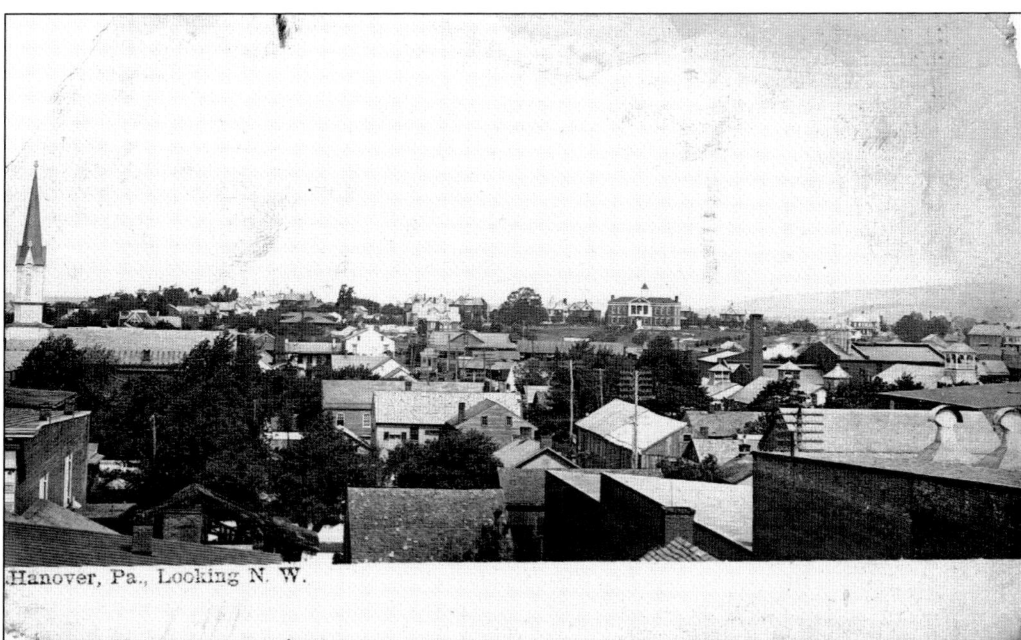

Here is a view looking northeast with St. Mark's Church steeple to the left and Eichelberger School in the far background in the center. This is a Browntone photograph taken by Swords Brothers.

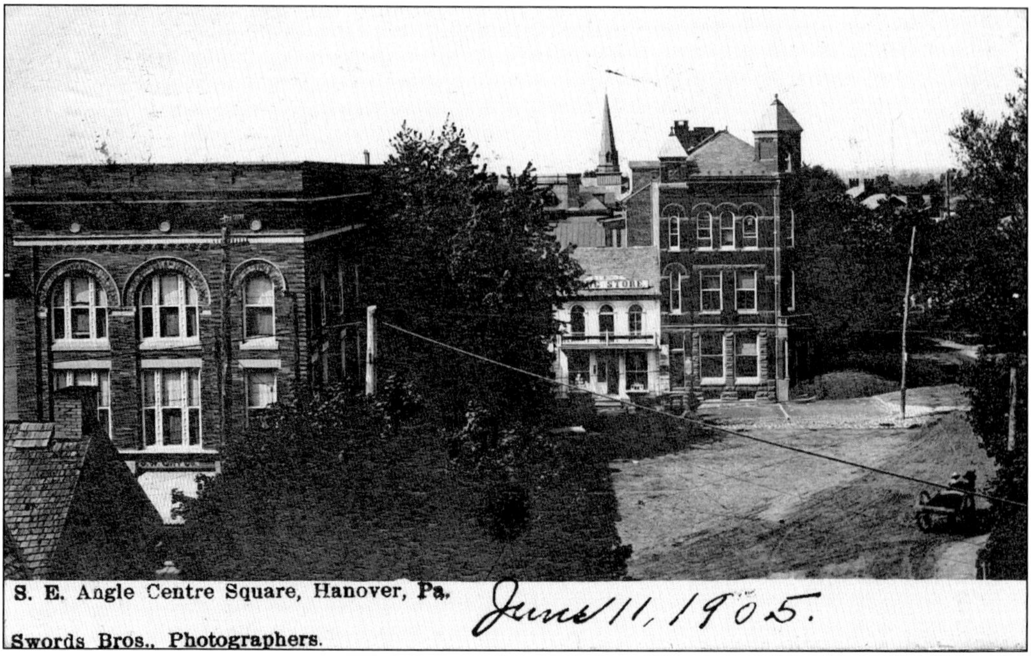

This view of Center Square, looking at the southwest quadrant, shows the Gitt building to the left, the spire of the Methodist church at Centennial Avenue and Frederick Street, and the first part of the People's Bank at the corner of Frederick Street. The postcard was mailed on June 12, 1905, and seems to be part of a set of at least six cards done at the same time by Swords Brothers early in 1905.

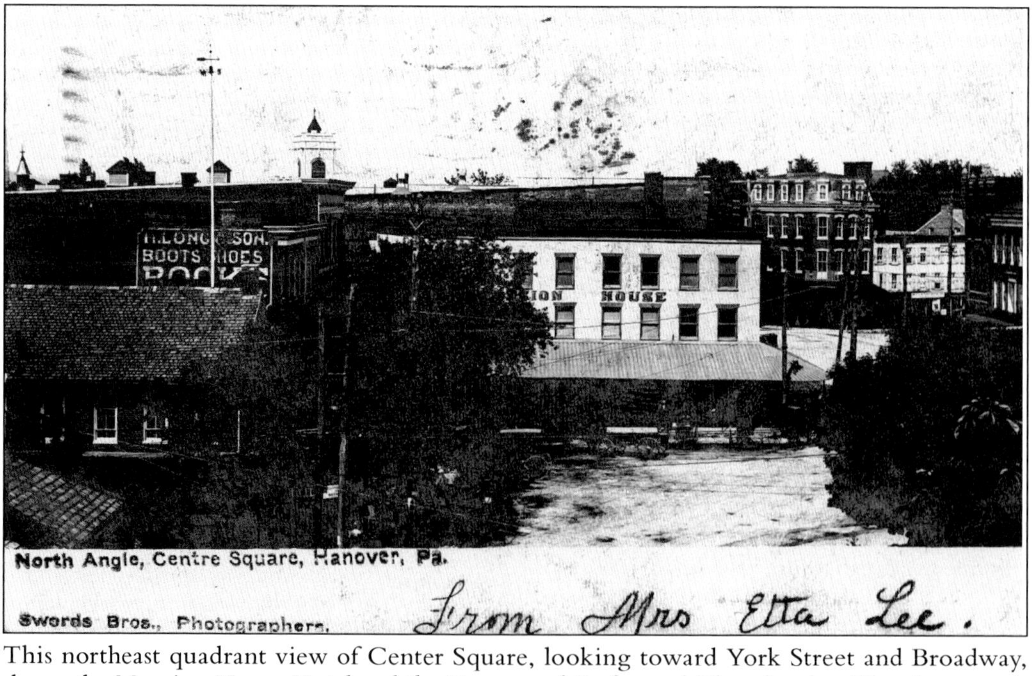

This northeast quadrant view of Center Square, looking toward York Street and Broadway, shows the Mansion House Hotel and the Emmanuel Reformed Church spire. The photograph is by Swords Brothers.

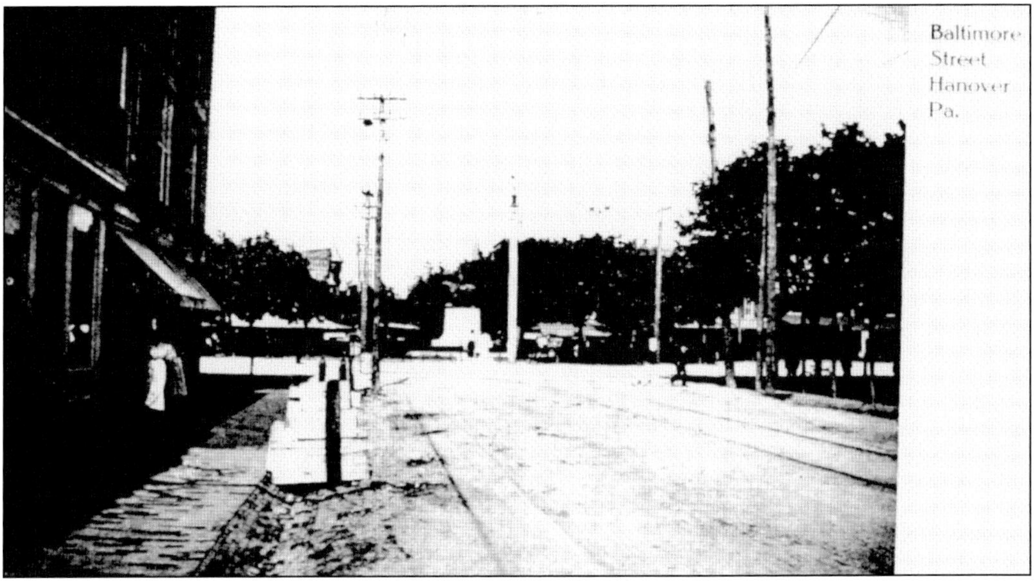

Because the monument is in the oval, this Baltimore Street scene with ladies with long dresses must date from after 1904. St. Mark's Lutheran Church spire on Carlisle Street is in the center background.

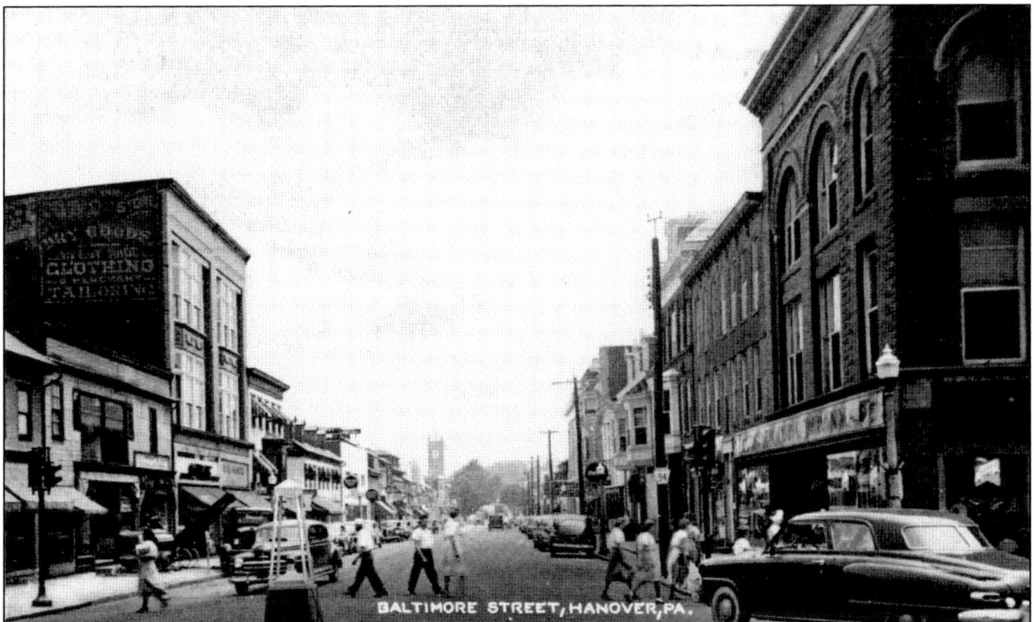

This Baltimore Street scene looks south, with St. Joseph's Catholic Church steeple in the background. The Gitt building is on the right, and the tall building on the left is the Carver store.

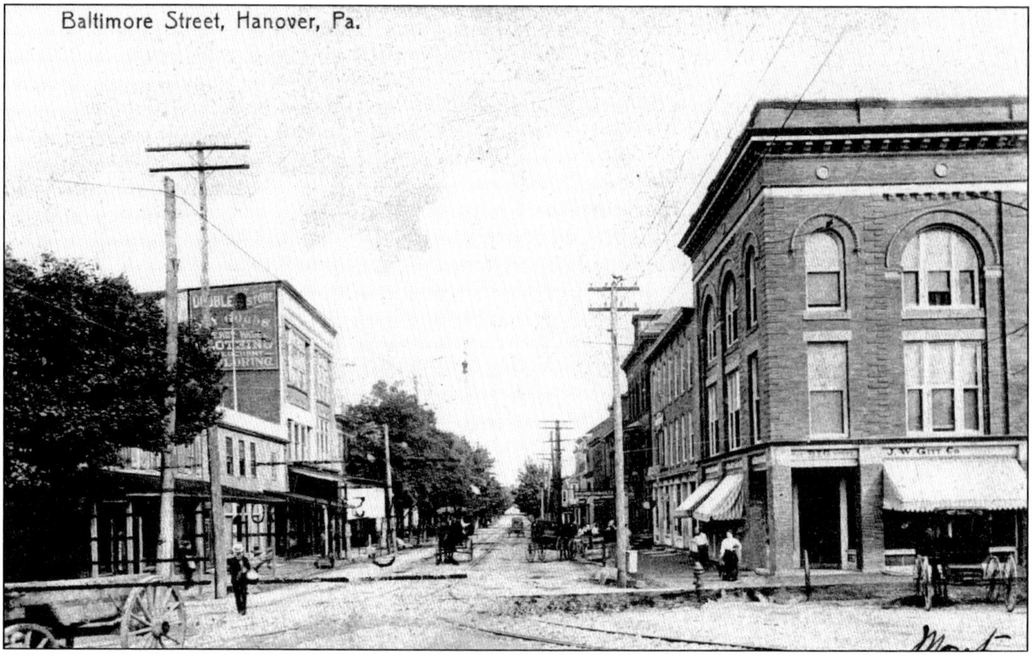

This view toward Baltimore Street shows the south side of Center Square in the foreground. The J. W. Gitt Company store is on the right. The card is postmarked August 1907.

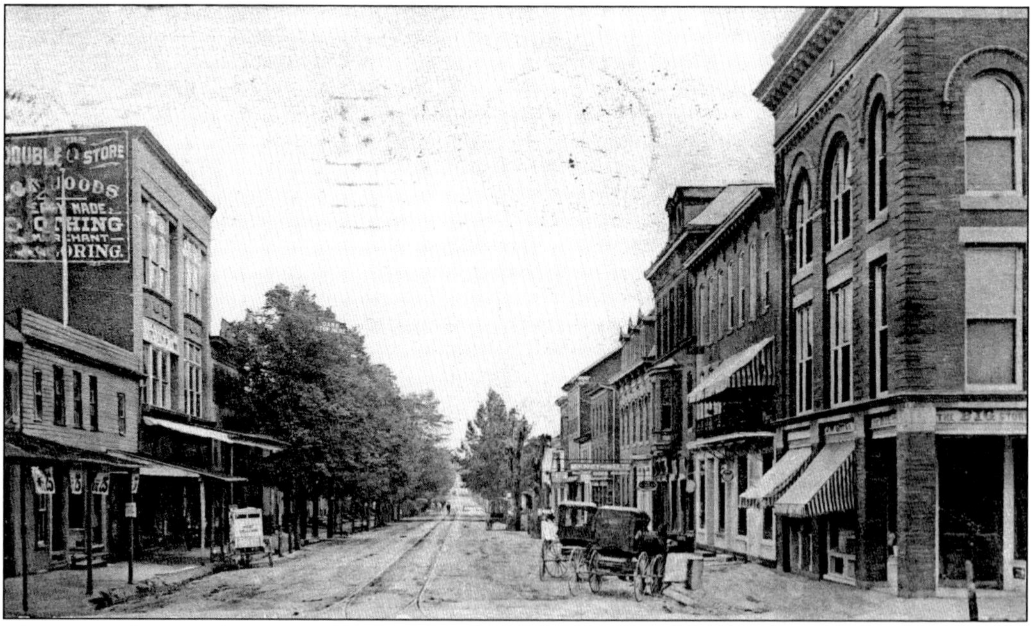

This scene shows Baltimore Street, facing south, as it exits Center Square. The corner building on the right is the Big Store, a department store later to become the J. W. Gitt Department Store. The tall building on the left side of the street was the Double O Store, later to be the N. B. Carver and Sons Department Store. The lettering on the rear of the white buggy on the left reads "meat delivered." This card was published by J. W. Fischer and is postmarked October 11, 1911.

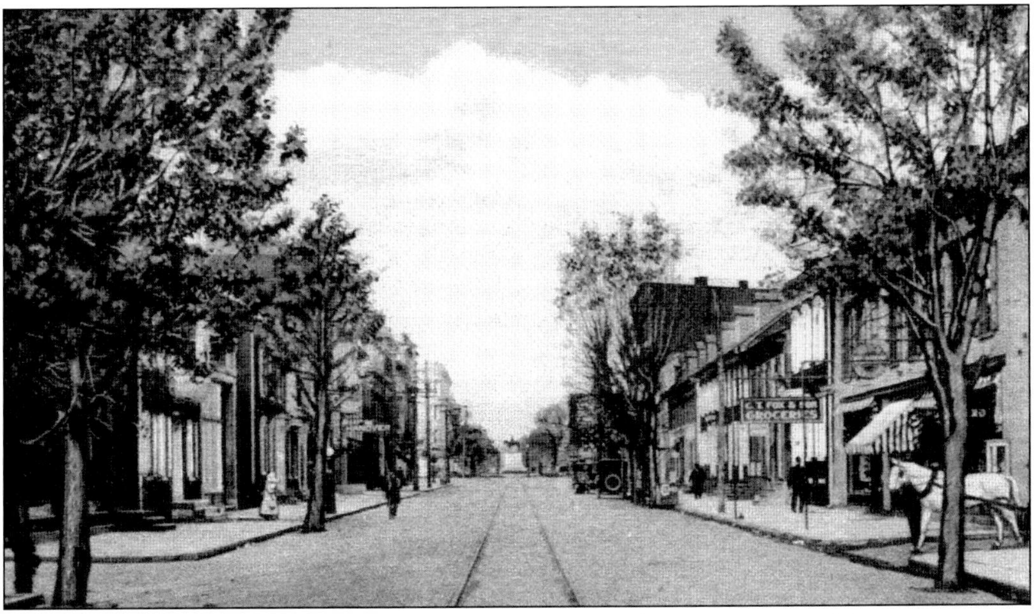

This Baltimore Street scene, looking north from West Walnut Street toward the square, shows C. T. Fox and Son Grocers on the right at 40 Baltimore Street, and the Hanover Theater at 29 Baltimore Street on the left. It was published by David Kaufman of Baltimore and was mailed June 6, 1934, but the scene on the front dates from much earlier.

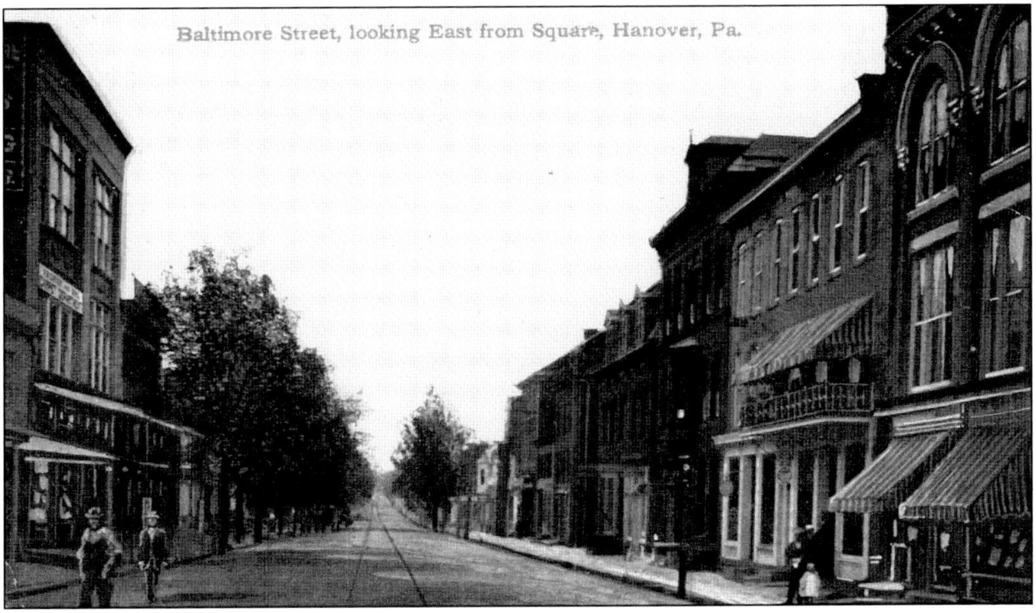

This view of Baltimore Street, looking south (not east as the postcard has printed) from the square, shows the Gitt building on the right and the Carver store on the left. The postcard was mailed October 25, 1911.

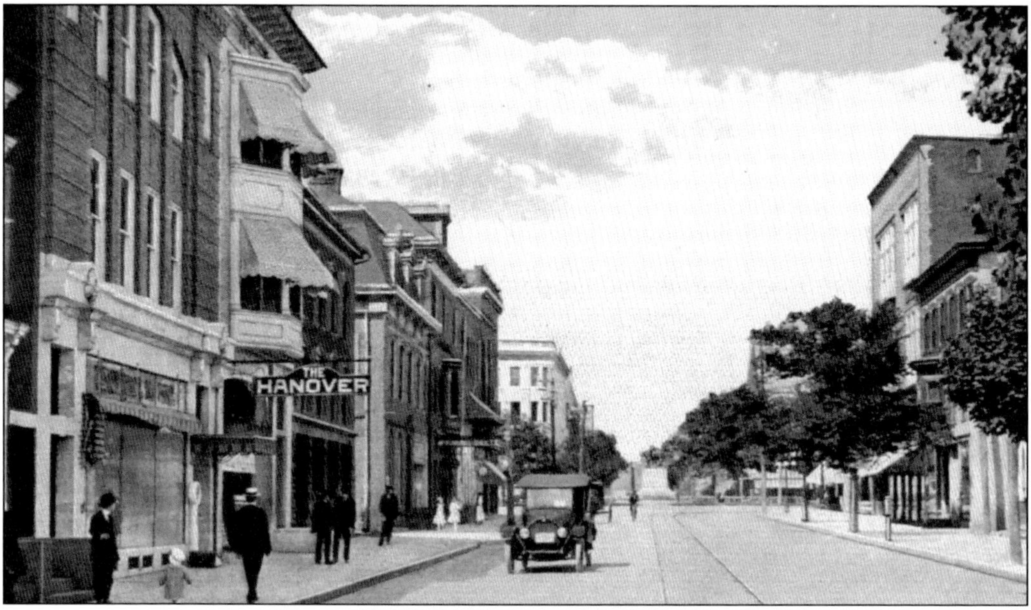

This *c.* 1915 image shows Baltimore Street looking north toward the Hanover Theater and the entrance to Farmers State Bank at the overhang below the awning.

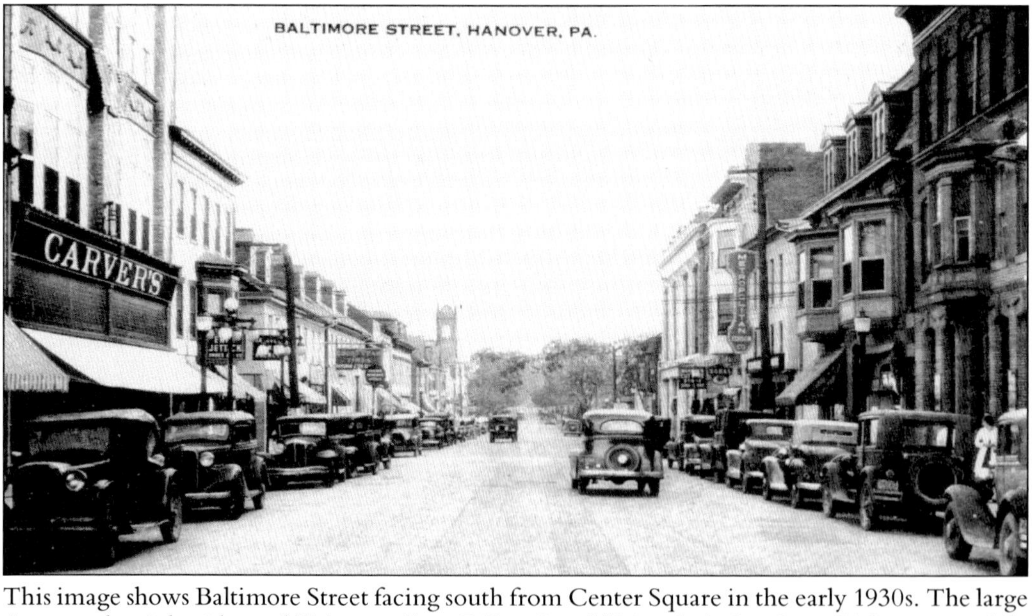

This image shows Baltimore Street facing south from Center Square in the early 1930s. The large signs on the right side read "Metropolitan Edison" and "Murphy's Cut Rate." The automobile traveling south appears to be a 1932 Plymouth. On the left side of the street is Carver's Department Store, Dave Anthony's "Enna-Jettick" shoe store, Haines the Shoe Wizard shoe store, and Goodyear Tire. In the background on the left side is the steeple of St. Joseph's Catholic Church. This card is a salesman's sample card from the Art-Vue Company of New York.

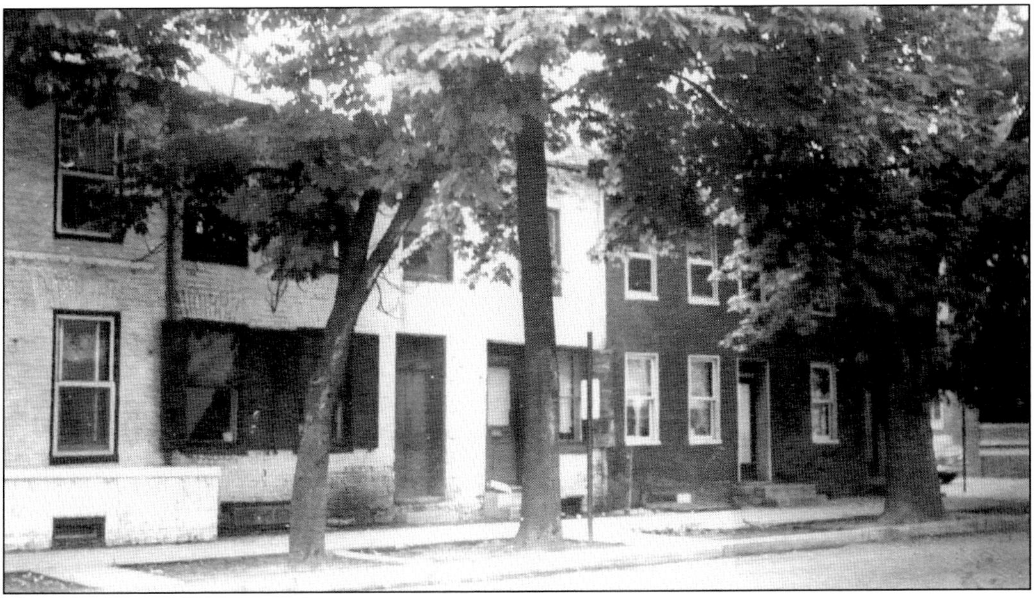

The house of the founder of Hanover, Richard McAllister, was at the northeast corner of Baltimore and Middle Streets. The McAllister house has been demolished, and the space is now occupied by the Hanover News Agency.

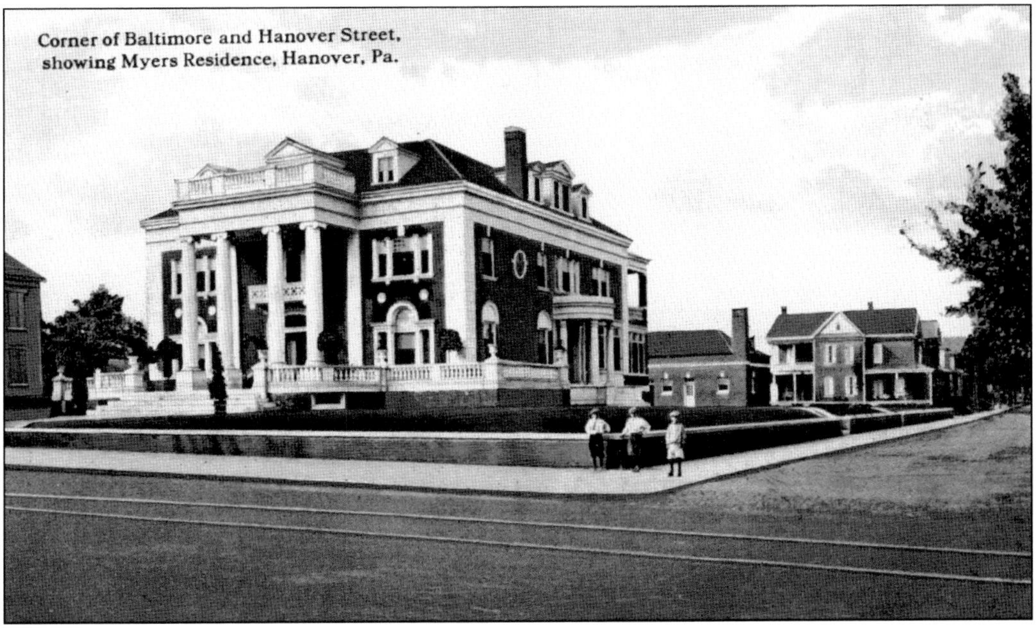

The home of Clinton and Ethel Myers was on the southwest corner of Hanover and Baltimore Streets. Clinton Myers was a co-founder of the Hanover Shoe Company. The house still stands and is now known as the Myers-Warehime mansion.

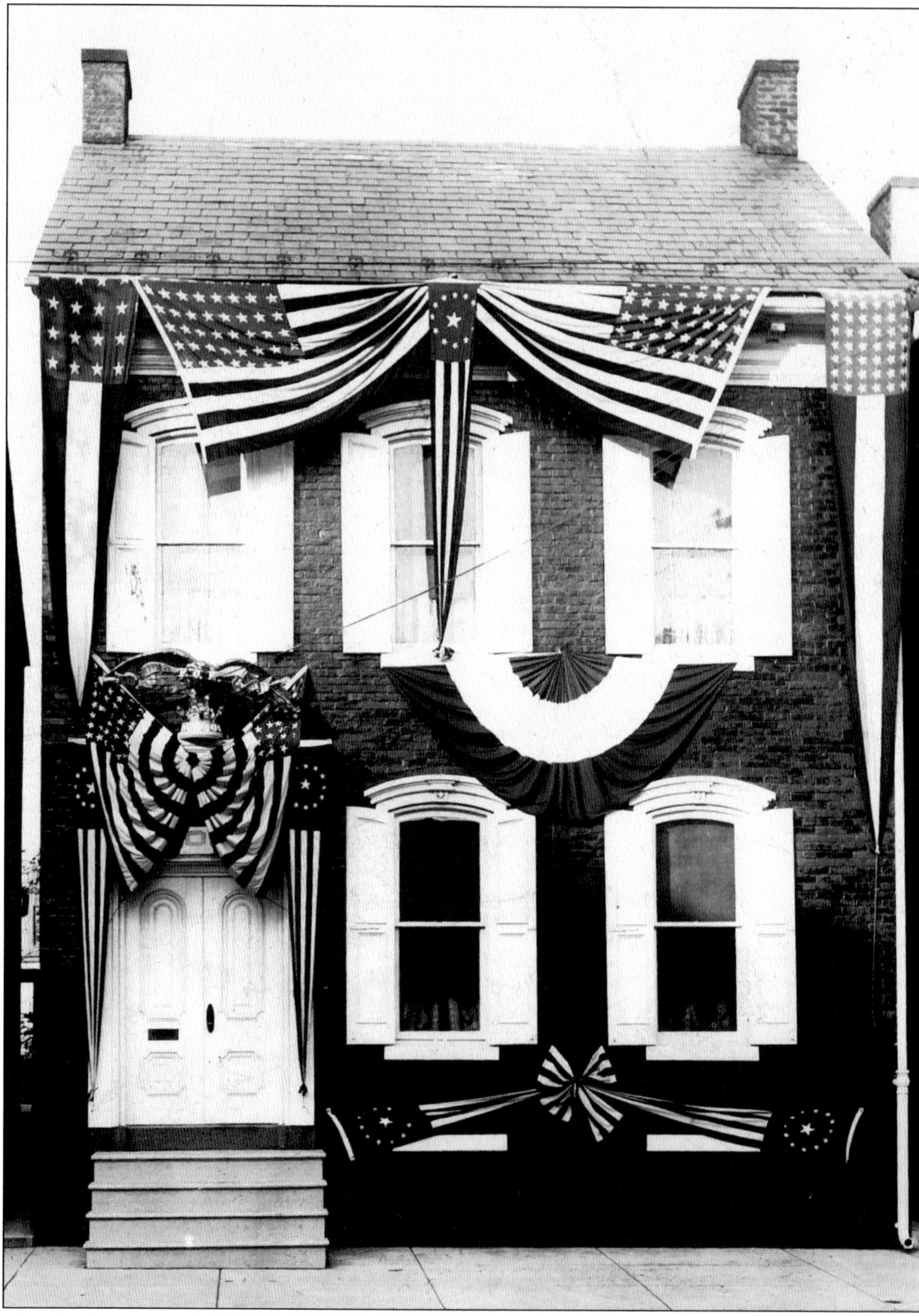

This building served as the lodge for the Fraternal Order of Eagles and was located at 38 Baltimore Street. Note the lodge insignia over the door. The stamp box indicates the card was made between 1904 and 1918.

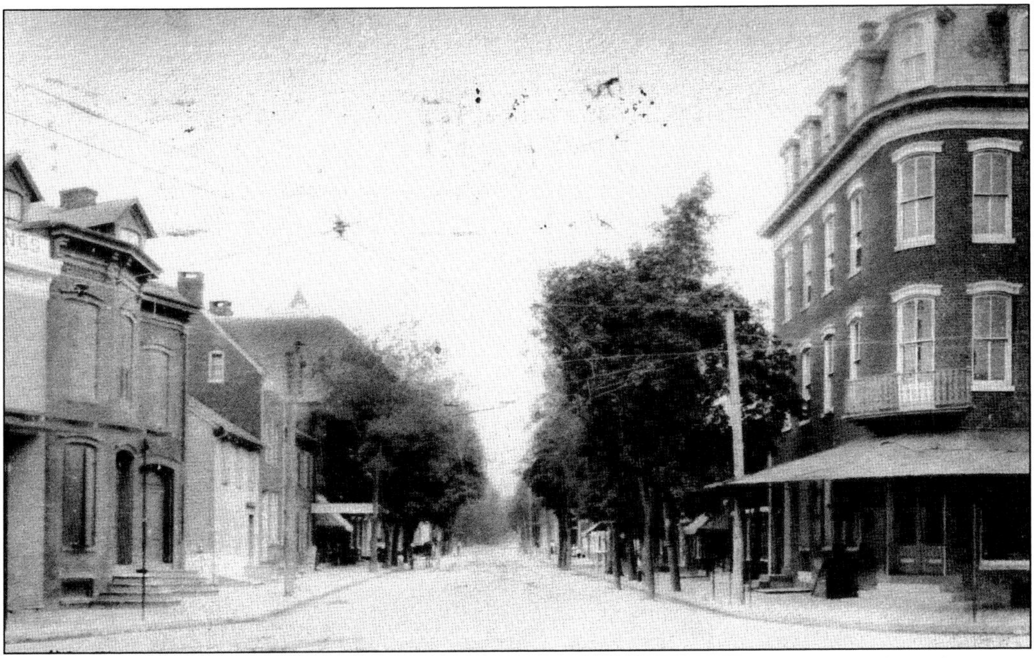

Abbottstown Street was later named Broadway. The brick building on the right still stands. It was known as the Sprenkle building and at one time housed the People's Bank. This color postcard from J. W. Fischer was mailed September 6, 1910.

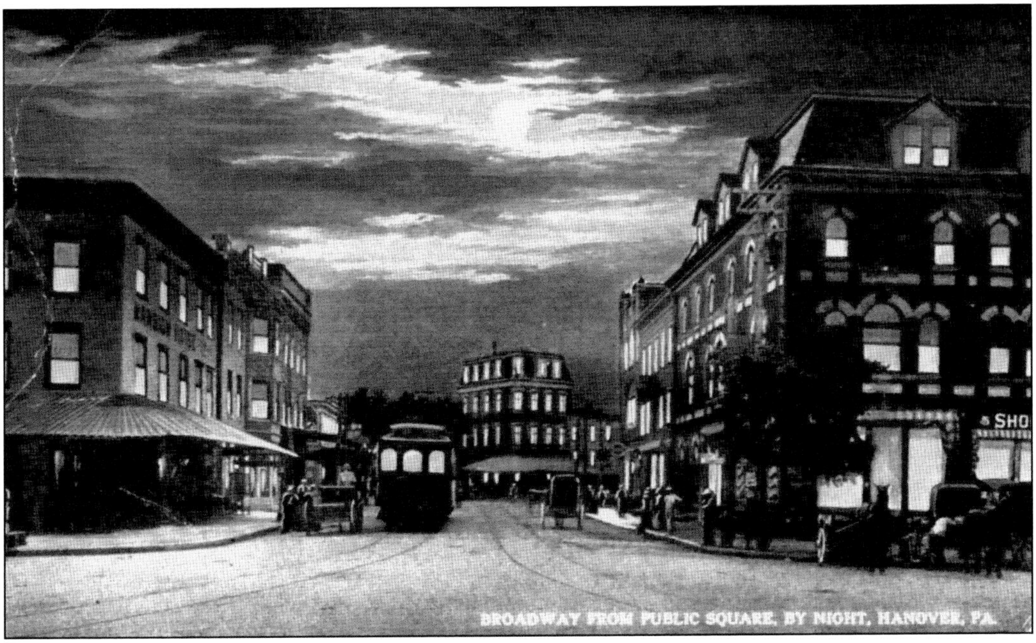

This night view shows Broadway from the public square, with the Mansion House Hotel on the left and the Sprenkle building at the York Street intersection. The trolly is awaiting freight and passengers for a return trip to York.

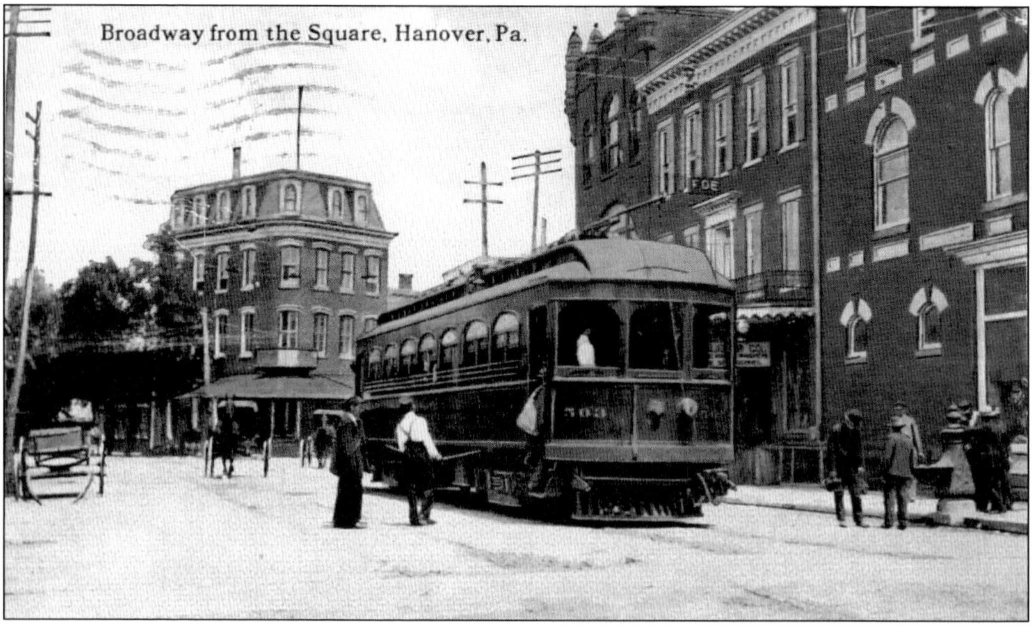

This image of Broadway from the square shows the Hanover terminus of the York trolley line. Note the F. O. E. sign on the building just above the front of the trolley. The tall building with the finials is the Tanger building on Broadway near York Street.

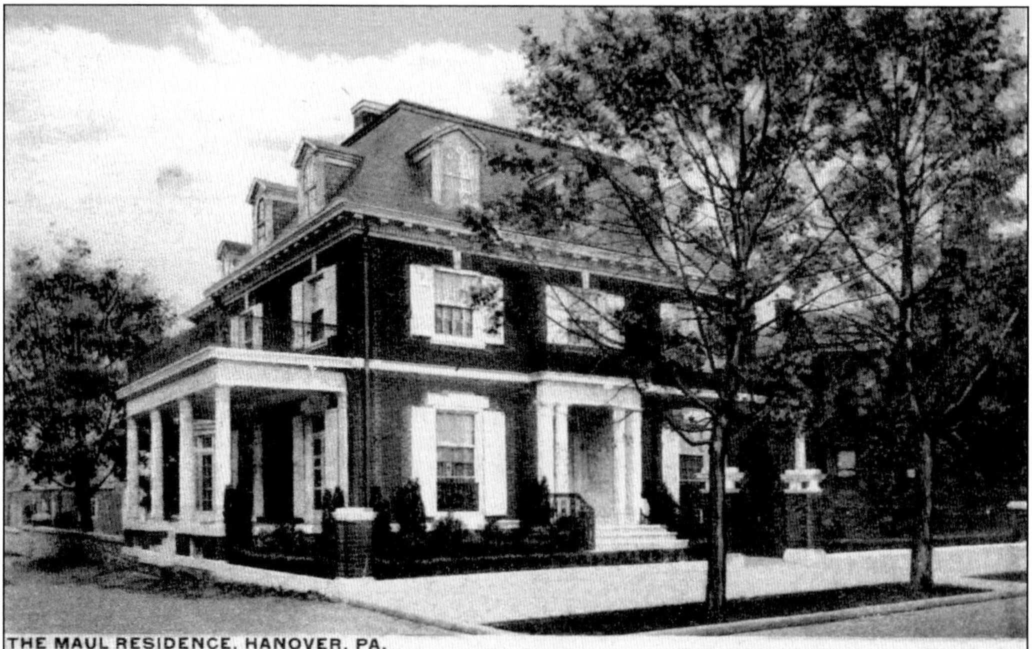

The Maul (Moul) residence, located at 216 Broadway, is now the home of Borough manager Bruce Rebert. This postcard by David Kauffman of Baltimore was postmarked March 26, 1922.

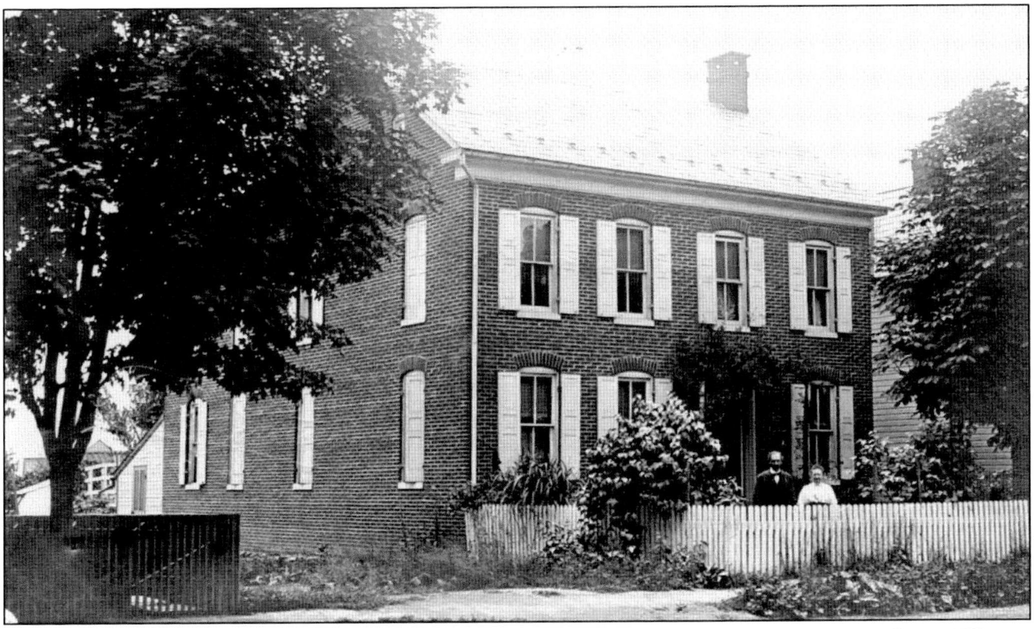

Eli and Lydia Flickinger were photographed in front of their residence at 643 Broadway. Eli was an agent for the Utica Heater Company. The card was postmarked June 30, 1909.

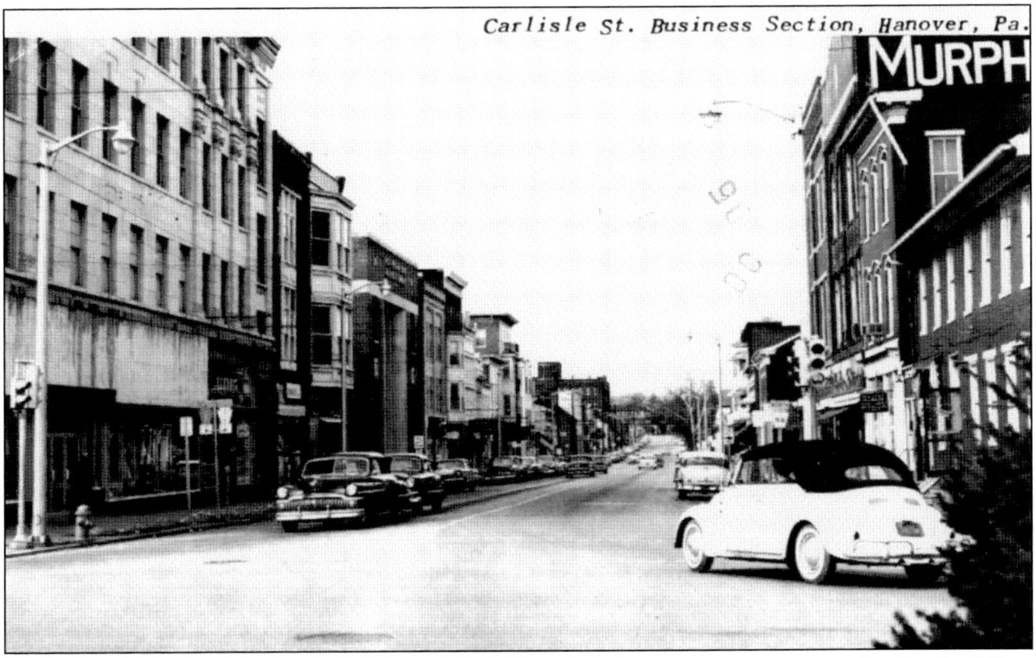

This is the business section of Carlisle Street looking north from the square. The first building on the left is the Sheppard and Myers building. The Hanover Shoe Factory building is in the center background.

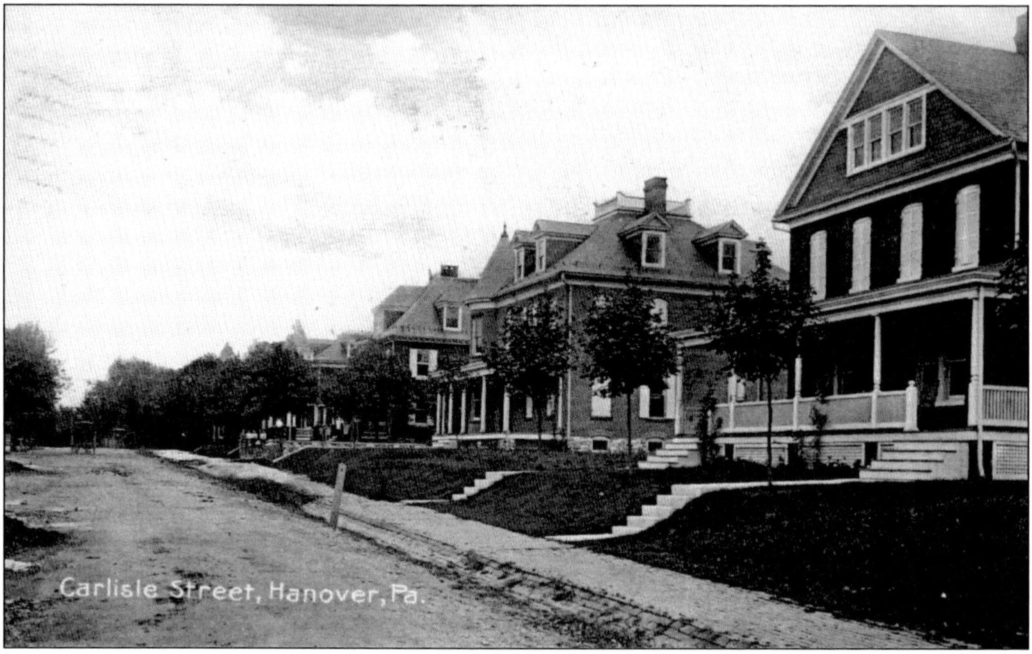

Bunker Hill is the area of Carlisle Street between Third Street and the top of the hill at Stock Street. This postcard of Carlisle Street, looking south toward Bunker Hill, was mailed July 24, 1911.

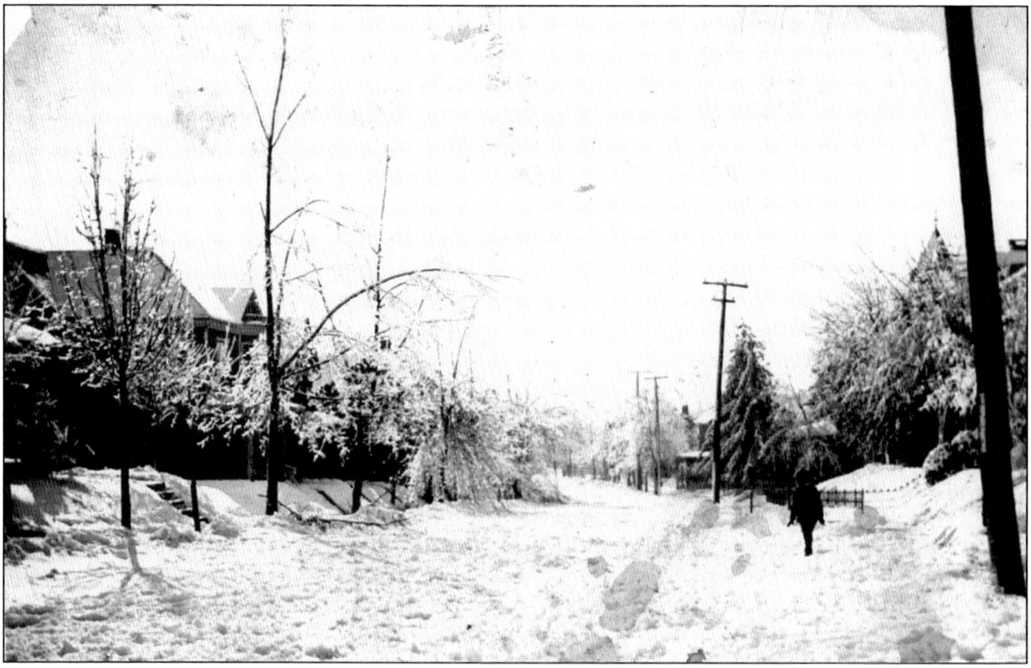

Bunker Hill on Carlisle Street is seen here covered in snow. The photograph was taken by Swords Brothers. The stamp box indicates the card was made between 1904 and the 1920s.

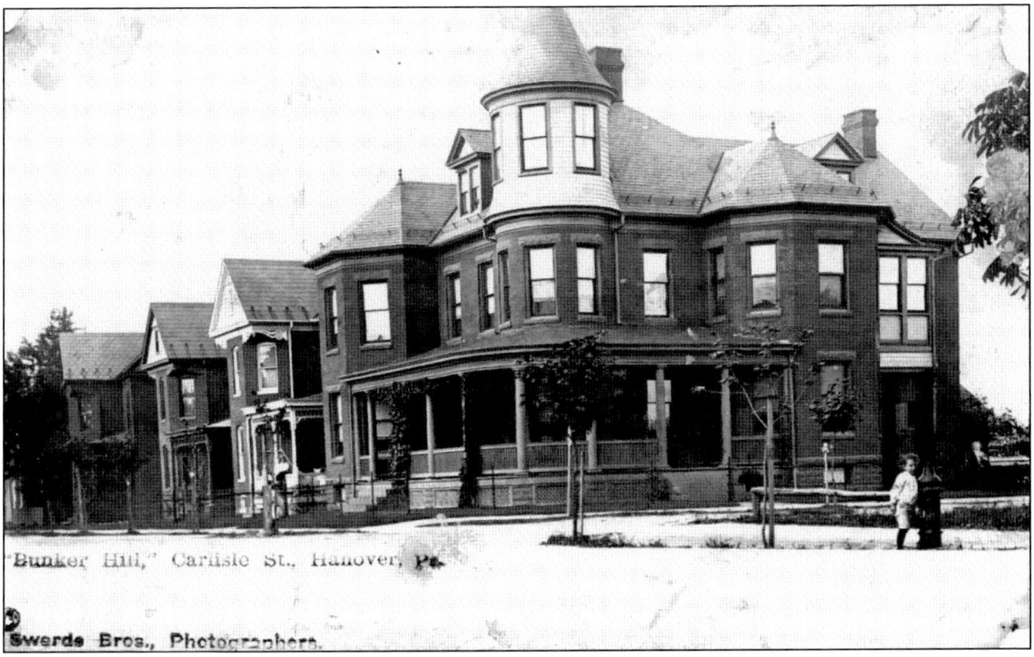

This view shows Bunker Hill on Carlisle Street looking north to Stock Street. The house was the Seibright property and later the home of James Gulden, a former president of the Hanover Area Historical Society. The photograph was taken by Swords Brothers and was printed between 1903 and 1906.

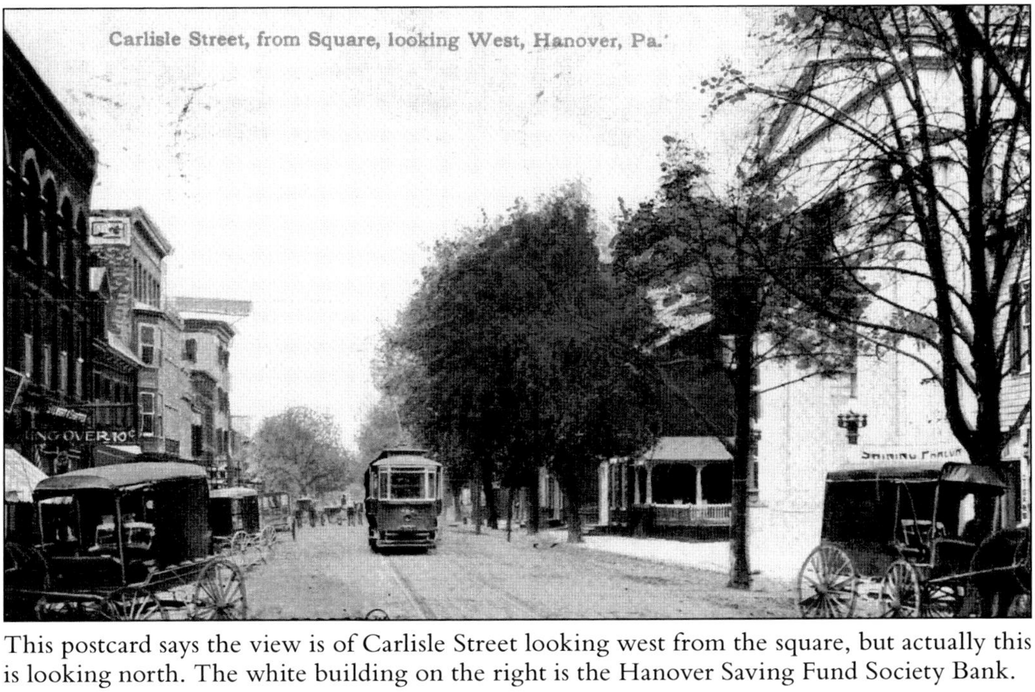

This postcard says the view is of Carlisle Street looking west from the square, but actually this is looking north. The white building on the right is the Hanover Saving Fund Society Bank.

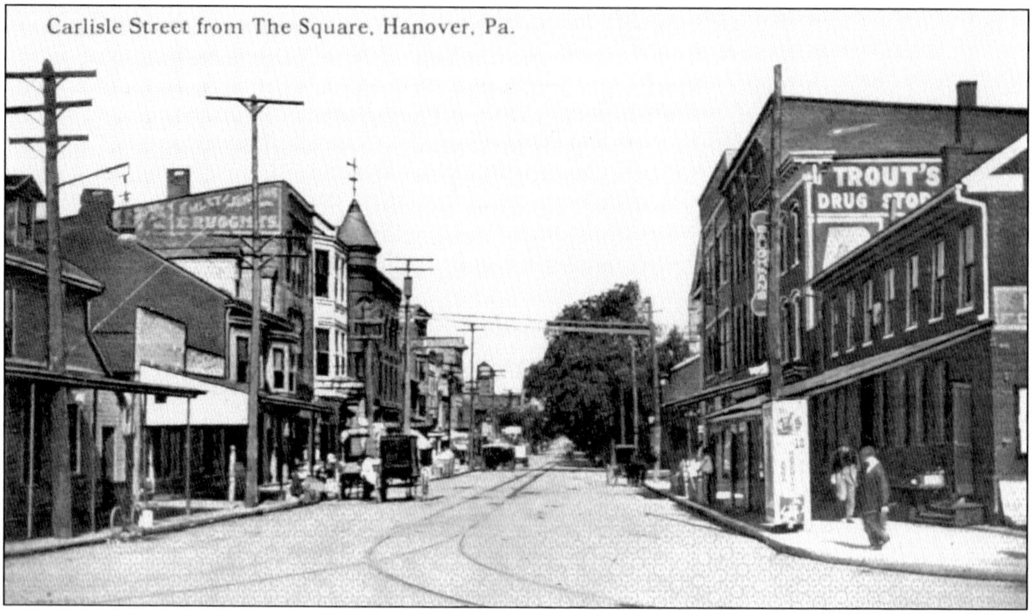

Carlisle Street is seen looking north from the square. This postcard was mailed June 22, 1912.

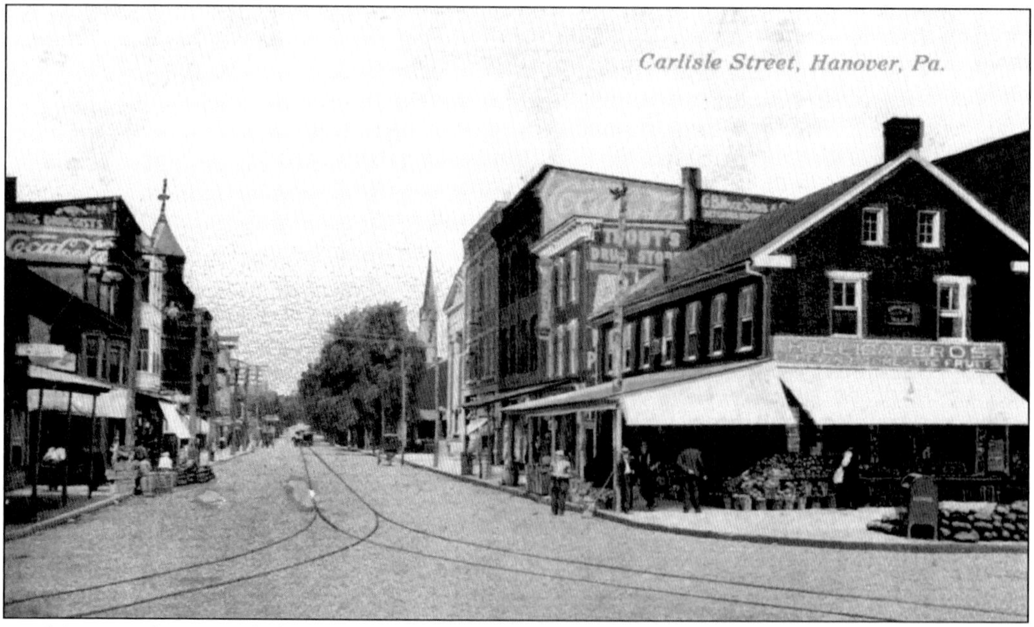

Looking north on Carlisle Street, the Holliday Green Grocery is on the corner with the St. Mark's Lutheran Church spire in the center background. The postcard has an interesting message on the back. The writer states that she "put up" 18 quarts of peaches that day and now they have 89 quarts "put up." The card was dated December 3, 1911. One wonders where she got fresh peaches in December.

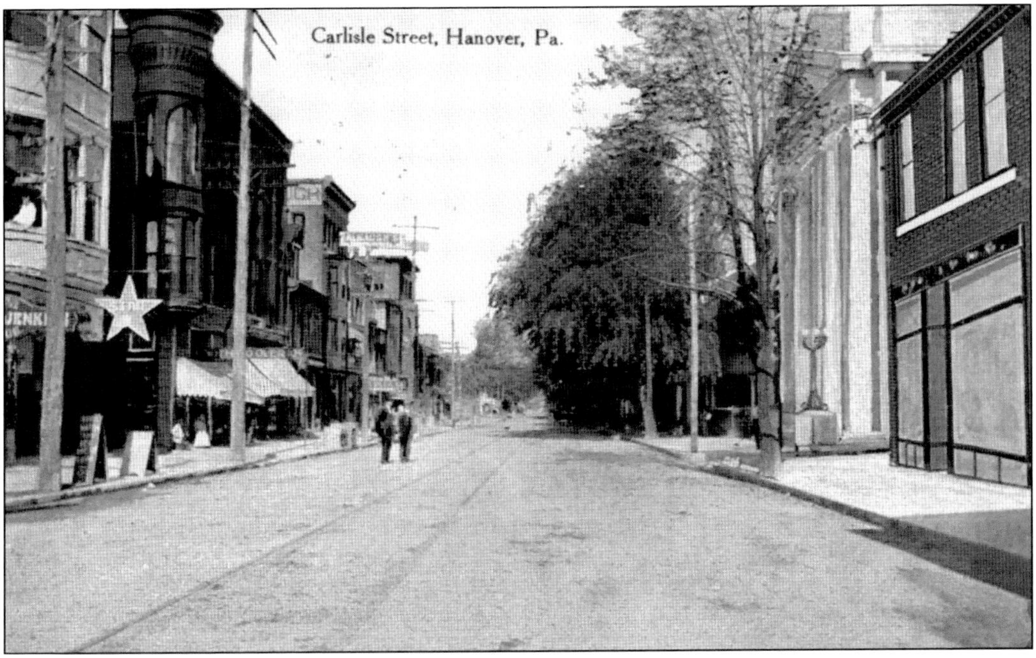

This view of Carlisle Street shows the Hanover Saving Fund Society Bank building on the right. On the left are the Star Theater and Hotel Aubaugh. The card was mailed November 9, 1910.

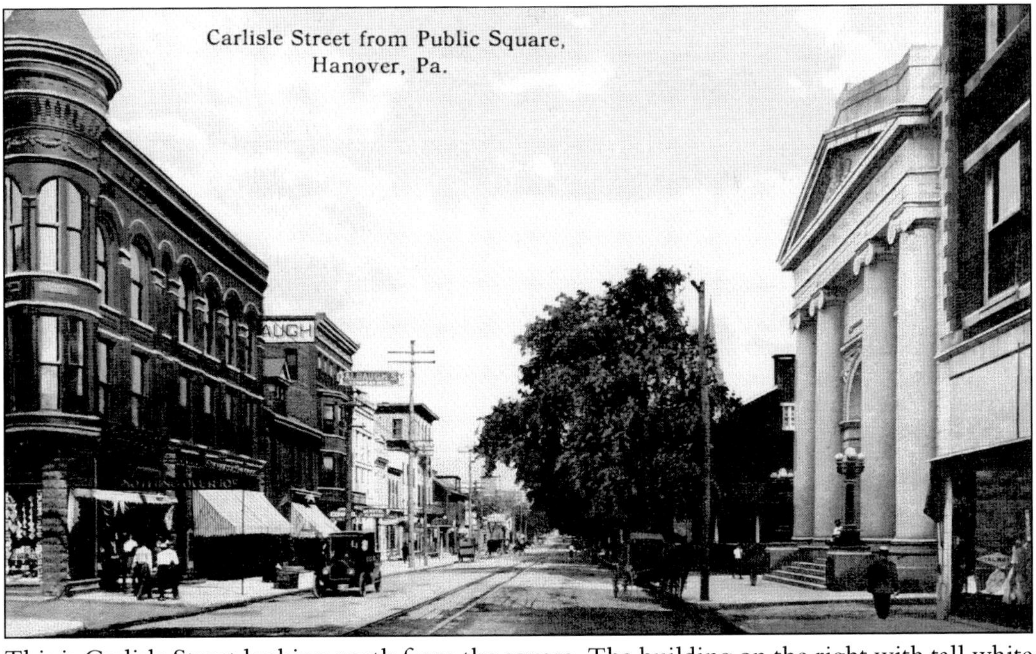

This is Carlisle Street looking north from the square. The building on the right with tall white columns was built as the Hanover Saving Fund Society Bank in 1906. The building with the sign, on the left side of street, was the Hotel Aubaugh. This was taken during the transition period from the horse to the automobile.

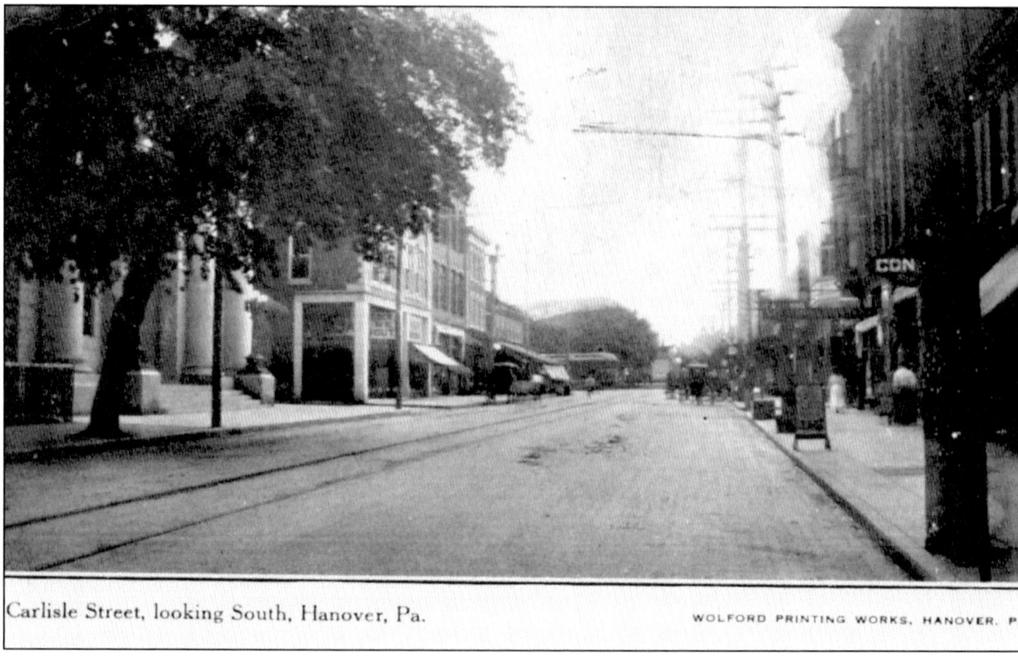

This image of Carlisle Street looking south toward Center Square was published by Wolford Printing Works of Hanover. On the right is Conrad's Shoe Store. On the left is the Saving Fund Bank and Baughman's Drugstore, with the Battle Monument in the center background. The card was mailed in May 1912.

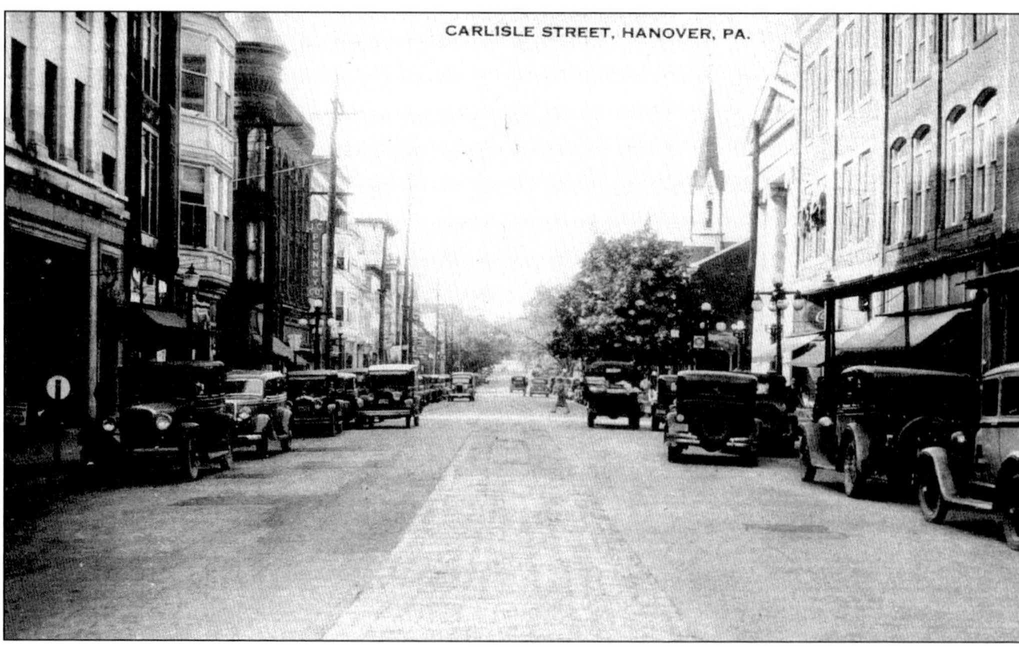

This view, looking north on Carlisle Street, shows St. Mark's Lutheran Church in the background and J. C. Penney on the left. The photograph is from the early 1930s. The card is an Artvue Card Company salesman's sample.

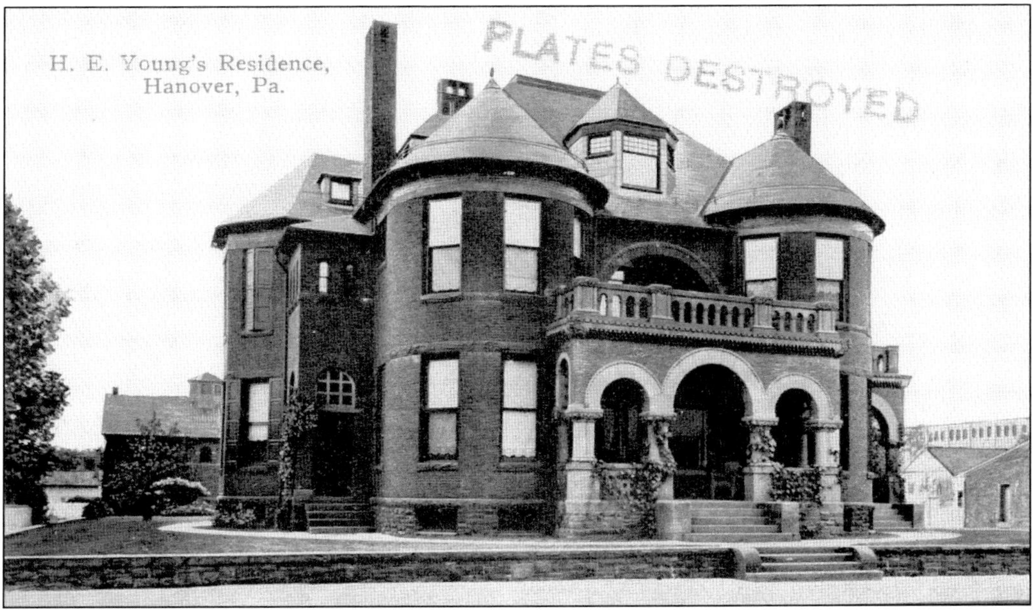

H. E. Young's residence was located in the second block of Carlisle Street. The building is still in use as commercial office space. The row of small windows on the right side is part of the Hanover Shoe Factory on Park Avenue. This postcard is a salesman's sample to jobber J. W. Fischer. Note the ink stamp says "plates destroyed," yet the original negative survives.

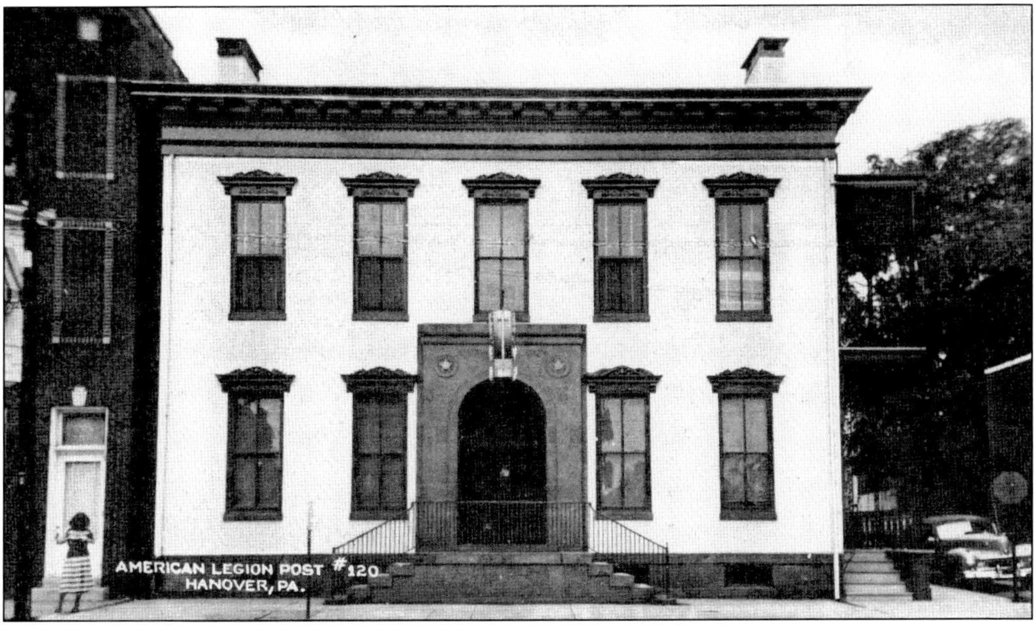

The American Legion Post No. 120 was located north on Carlisle Street at Park Avenue. The legion post is still at the same location, though now in a new building.

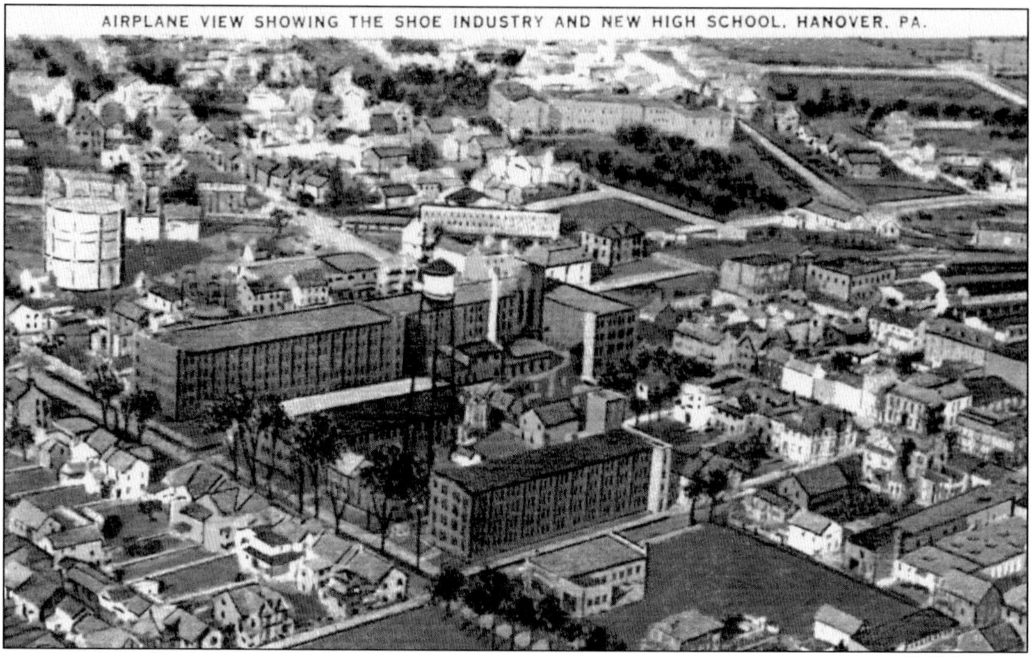

An aerial view shows the shoe industry and new high school in Hanover. This postcard was published by E. Madciff of Hershey, Pennsylvania.

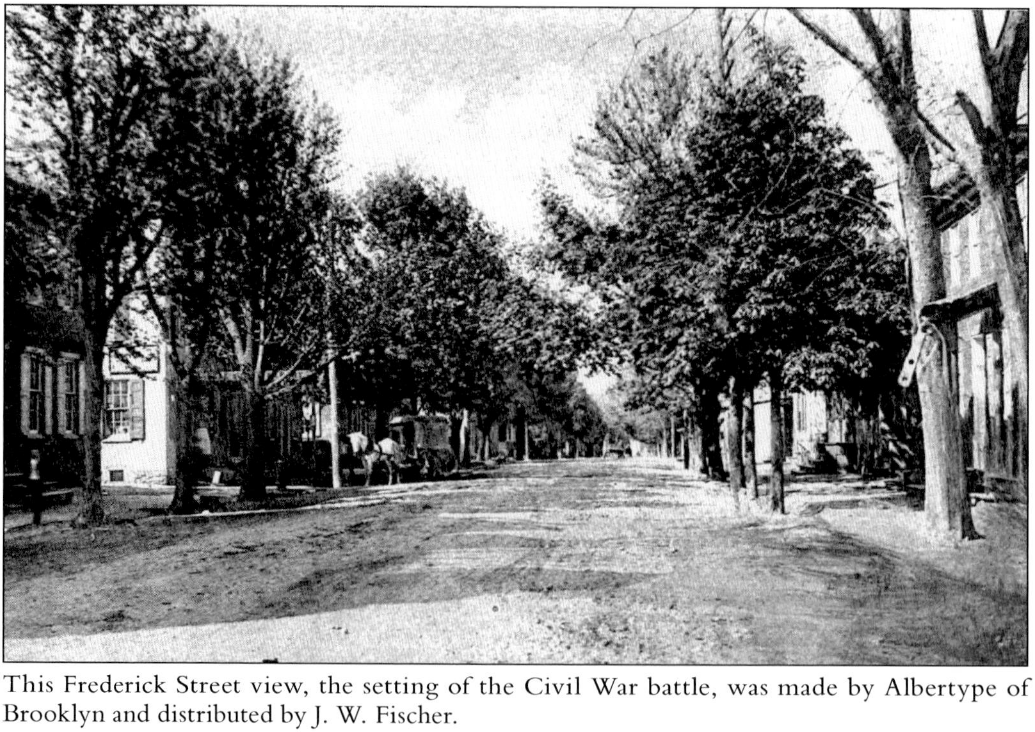

This Frederick Street view, the setting of the Civil War battle, was made by Albertype of Brooklyn and distributed by J. W. Fischer.

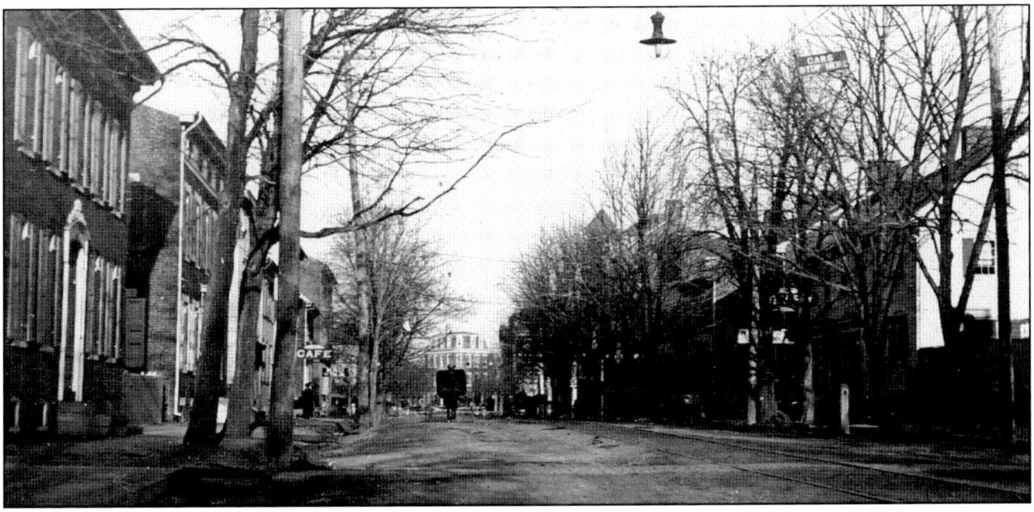

The view of Frederick Street looks east from North Franklin Street toward Center Square. The Sprenkle building is at the intersection of York Street and Broadway in the center background.

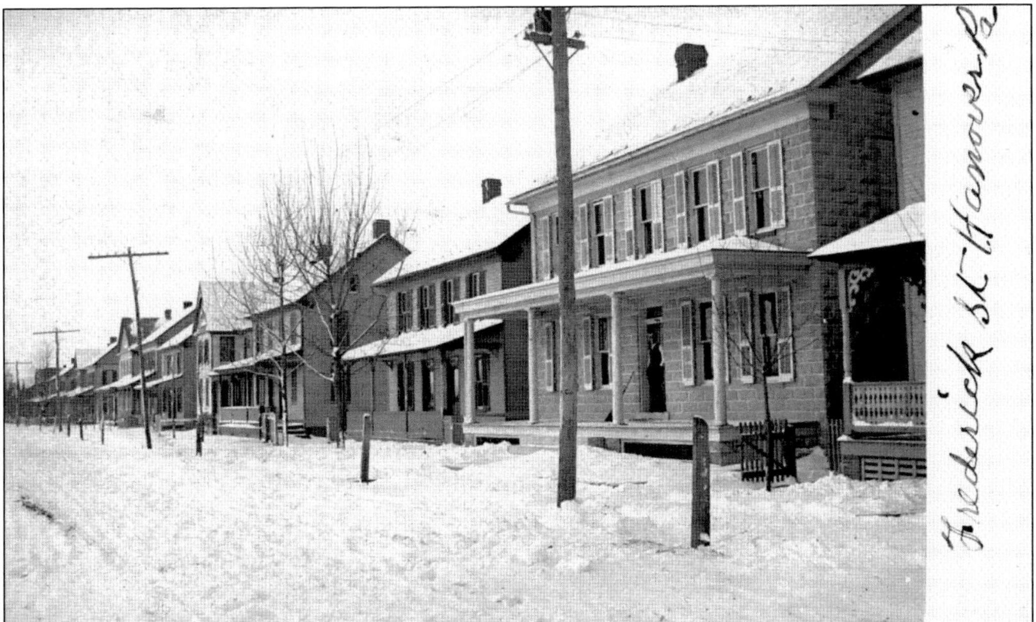

This is a photograph of the "Pennville suburb" of Hanover along Route 194 to Littlestown. There was quite a bit of snow that year!

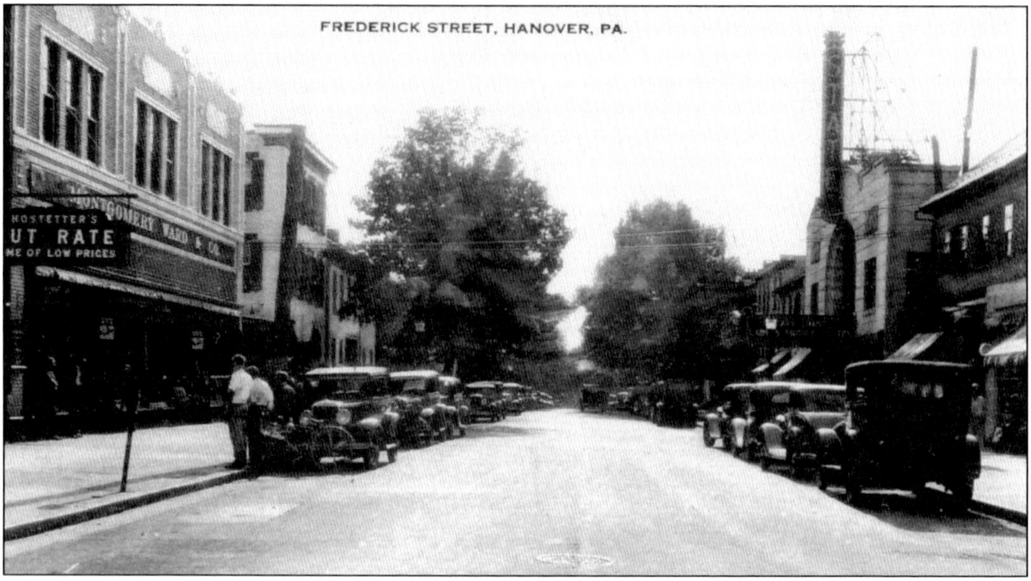

The second building on the right in this Frederick Street view is the State Theater, still standing but now in very poor condition. On the left is Hostetter's Drugstore, which is still there but now vacant. The Montgomery Ward store, an art deco building, is still standing but with no tenants. The next building, which looks to be leaning to the front, was Swopes Butcher Shop, now long gone and replaced with a municipal parking lot. This Artvue salesman's sample card dates from the late 1920s to early 1930s.

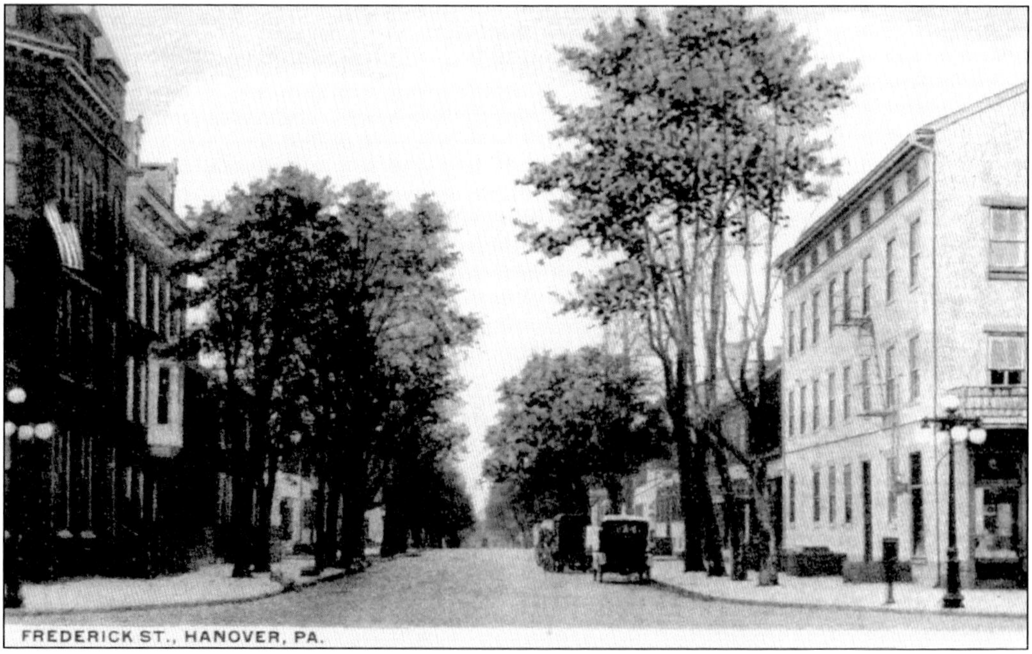

This view, looking west on Frederick Street, shows the People's Bank on the left with the flag and the Central Hotel on the opposite side.

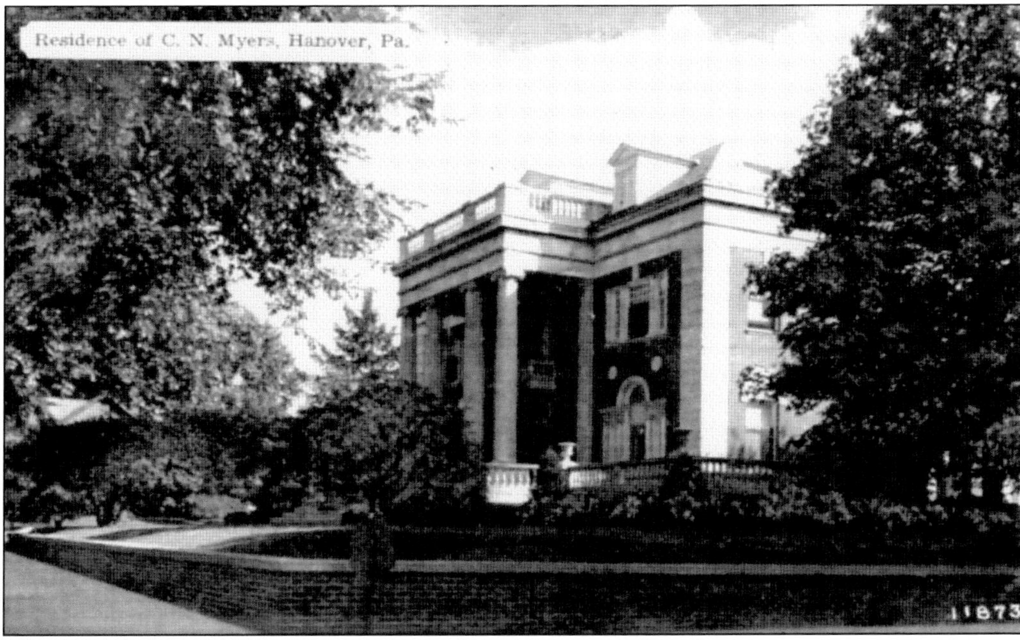

The residence of C. N. Myers, one of the co-founders of the Hanover Shoe Company, is at the southwest corner of Baltimore Street and Hanover Street. This card was made for C. H. Stallman and Son of Hanover.

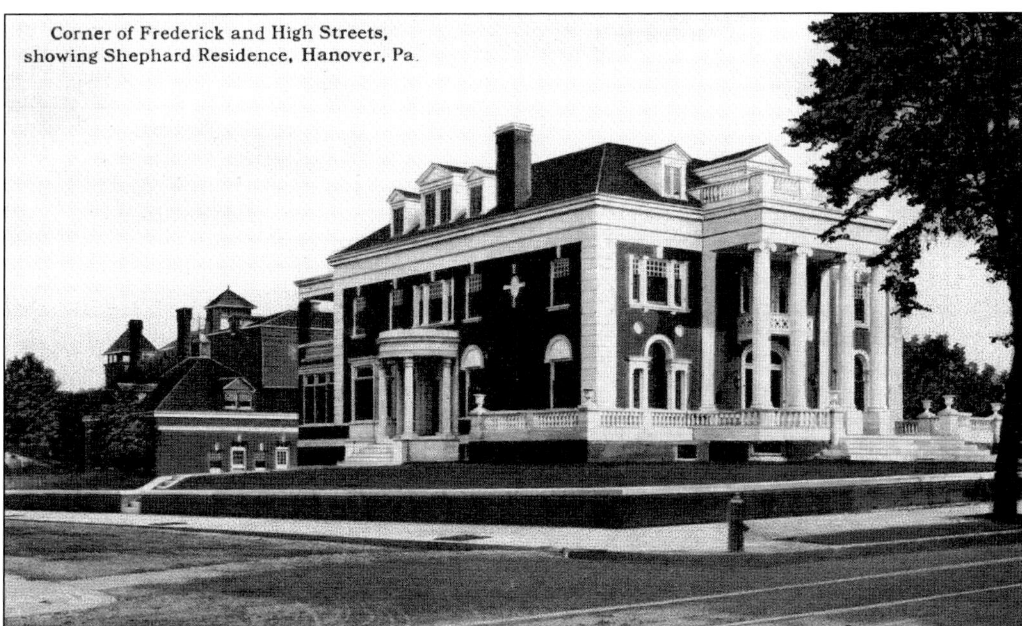

The Sheppard residence is at the northeast corner of Frederick Street and High Street. Sheppard was a co-founder of the Hanover Shoe Company. The building with the cupolas in the left background is the Hanover Opera House.

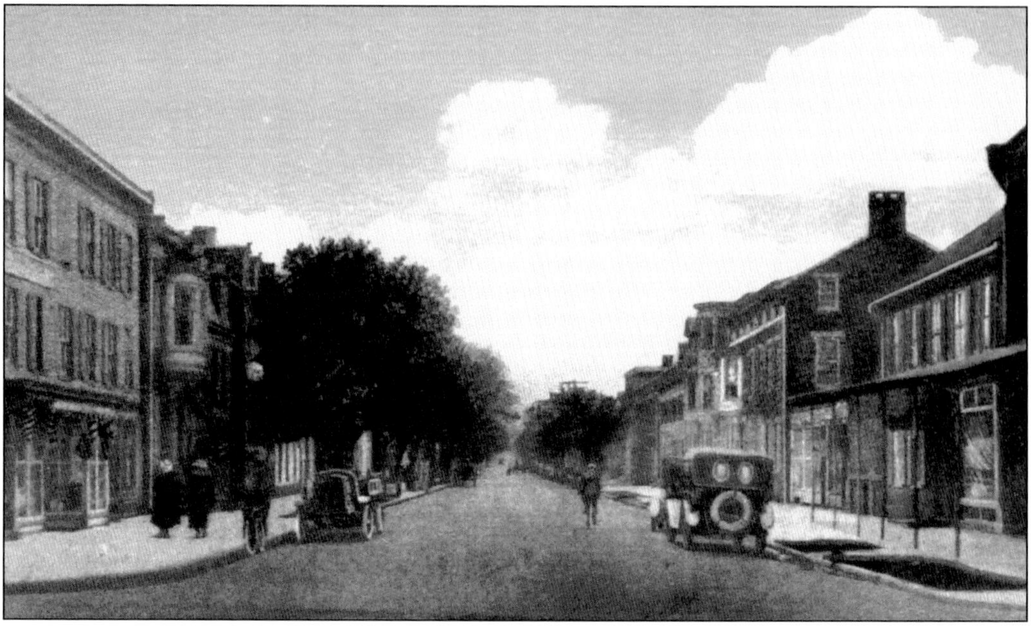

This view of York Street looks south from Broadway toward Walnut and Middle Streets. The building with the bay window on the left was the home of Dr. H. C. Ruth, dentist, the grandfather of the owner of this card collection. The picture was taken before the Hotel Richard McAllister was on the site of the right foreground.

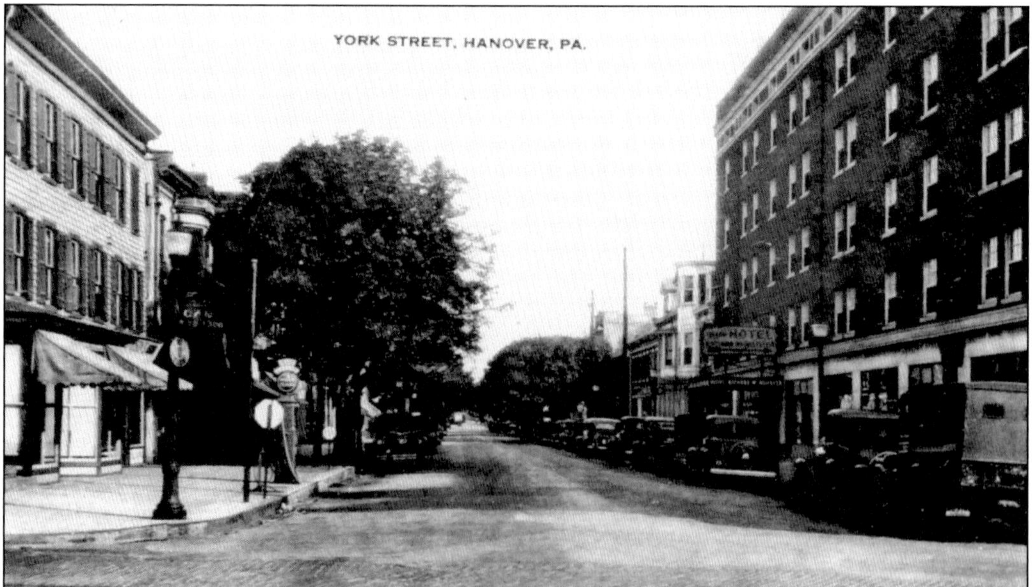

Looking down York Street from Broadway, the Hotel Richard McAllister is on the right. The photograph was taken in the late 1920s.

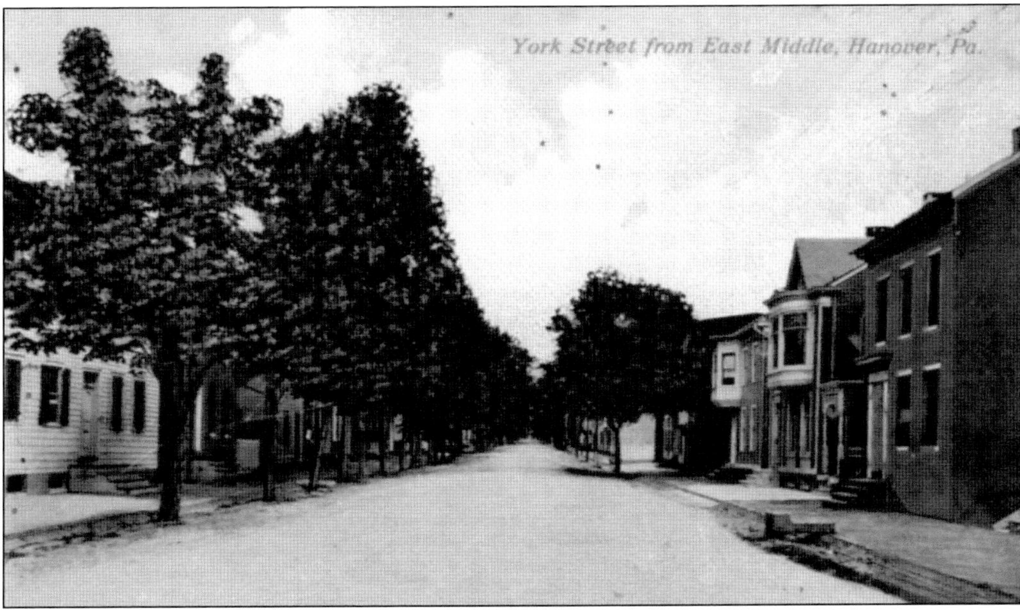

York Street is viewed looking from East Middle Street toward Hanover Street. This postcard was mailed June 9, 1922. Most of the houses are still standing.

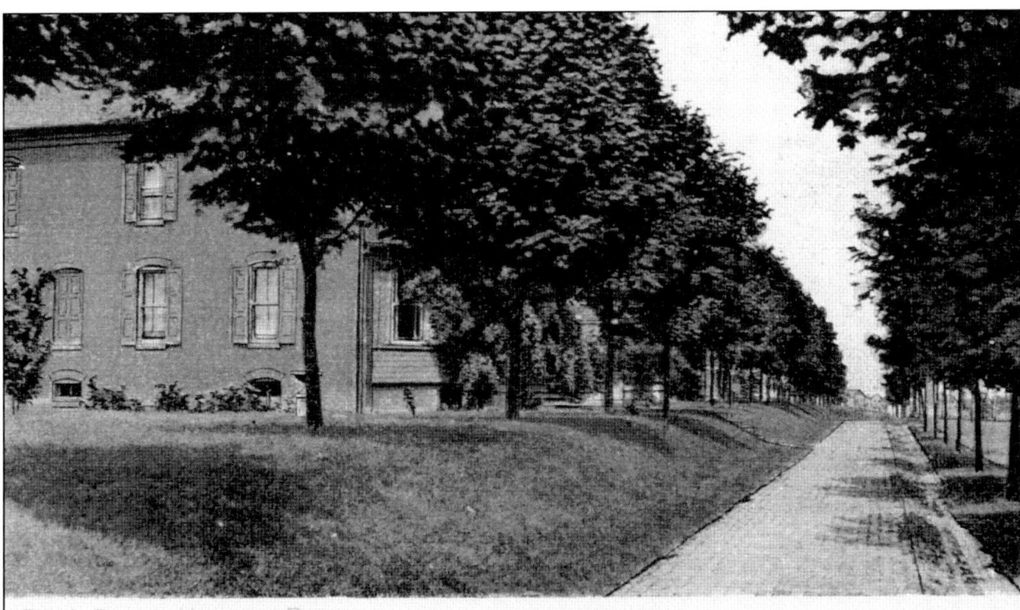

This view of Stock Street, between what is now Penn Street and Charles Street, looks west toward Carlisle Street. Note the neat brick pavement, gutter, and rows of trees. The houses remain, but the trees are gone.

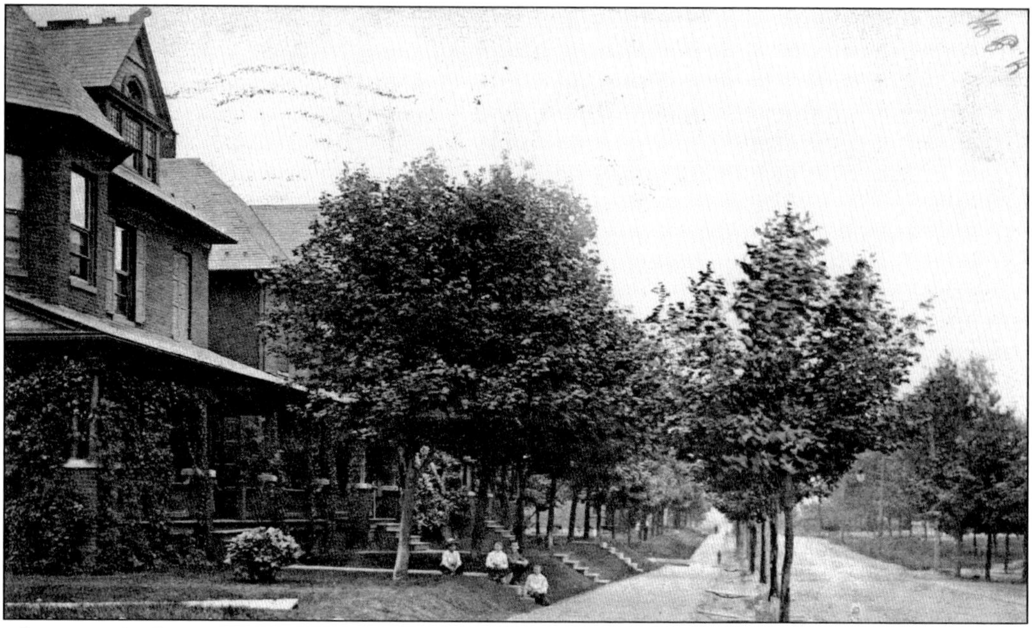

This scene looks west on Stock Street toward Carlisle Street. The postcard was mailed February 18, 1909, with a very enlightening message from one man to another man: "Dear Harry: We are all well. My sister is big and fat and I love her more every day. I wish you could see her. Good by. From Norman." This well-mannered writer was perhaps a child.

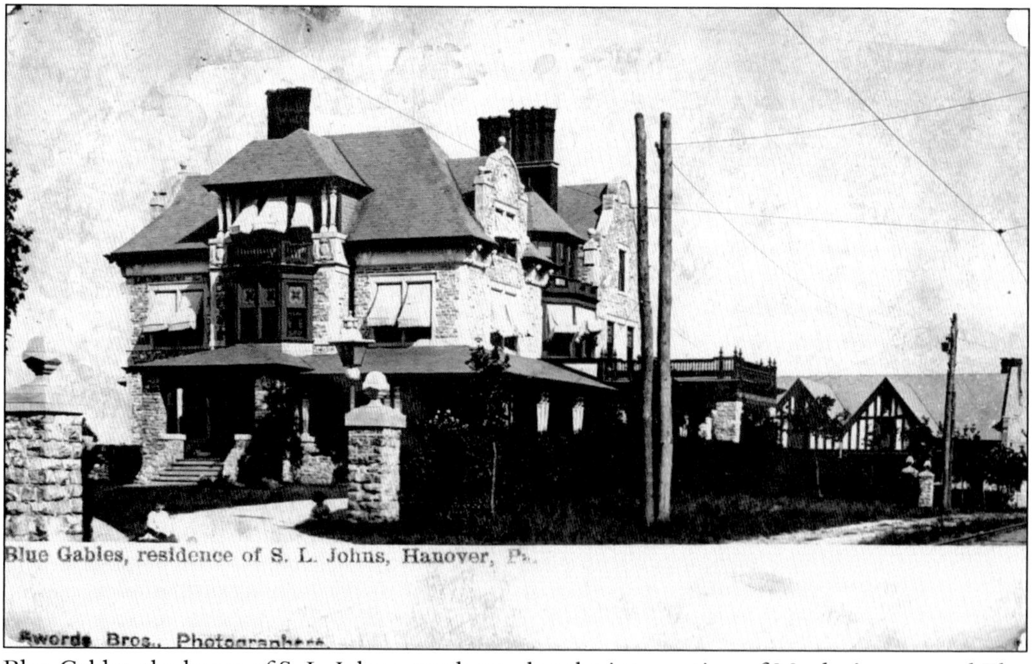

Blue Gables, the home of S. L. Johns, was located at the intersection of Maple Avenue and Elm Avenue at the edge of McSherrystown. In later years, the home became a fine dining restaurant and later was destroyed by fire. The photograph is by Swords Brothers. The stamp box indicates the card was printed between 1903 and 1906.

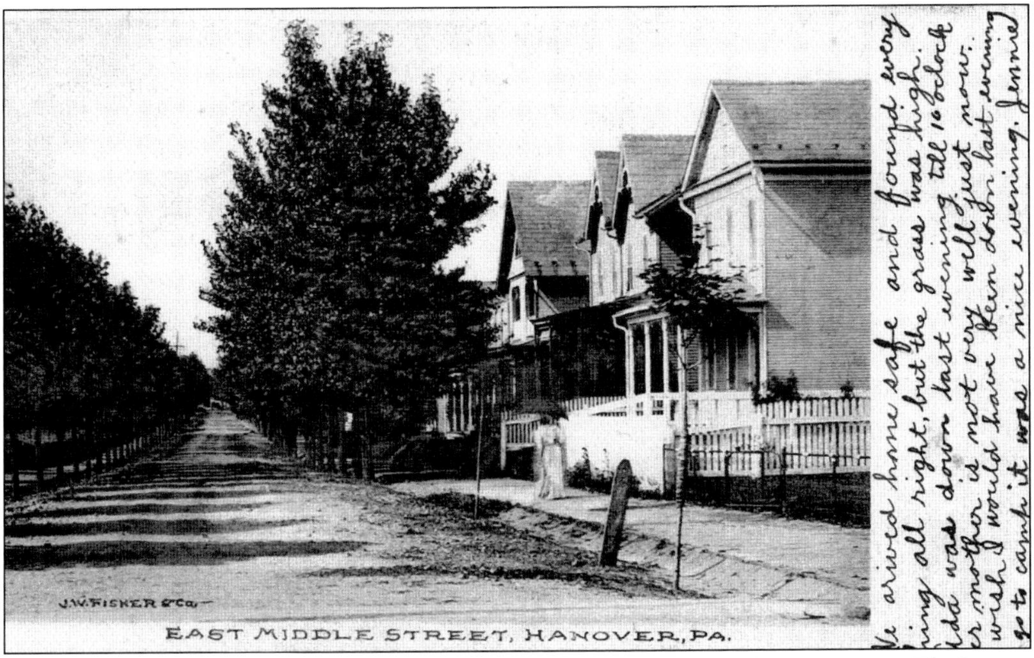

The view is East Middle Street looking west between Locust Street and Baer Avenue. The houses are still standing but the trees are gone. The card was mailed August 6, 1906.

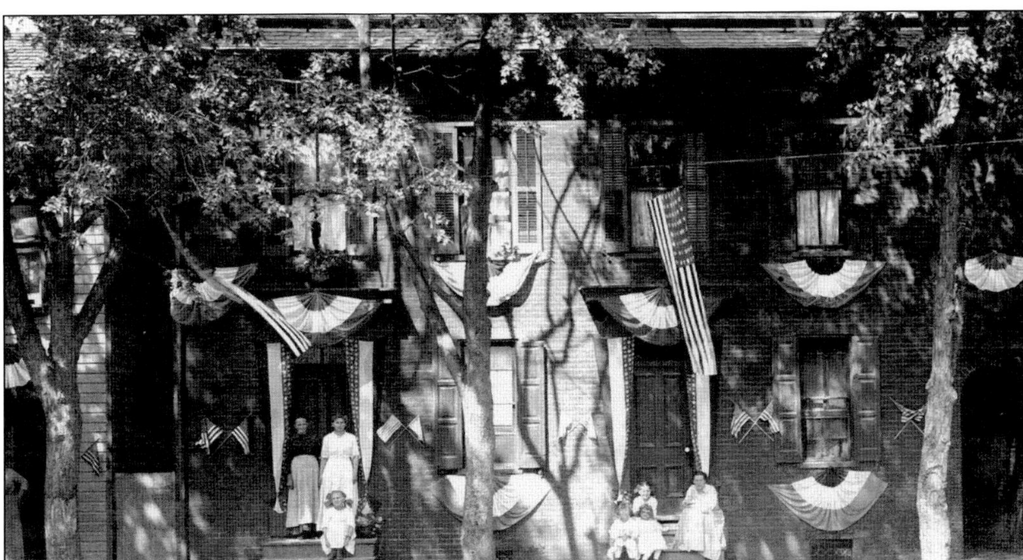

Early 1900s homes on Baltimore Street were decorated for festivities, perhaps the 1915 centennial.

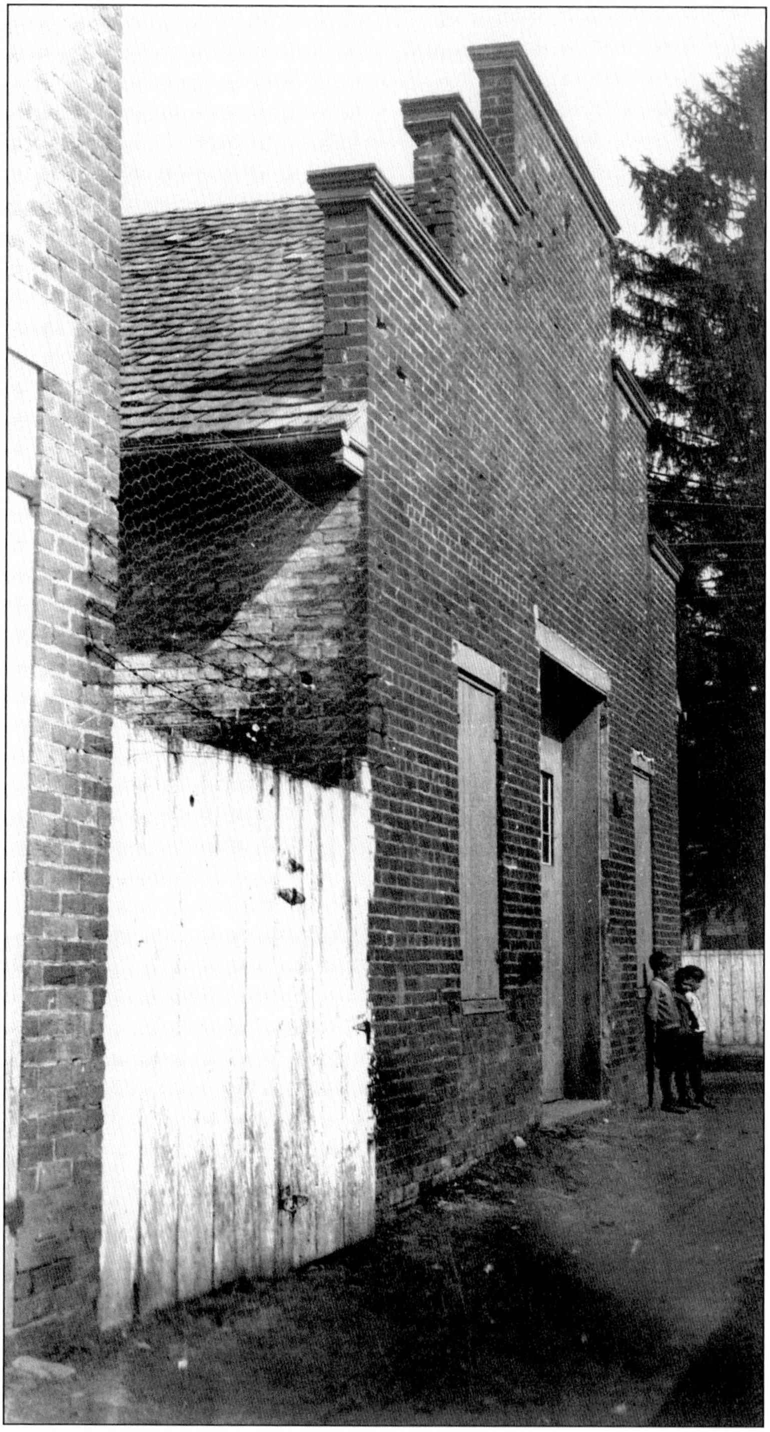

Marion Hall, at 107 East Walnut Street, was built in 1860 as an armory and drill site for the Hanover Marion Rifle Militia. It served as one of three field hospitals after the Battle of Hanover on June 30, 1863. It was torn down in March 1996 to provide additional parking for Trinity Church on York Street.

Three

RURAL SCENERY

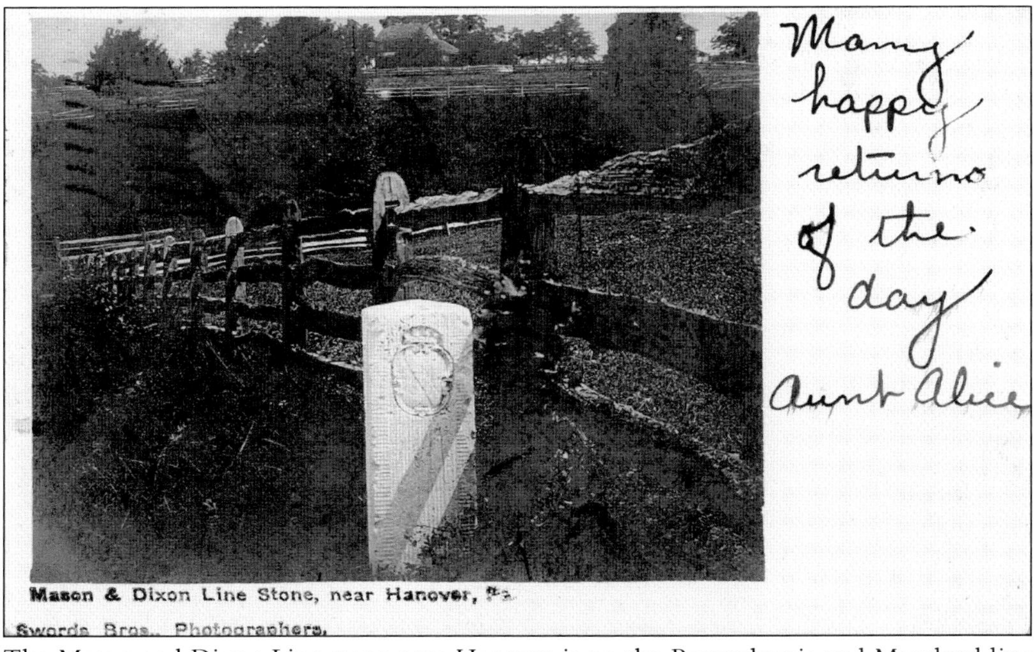

The Mason and Dixon Line stone near Hanover is on the Pennsylvania and Maryland line south of Hanover, just off the Baltimore Pike. The stone has now been secured in a protective enclosure. This postcard was mailed September 18, 1905.

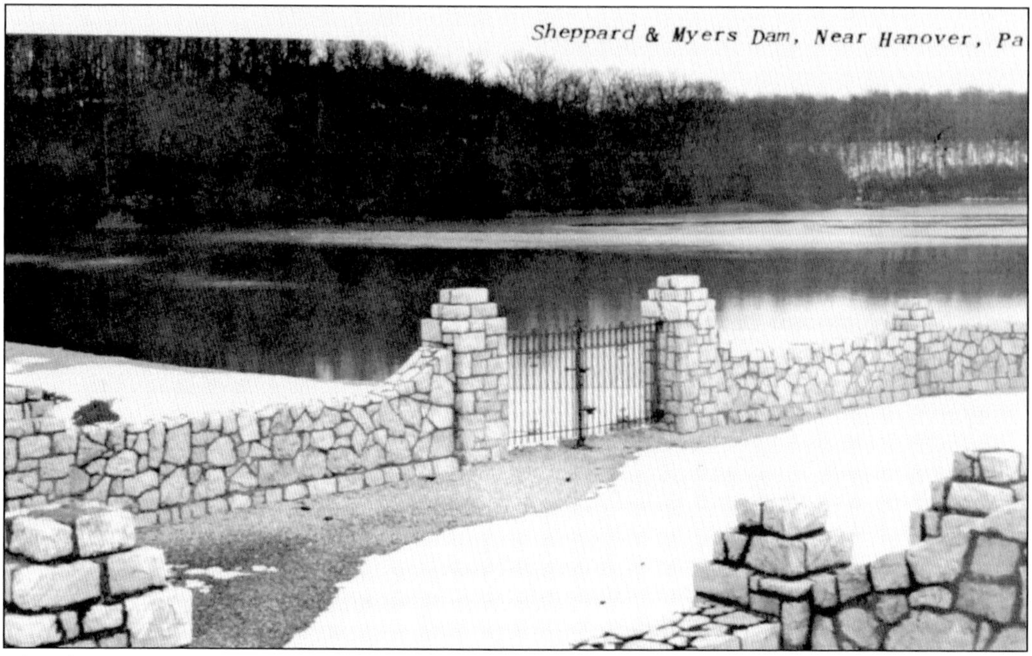

The Sheppard and Myers Dam, a municipal water supply, is near Hanover. This postcard was printed by Merrimack Post Card Company of Haverhill, Massachusetts.

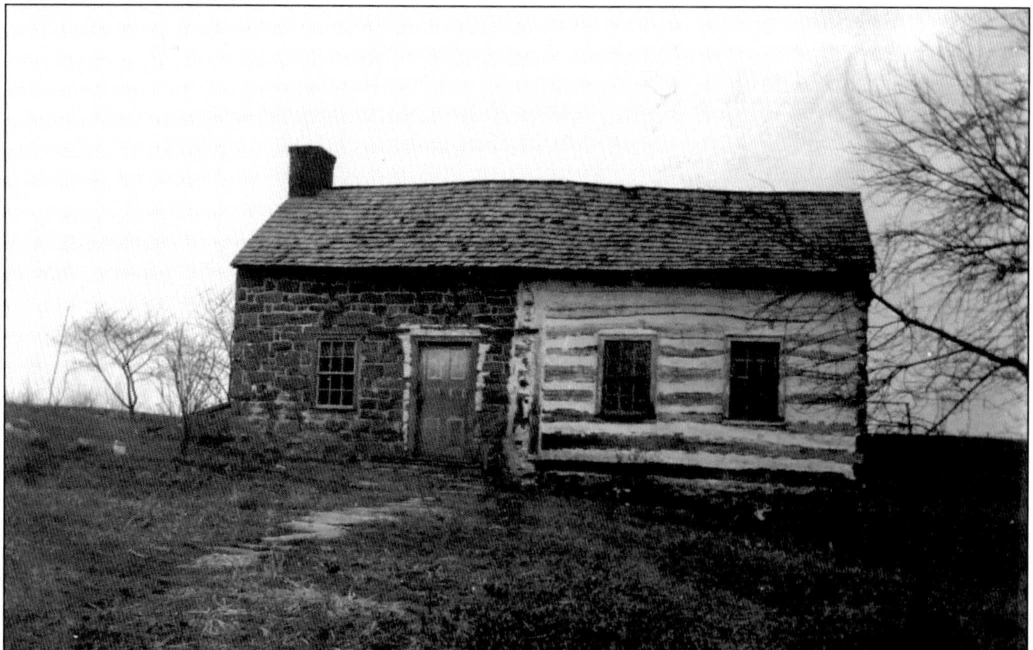
This log cabin in the Pigeon Hills is said to have been the home of the family of Harry Auchey, who had an orchard business. This card was mailed by Amanda Auchey on March 24, 1911.

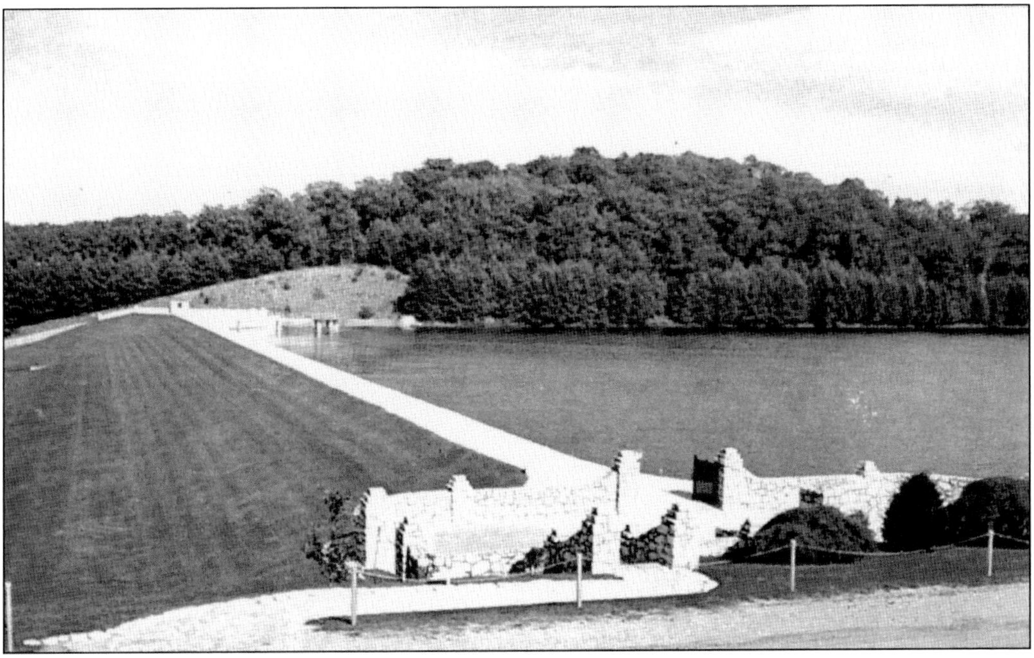
The Sheppard and Myers impounding dam was built in 1932, following a severe drought, to hold the water supply for Hanover.

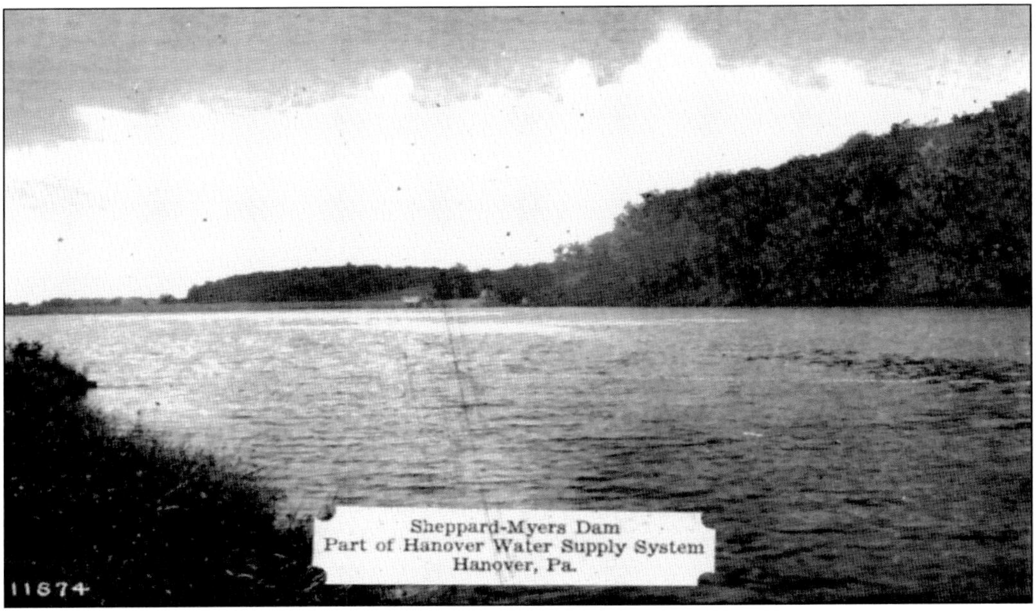

The Sheppard and Myers dam is part of the Hanover water supply system.

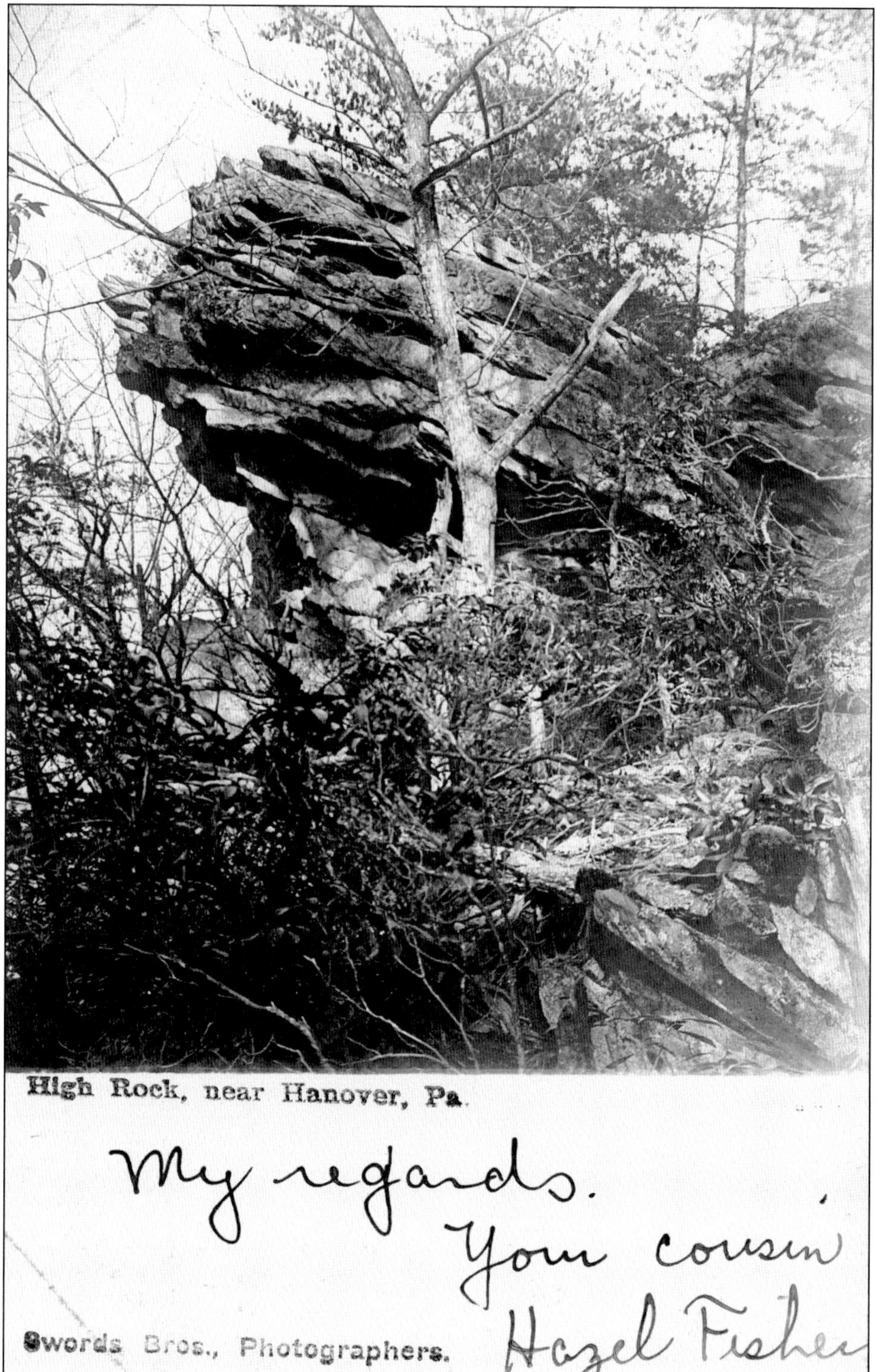

High Rock is a promontory on the north side of the Pigeon Hills. This photograph is by Swords Brothers.

Four

Society

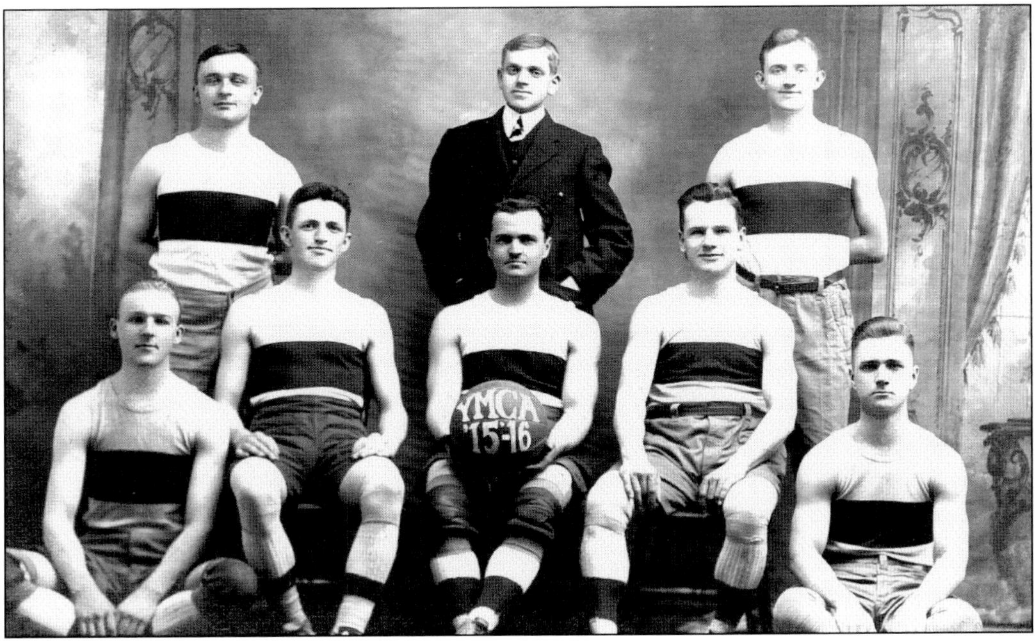

This is a YMCA basketball team for the year 1915–1916.

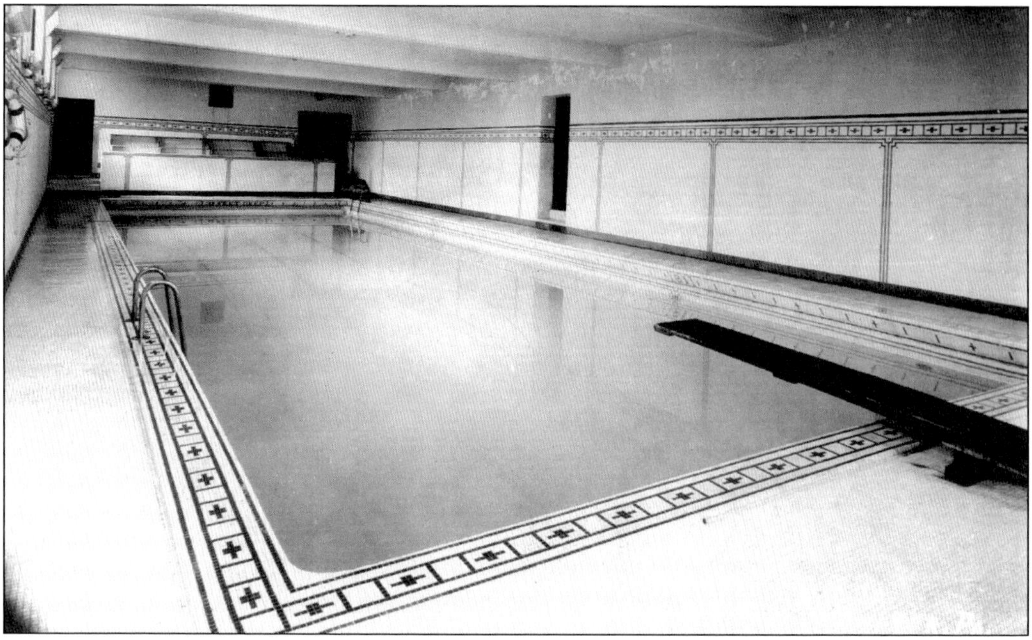

The YMCA swimming pool was located in the Y's facility at 20 York Street.

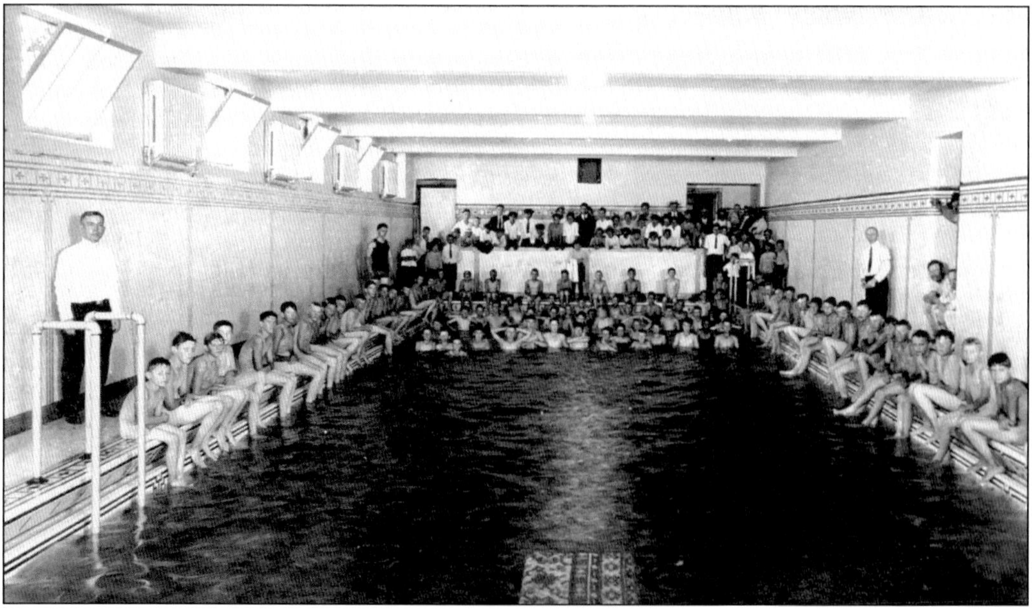

The YMCA swimmers were at the pool located at 20 York Street. At the time, in the 1930s, the practice was to swim nude.

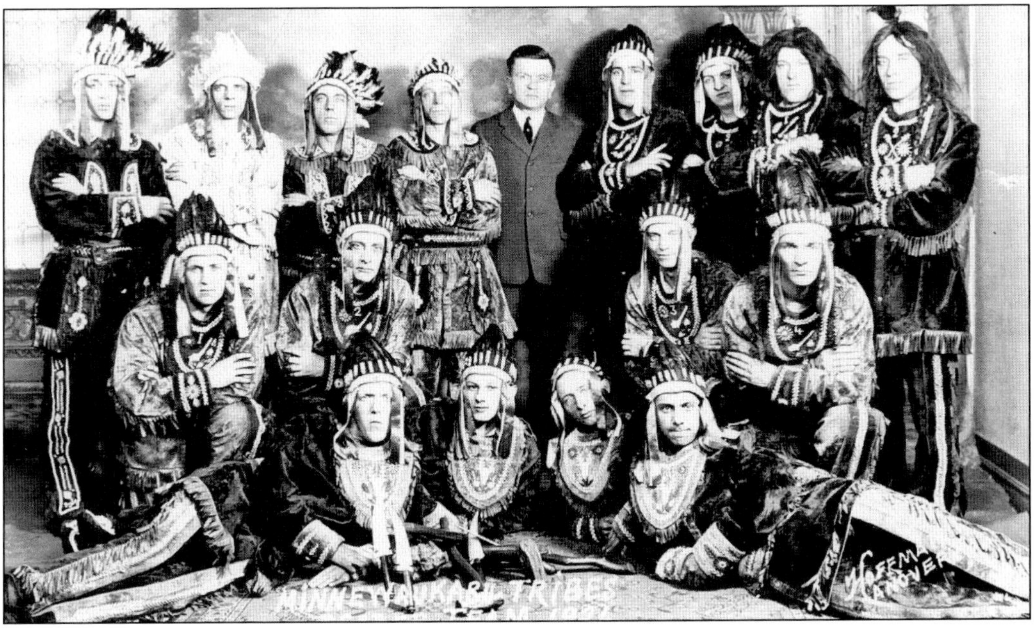

The Minnewaukaru Tribe Degree Team 1926 of the Independent Order of Red Men was a social organization that had its headquarters in the Melhorn building at 18–20 Carlisle Street. This photograph was by Hoffman Studio.

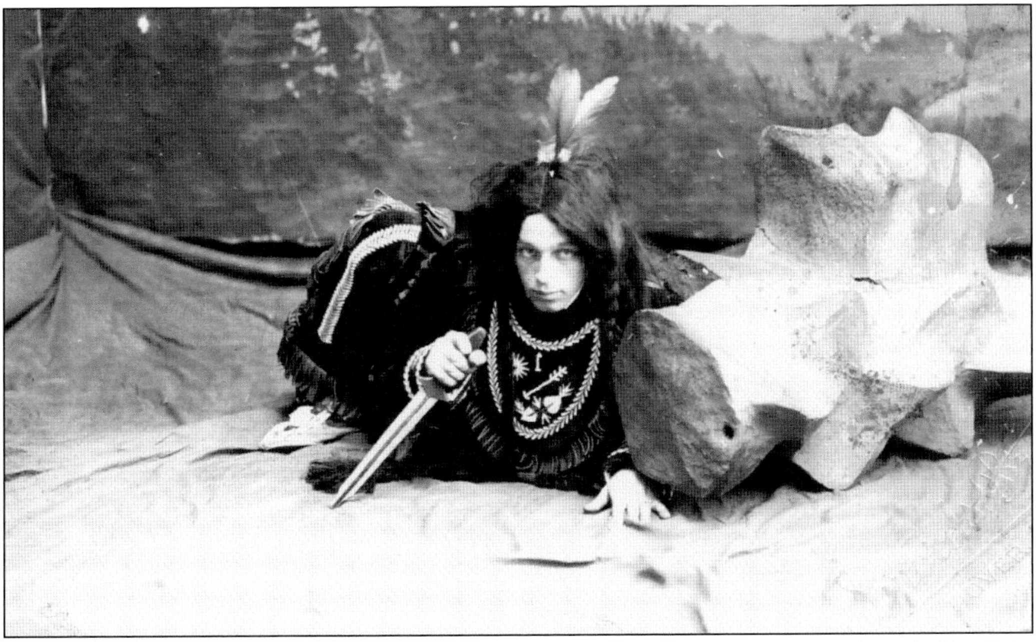

Pictured here is a member of the Independent Order of Red Men Minnewaukaru Tribe. The order was a social organization with a meeting room in the Melhorn building at 18–20 Carlisle Street. This photograph was by Swords Brothers, and the stamp box indicates the card was made between 1904 and 1918.

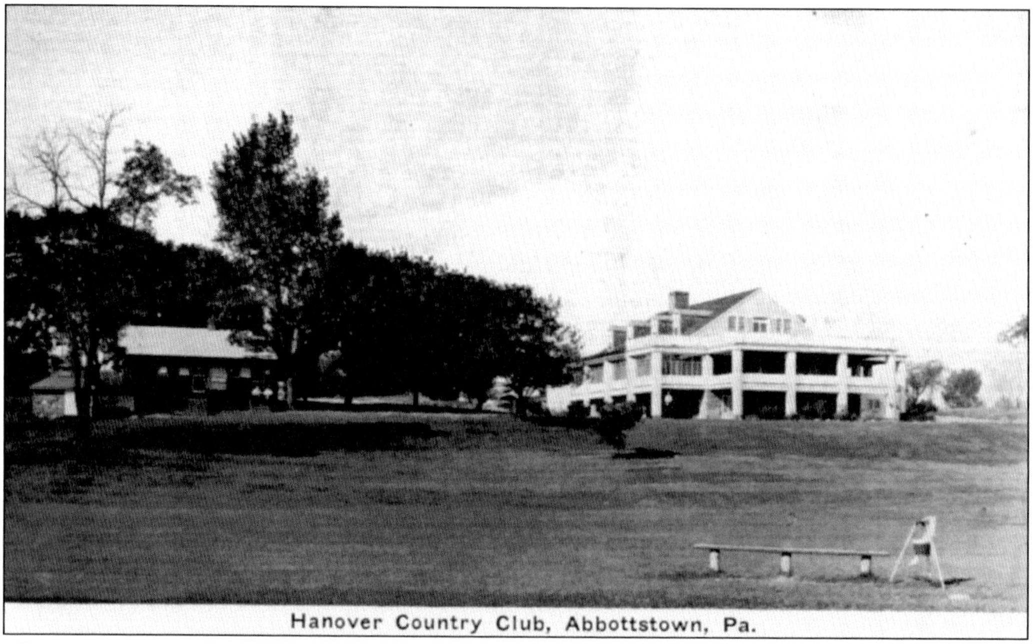

The Hanover Country Club in Abbottstown is on Route 30 east of Abbottstown. The card was published by Spangler's Restaurant, which is just off Route 15, east of Gettysburg.

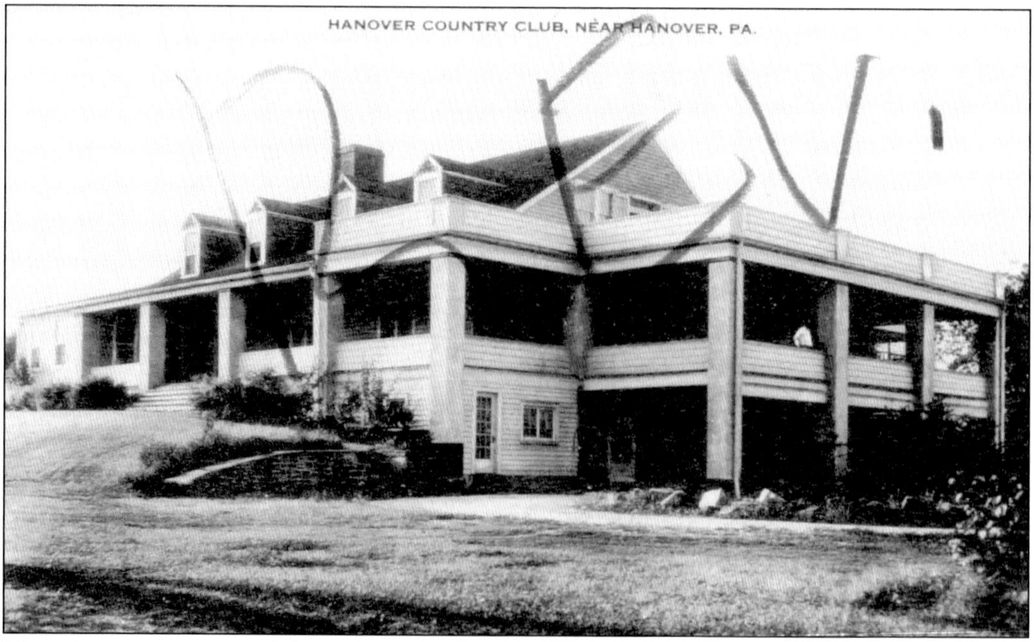

The Hanover Country Club is located on the east side of Abbottstown. The back of this card is blank. It was a salesman's sample by Artvue Card Company.

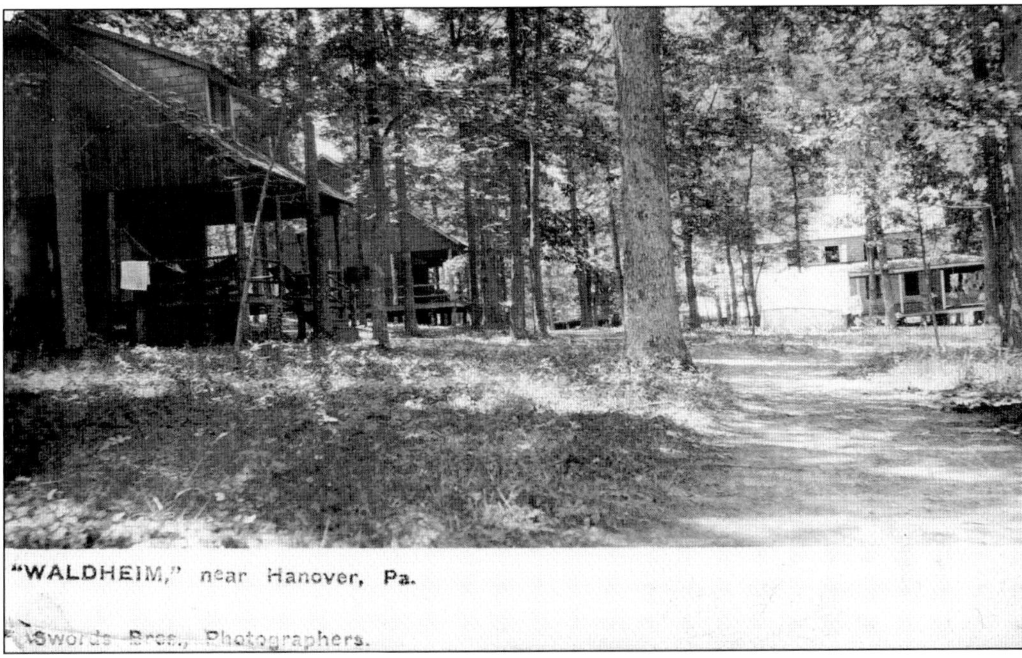

Waldheim, near Hanover, is a community of summer cottages at Dick's Dam on the Conewago Creek near Hampton. This photograph in browntone was by Swords Brothers. The card was printed between 1904 and the 1920s.

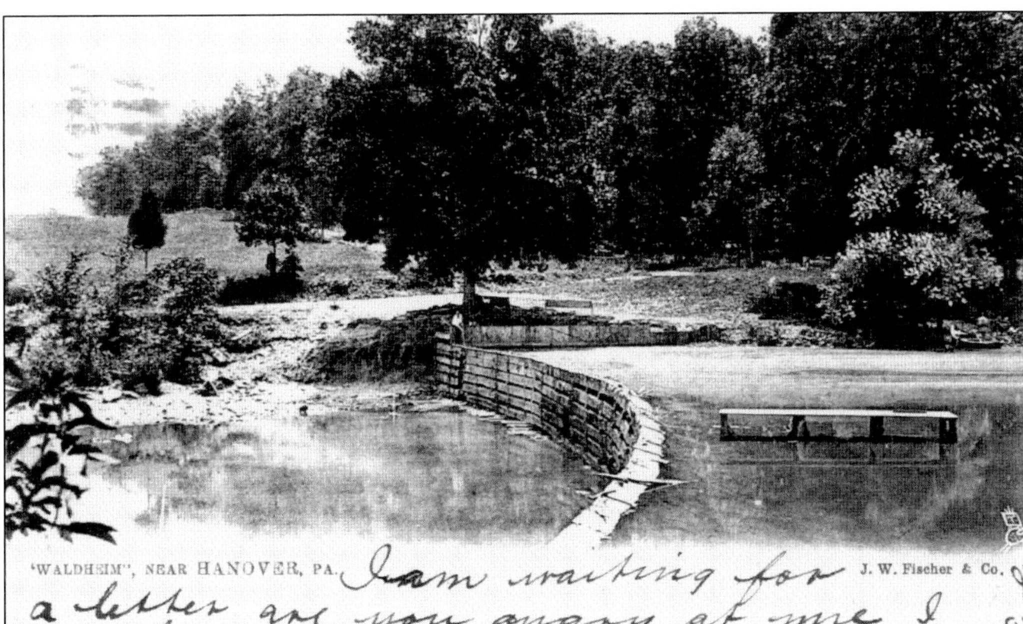

This postcard offers another view of Waldheim.

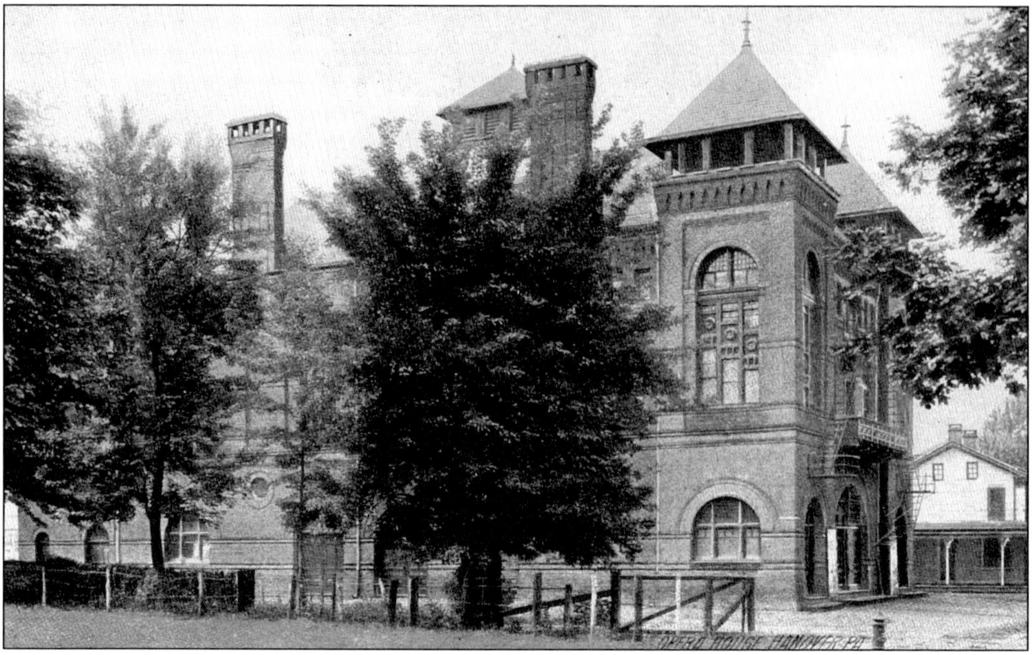

The Hanover Opera House was located at the southwest intersection of North Franklin and West Chestnut Streets.

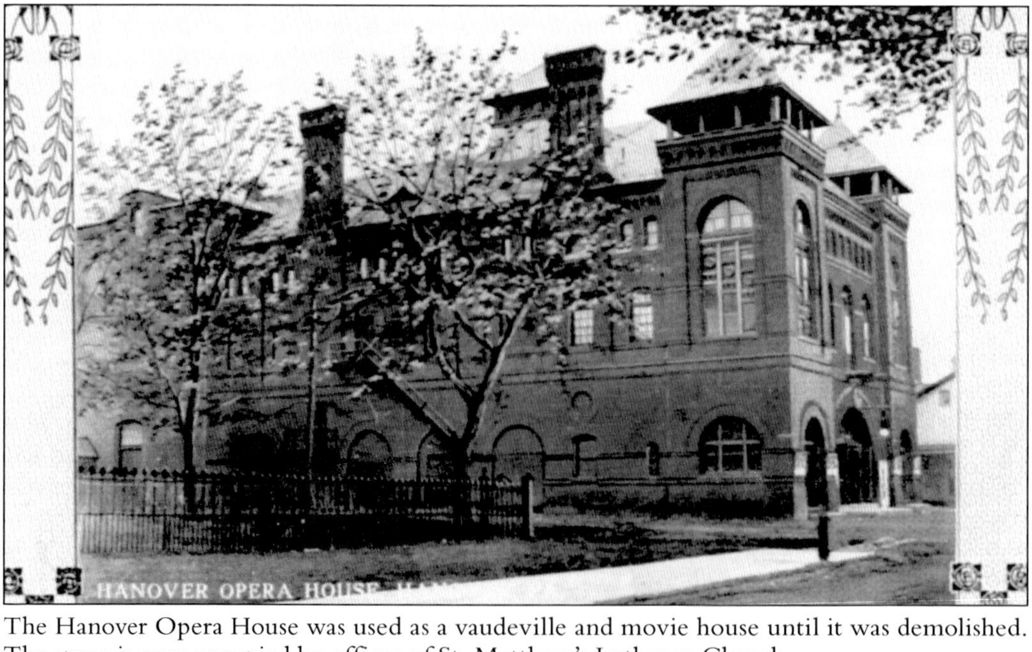

The Hanover Opera House was used as a vaudeville and movie house until it was demolished. The space is now occupied by offices of St. Matthew's Lutheran Church.

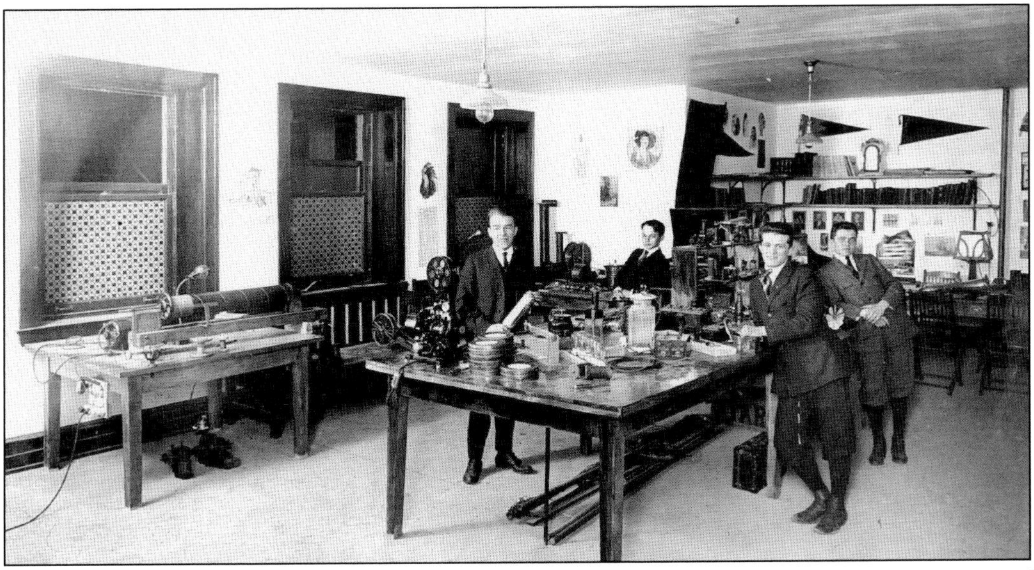

The Hanover Scientific Club, a group of young men interested in advancing the technology of the day, met in the Sheppard and Myers building on Center Square in 1917.

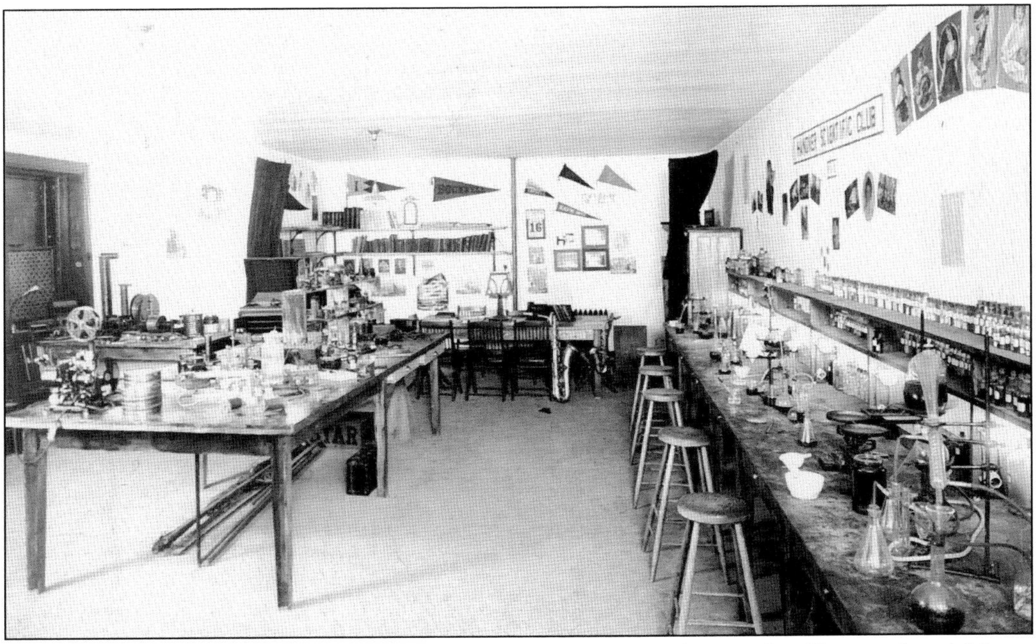

This picture of the Hanover Scientific Club in 1917 was taken at the Sheppard and Myers building on the corner of Center Square and Carlisle Street. This card was from the former E. J. J. Gobrecht collection.

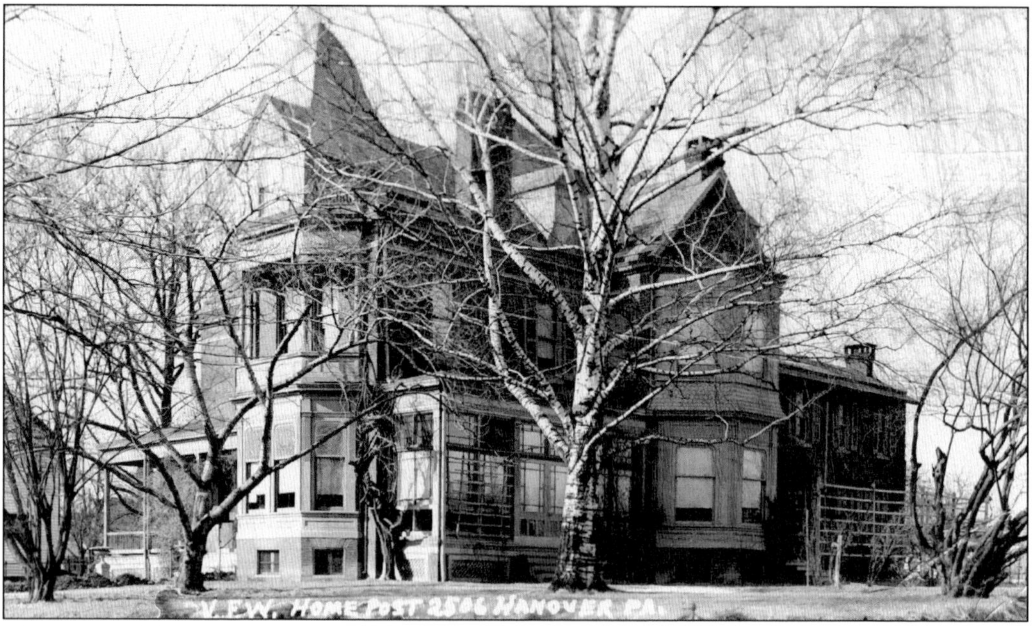

The home of the Veterans of Foreign Wars Post No. 2506 was at 314 York Street.

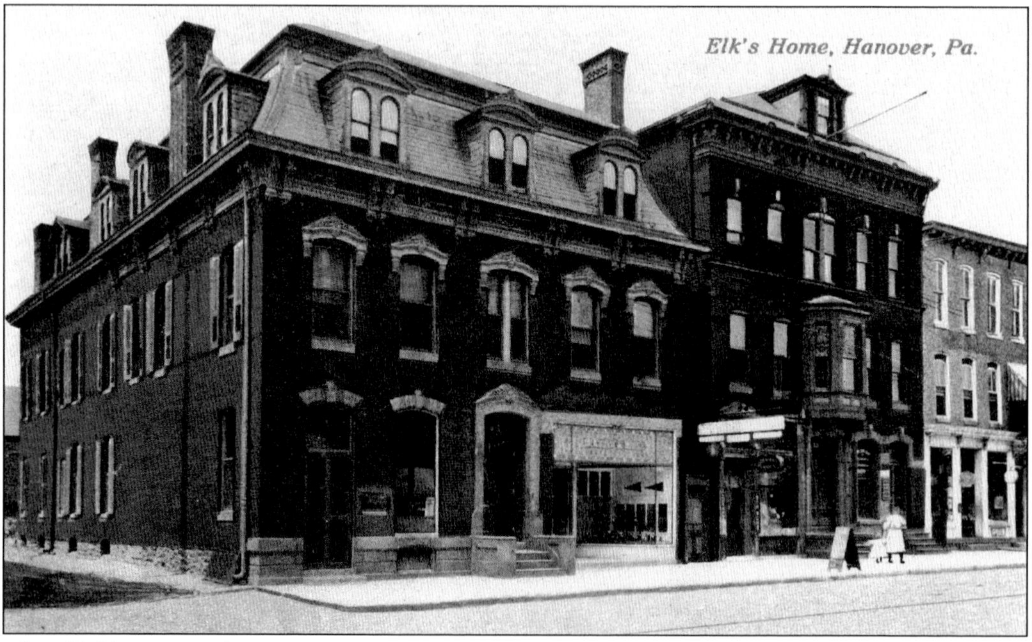

The Elks' home was located in the first block south of the square on Baltimore Street. The brick building to right of the Elks' was the Farmers State Bank. The Elks' and Farmers State Bank buildings were demolished and the space is now occupied by Rite-Aid.

Five

Transportation: Trains and Trolleys

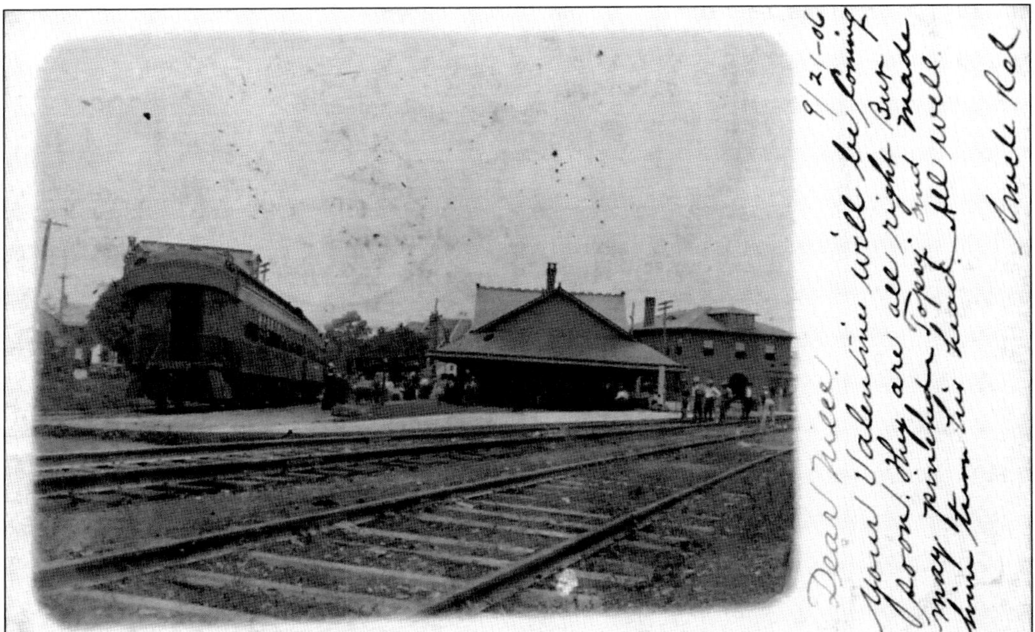

This view of Union station looks west from the Western Maryland Railroad tracks. The passenger car on the left is on the Pennsylvania Railroad tracks. The building to the right of the station was at one time the Western Maryland Railroad office and the office of the railroad telegraph operators. The square building in back of the station is the Edward E. Young Memorial Library, and the building in back of the railcar is the Colonial Hotel.

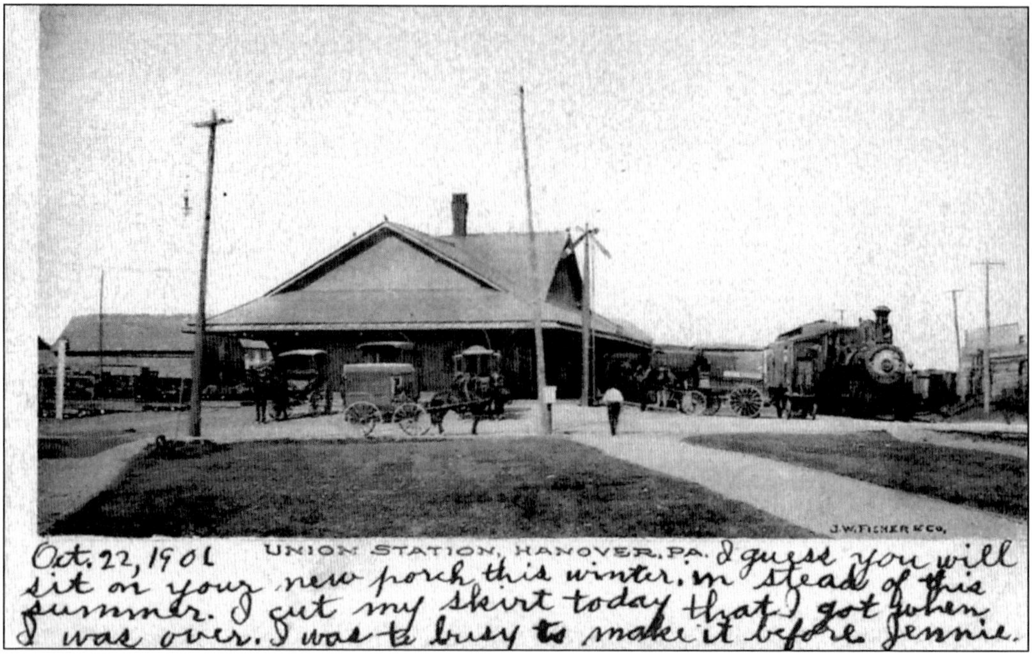

Union Station got its name because it handled two railroads, the Western Maryland Railroad on the north side and the Pennsylvania Railroad on the south side of the station. The building still stands and is now an insurance office. This card was postmarked October 23, 1906.

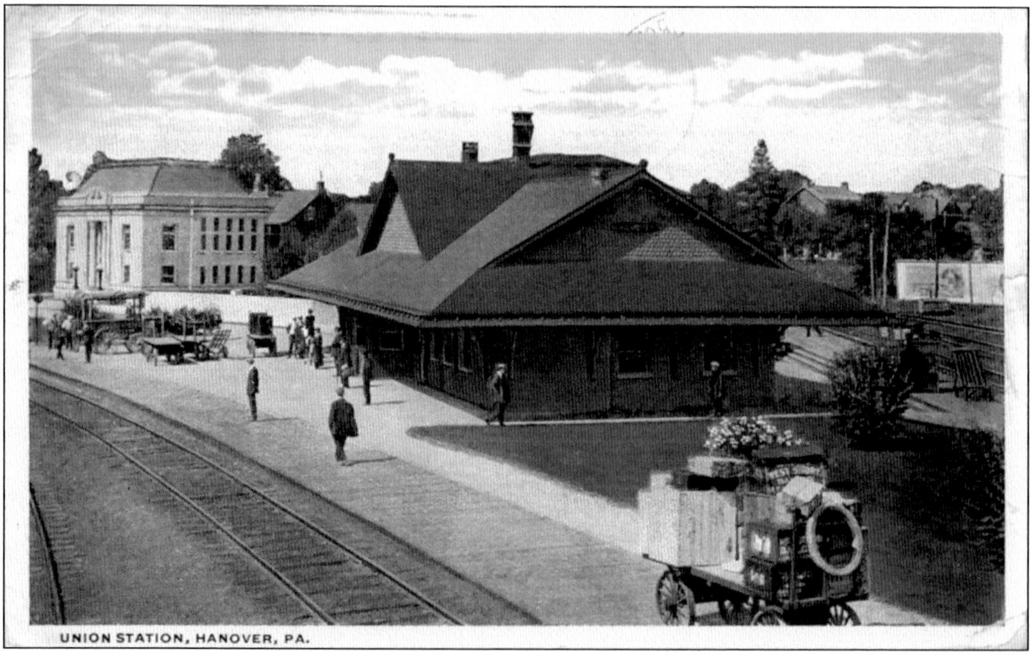

The view of Union Station looks west along the former Pennsylvania Railroad tracks toward Carlisle Street. The building on the left is the Edward E. Young Memorial Library. This card was mailed June 22, 1925.

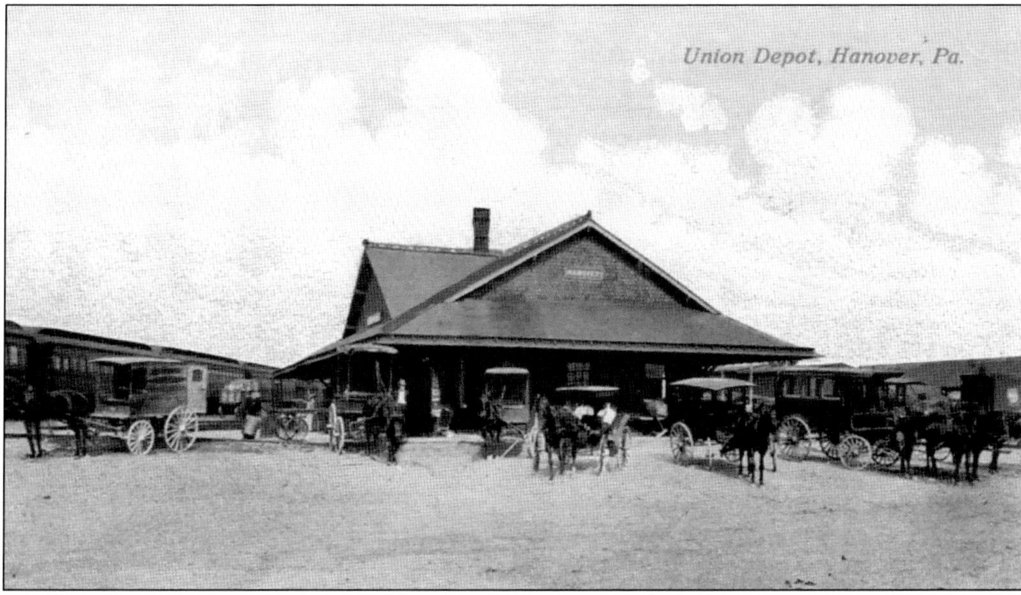

The photograph shows Union Depot looking east from Library Place. The train standing to the left of the station is a Western Maryland passenger train. A sad message on the back of the card reads as follows: "Dear Mary: I will let you know that we will come in on Saturday if it's not too ugly, as Johnny cut the end of his finger off and cut another one bad. The piece of finger was lying down on the wash house floor, so we must bring him in to have it dressed. Dr. Keagy was out last nite and dressed it. All kinds of bad luck. Good by, Mother." This card was mailed on February 20, 1916.

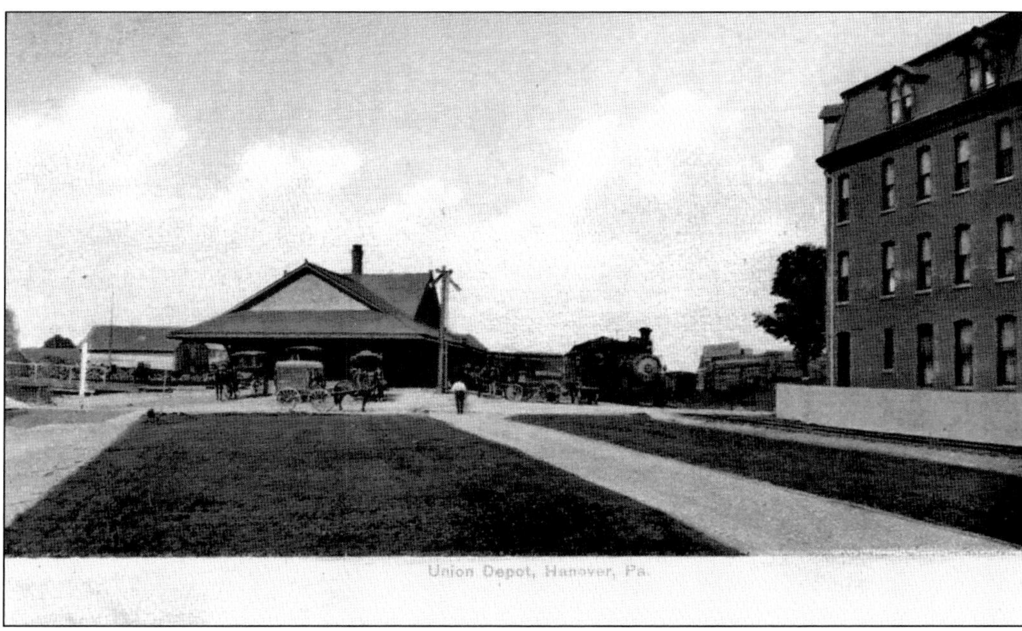

This is a view of the railroad station and the former Pennsylvania Railroad tracks that went to Frederick, Maryland. The former Western Maryland Railroad is on the opposite side. The building on the right is the Colonial Hotel.

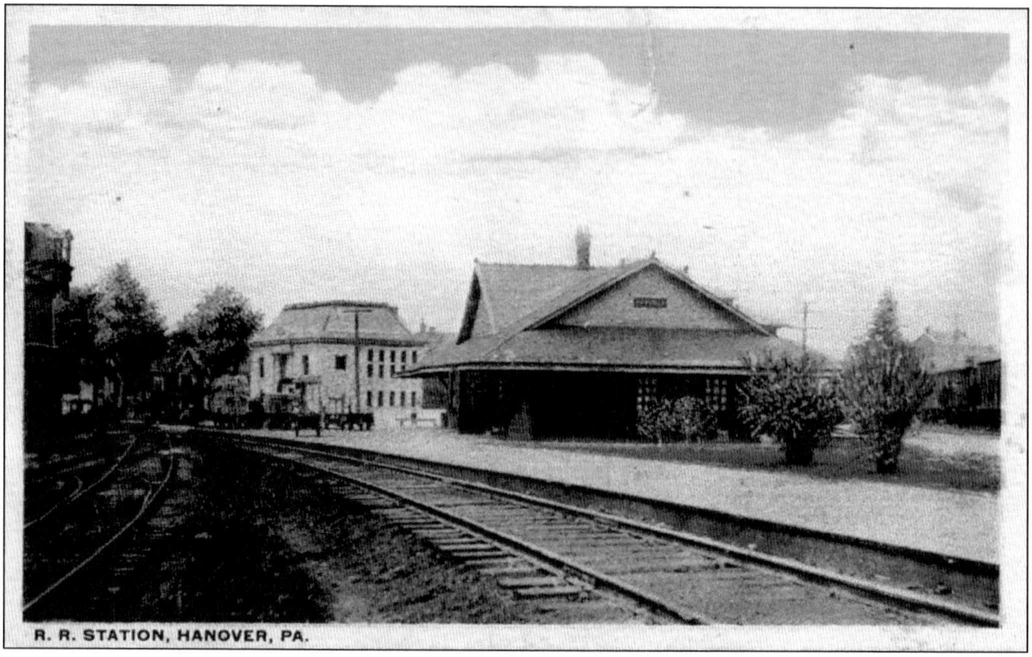

The Union Depot train station is in the foreground, and the Hanover Public Library is behind it on the west side of Railroad Street.

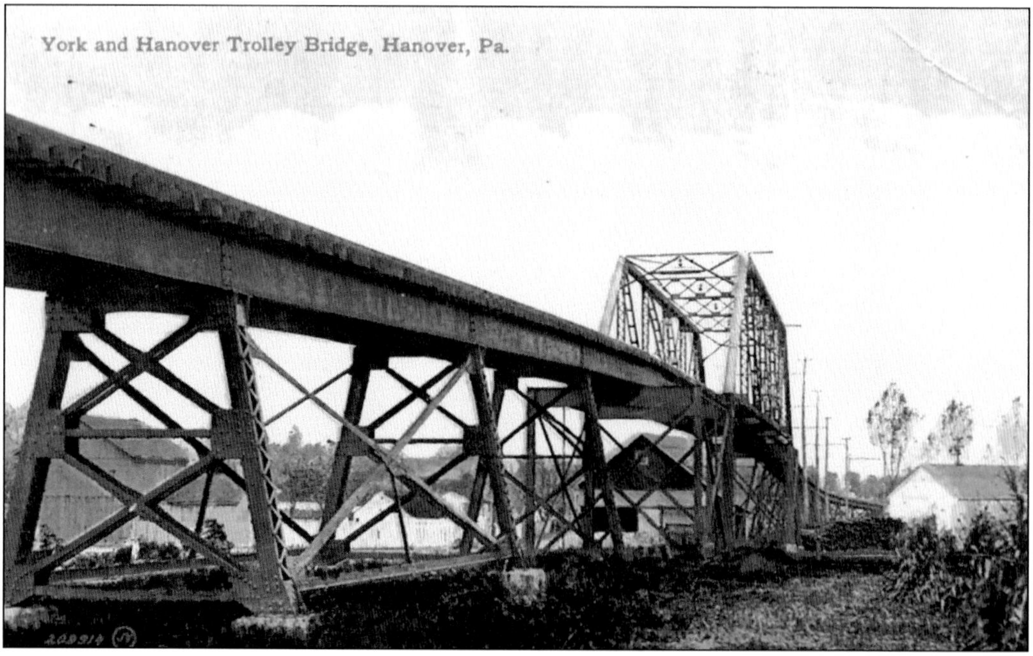

The York and Hanover Trolley Bridge carried the trolley over the Pennsylvania Railroad and the Western Maryland Railroad tracks in the east end of Hanover. This view looks toward Hanover. The card was mailed in 1911.

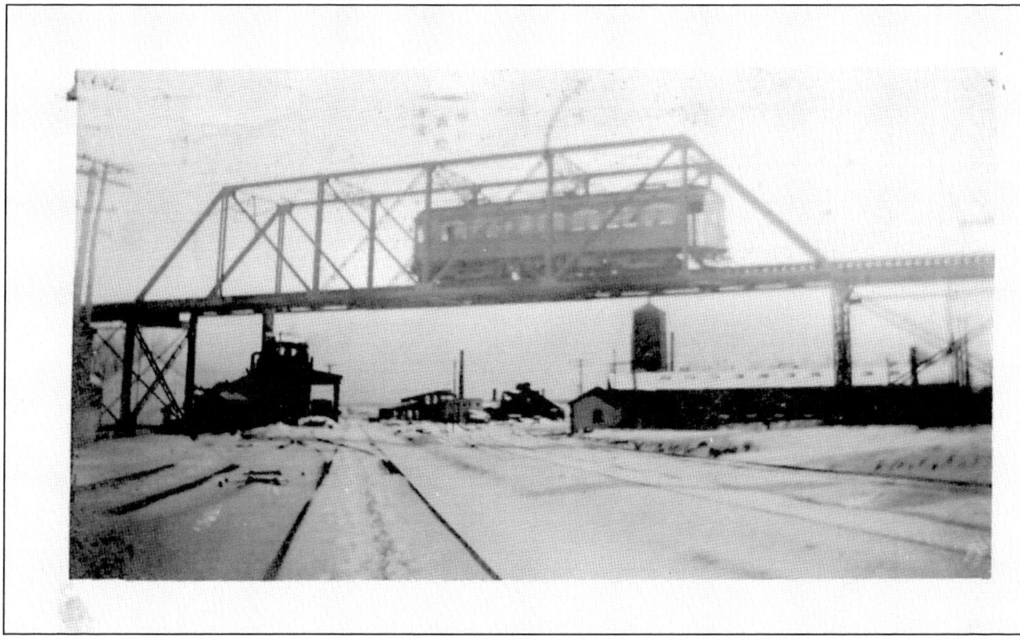

A Hanover and York Street Railway Company trolley car crosses the bridge over the tracks of the Western Maryland and Pennsylvania Railroads. The Hanover Wire Cloth Company buildings are on the right.

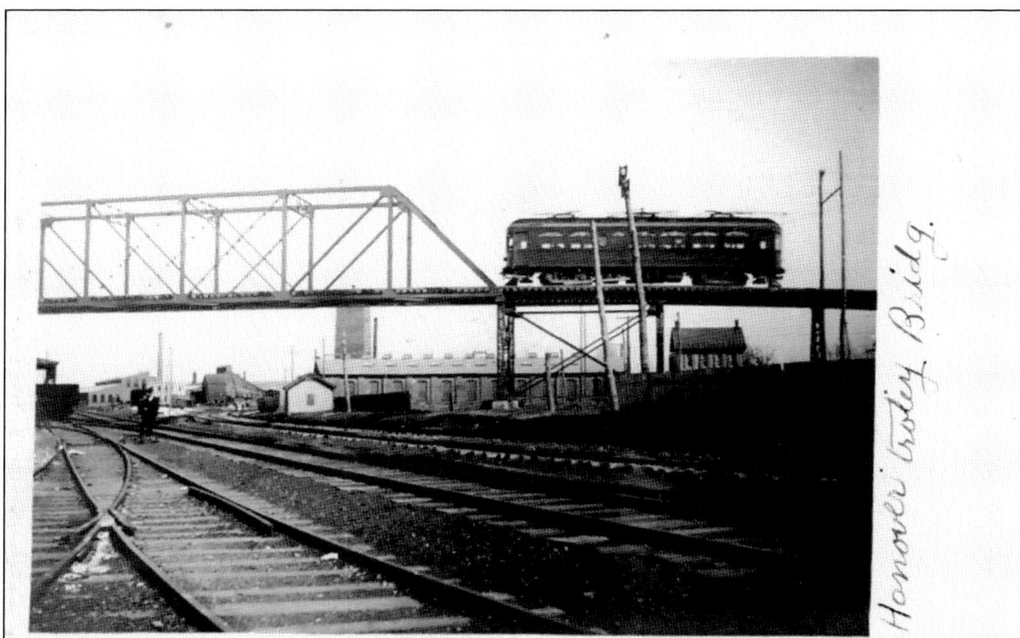

A Hanover and York Street Railway Company car crosses over the railroads. This view faces from Broadway looking toward Middle Street. The tower beneath the trestle bridge is the paint drying tower of the Hanover Wire Cloth Company in the 400 block of East Walnut Street. The buildings to the left were the W. F. Kintzing and Company Machine Works, and later the Revonah Spinning Mills.

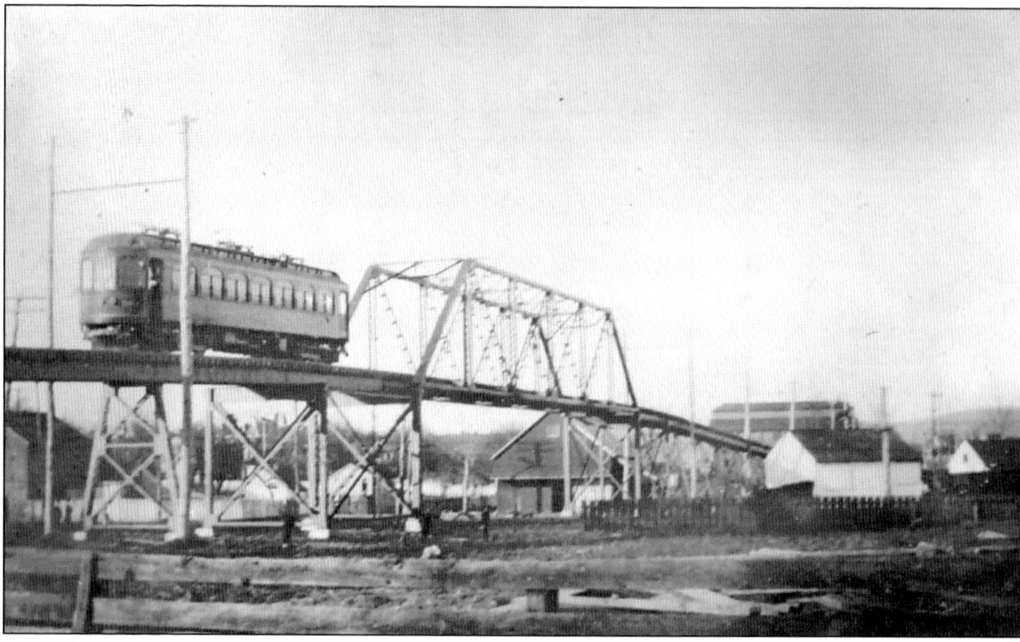

A trolley crosses the bridge over the railroad tracks. This postcard is postmarked 1908.

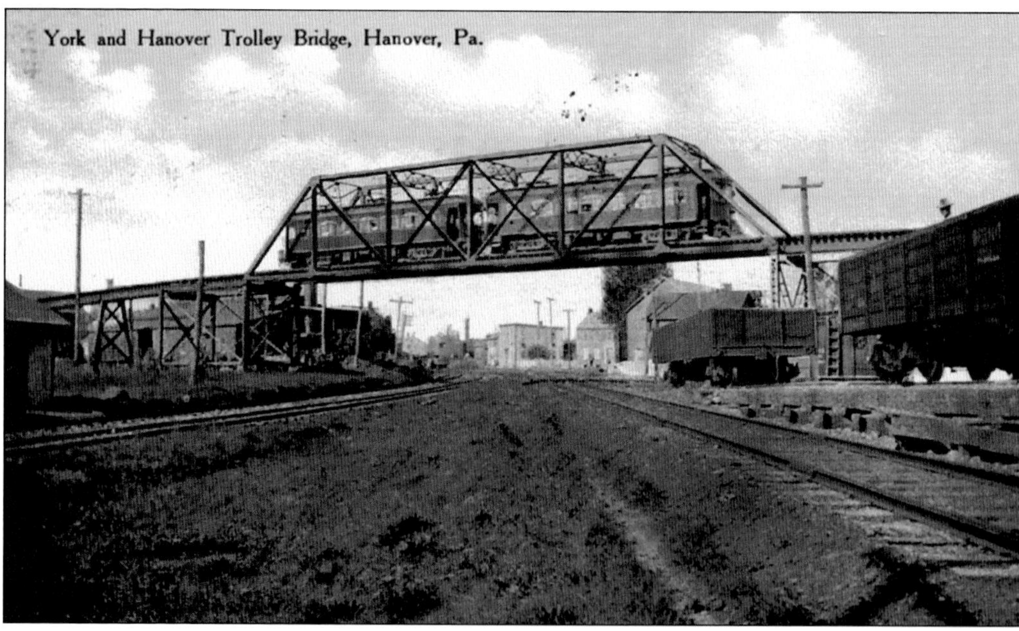

A two-car train of the 500 series cars rumbles across the trolley bridge over the railroad tracks from Walnut Street in Hanover. The tracks on the right belong to the Pennsylvania Railroad, and those on the left belong to the Western Maryland Railroad. This card is by C. T. Photocrome Company of Chicago and has a divided back. It is postmarked July 2, 1910.

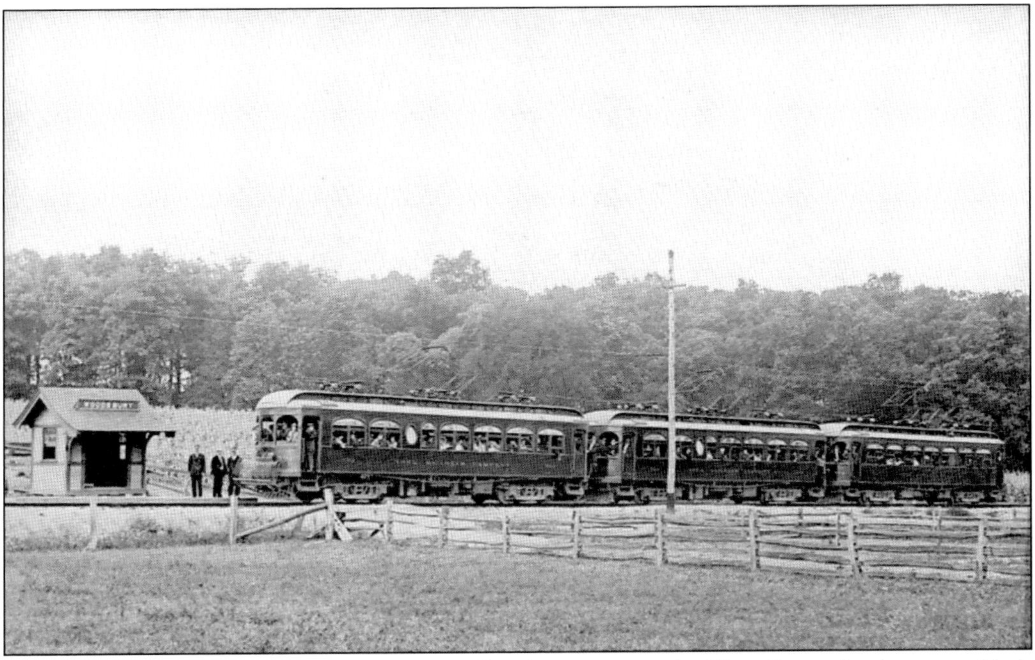

A three-car train of the York-Hanover trolley line stops at the Woodbury Station near York shortly after the line opened in 1908.

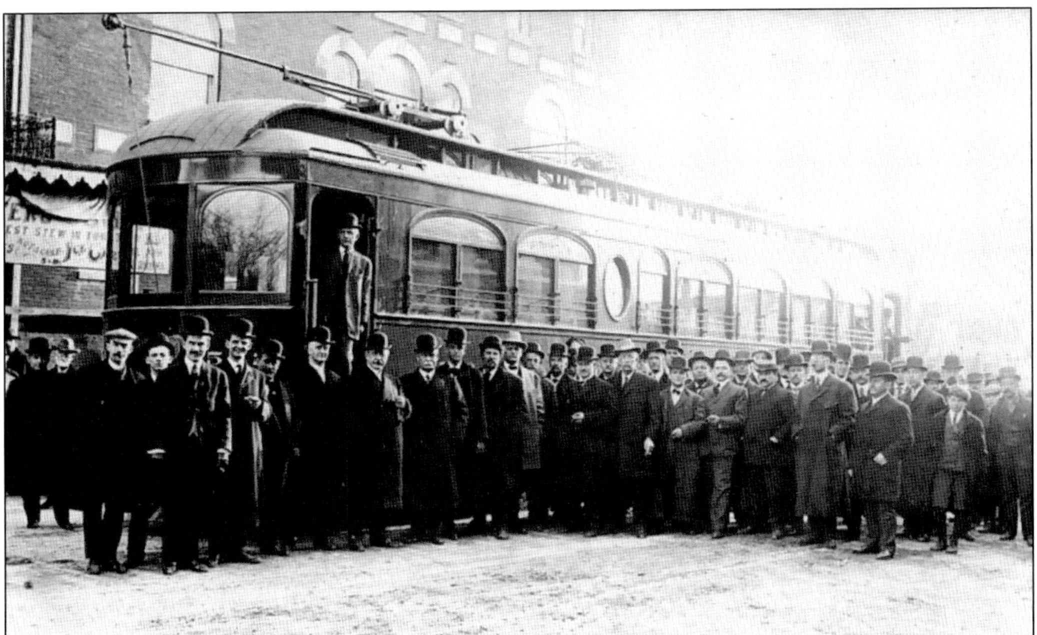

The York Railways Company trolley line was extended to the Hanover square. This scene shows the inaugural trip to Hanover on February 28, 1908, with dignitaries standing in Center Square in front of the Hotel Hanover on the southeast quadrant of the square. The photograph was taken by Swords Brothers, whose insignia is pressure-stamped on the front of the card.

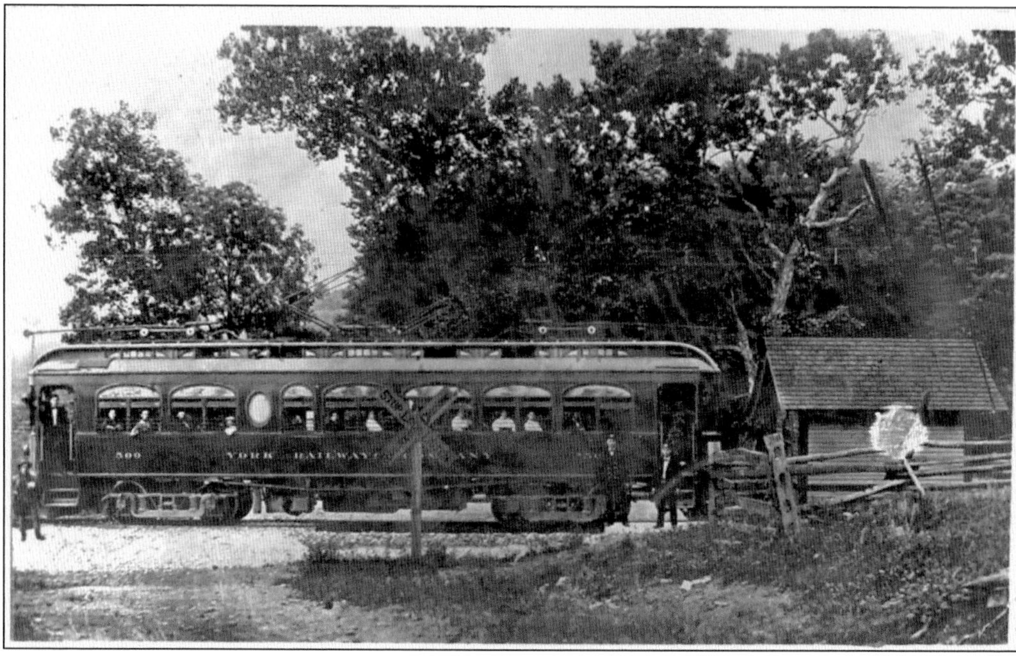

The York-Hanover trolley line is seen here before it was converted from 6,000 volts AC to 600 volts DC.

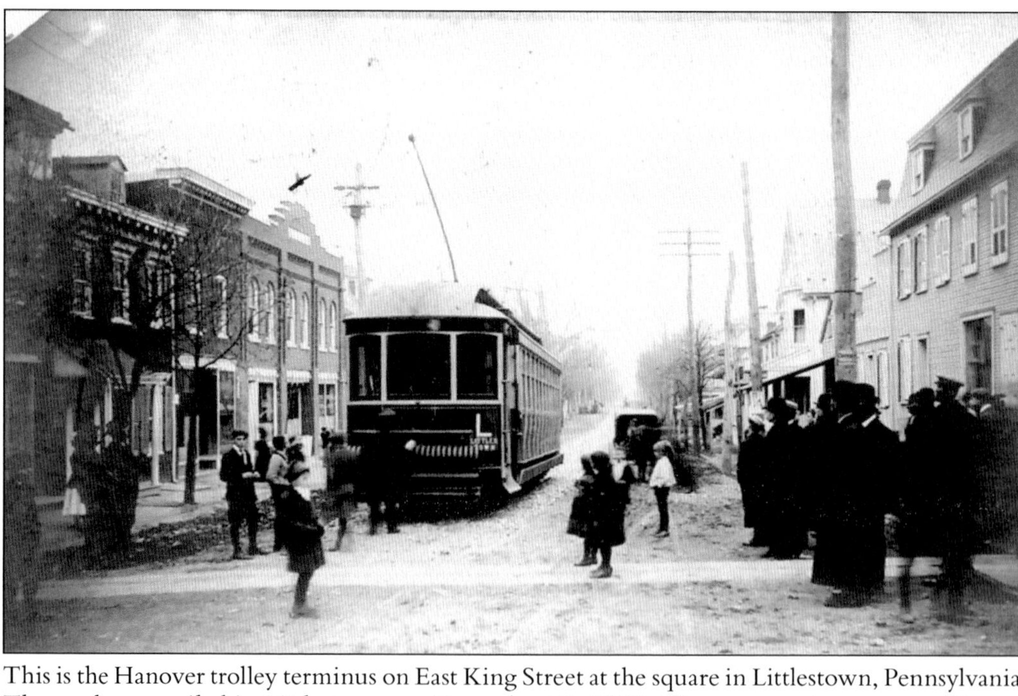

This is the Hanover trolley terminus on East King Street at the square in Littlestown, Pennsylvania. The card was mailed in Littlestown on December 31, 1908. The message in part says, "I want you to see our new trolley car which now comes to the center of town. Cecile."

Six

Industry and Commerce

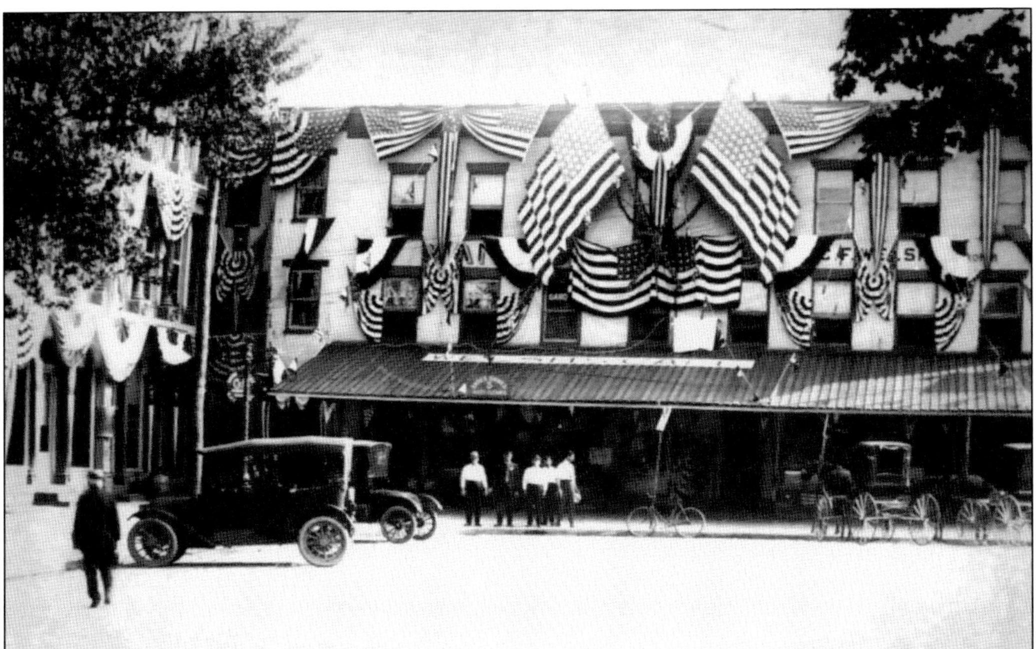

The Mansion House Hotel, C. F. Welsh, proprietor, on Center Square is decorated for the September 1915 centennial week. This hotel later became Murphy's Five and Ten and is now the Hanover Shoe retail outlet location.

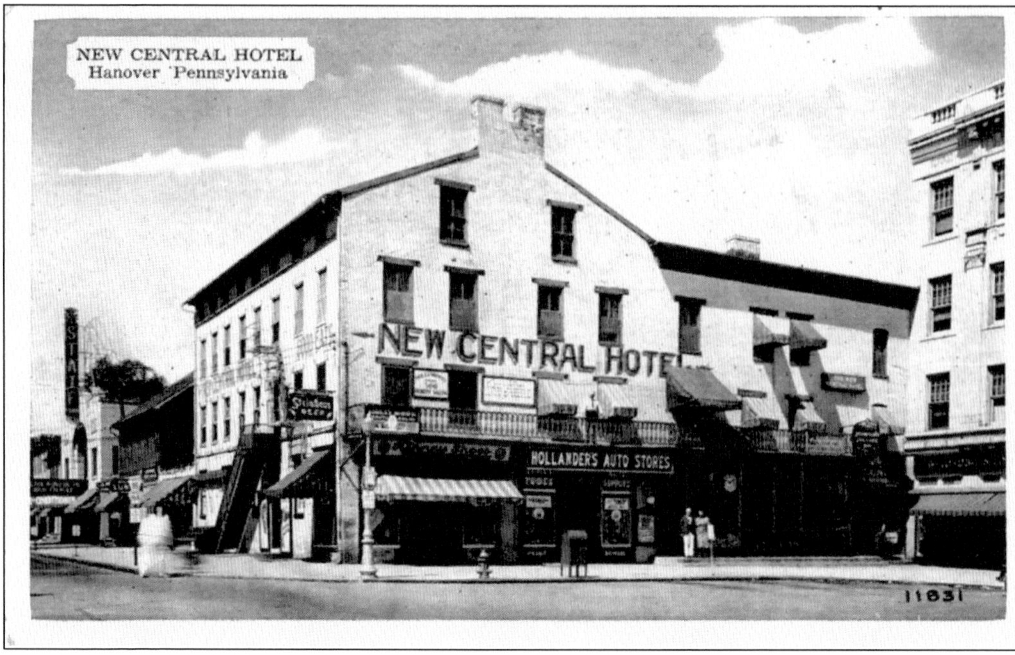

The New Central Hotel was on the northwest corner of Frederick Street and Center Square. Built in 1810, a portion served as union headquarters in the Civil War Battle of Hanover. The state movie theater is on the left. The card was published by C. J. Reeder, proprietor of the Central Hotel.

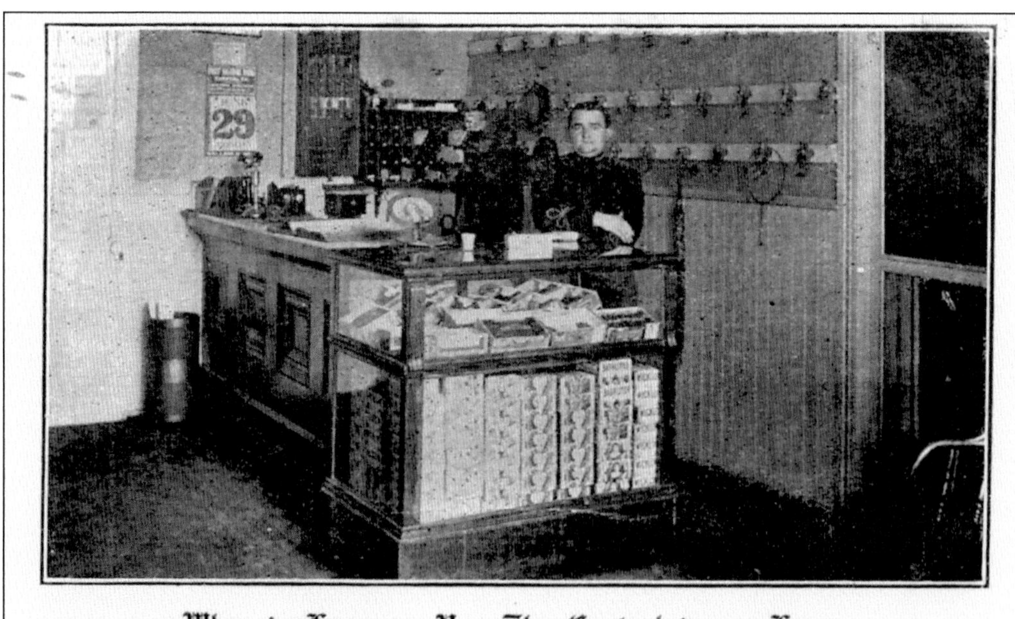

"When in Hanover, PA, the Central is my home" refers to the New Central Hotel on Center Square. The card was mailed on April 1, 1910.

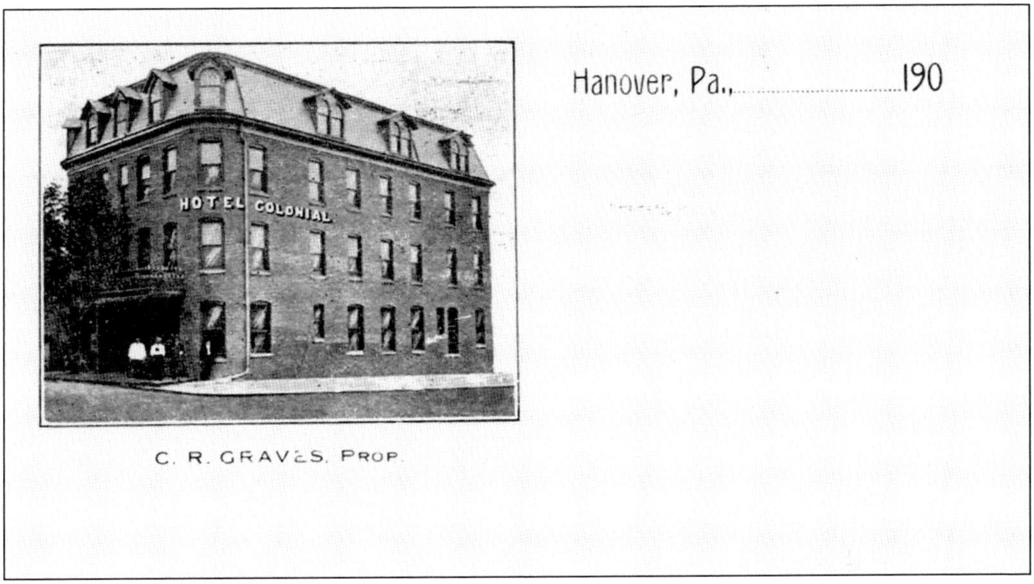

The Hotel Colonial is located at the intersection of Railroad Street and Library Place at Union Station. It served the travelers of both the Western Maryland and the Pennsylvania Railroads. The back indicates that this was a "private mailing card—authorized by act of congress May 19, 1898."

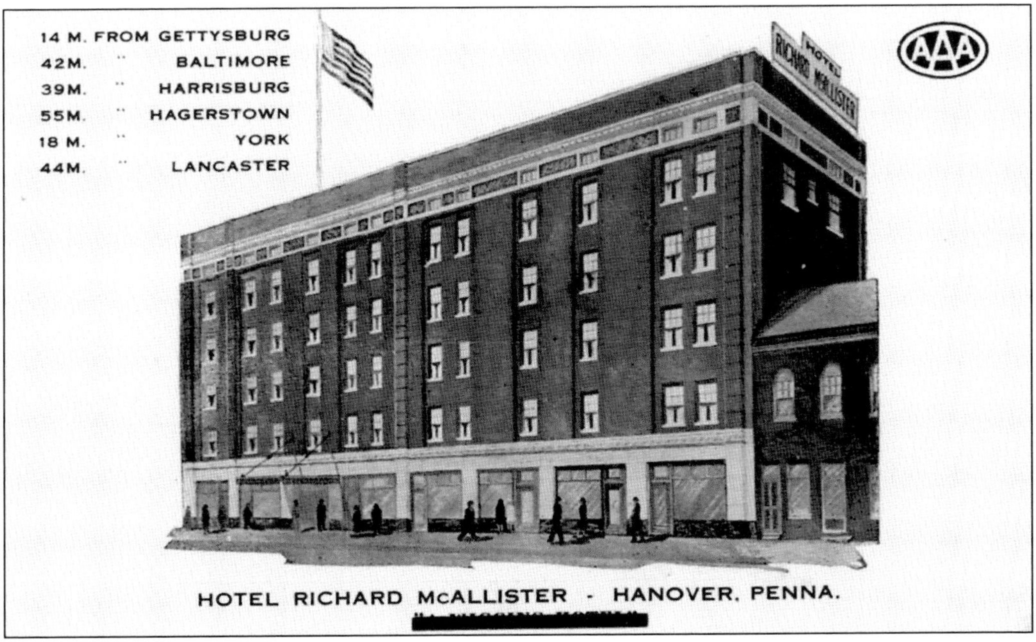

This promotional postcard shows Hotel Richard McAllister, located on York Street. Note the large roof sign on the right side of the building. The text on the bottom of the card, "A Wiggin's Hotel," is blacked out. The building was later converted to the Homewood Retirement Center and is now a center for social welfare agencies and housing.

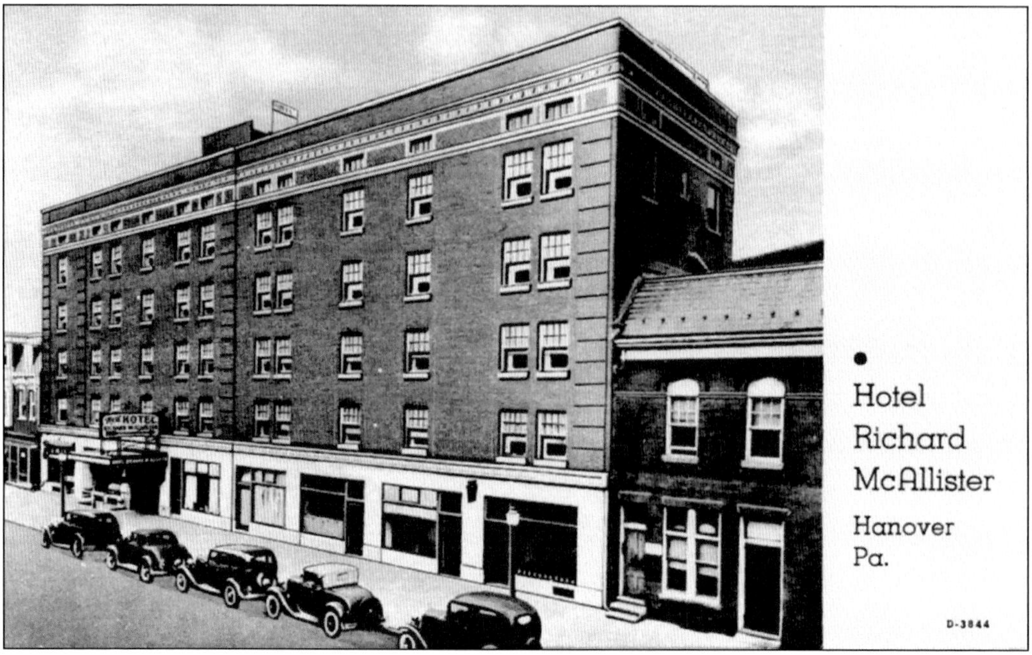

This Hotel Richard McAllister card was a "freebie" for hotel guests.

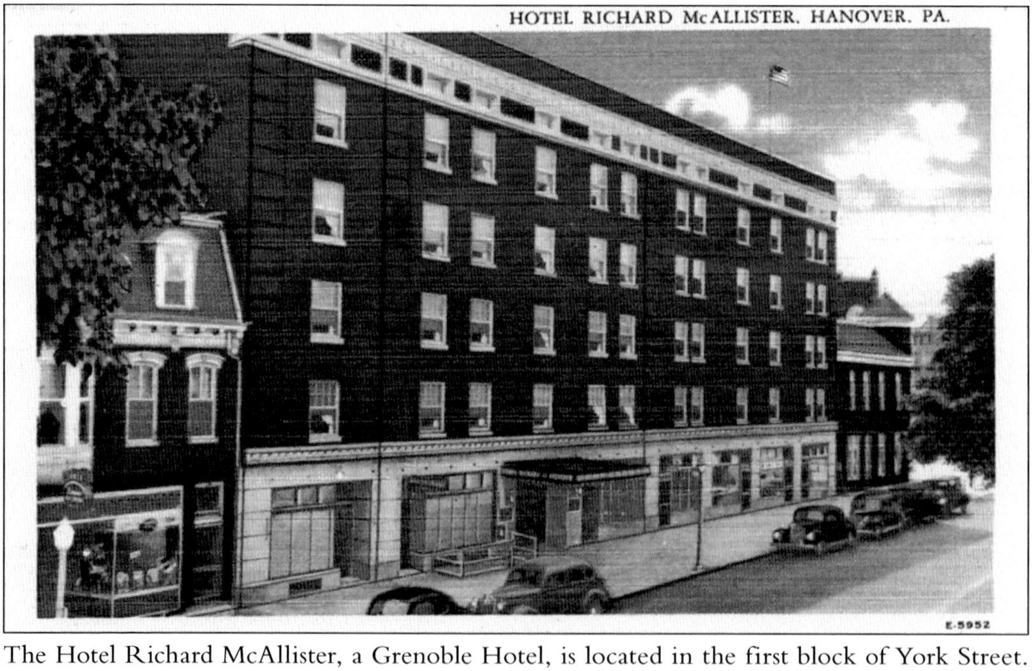

The Hotel Richard McAllister, a Grenoble Hotel, is located in the first block of York Street. This was a free advertising card supplied to hotel guests. The card was published by Walmer, Harrisburg, Pennsylvania. The cars on the street indicate the card was printed in the 1930s.

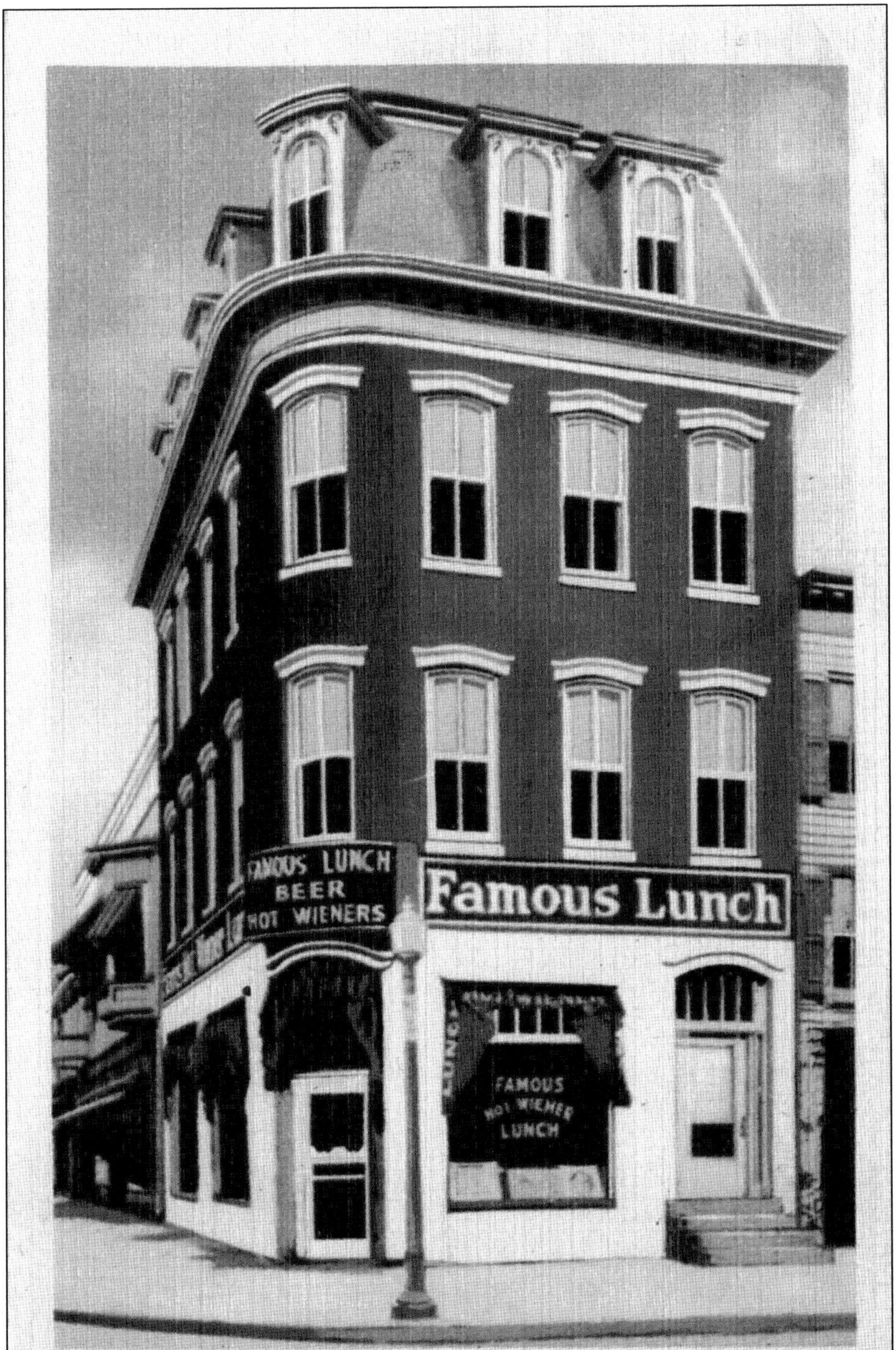

Famous Hot Wiener Lunch, Cor. York St. and Broadway, Hanover, Pa.

The Famous Lunch is located at the intersection of York Street and Broadway, just off the east exit of Center Square. In the building's early years, it was known as the Sprenkle Building, and it also housed People's Bank.

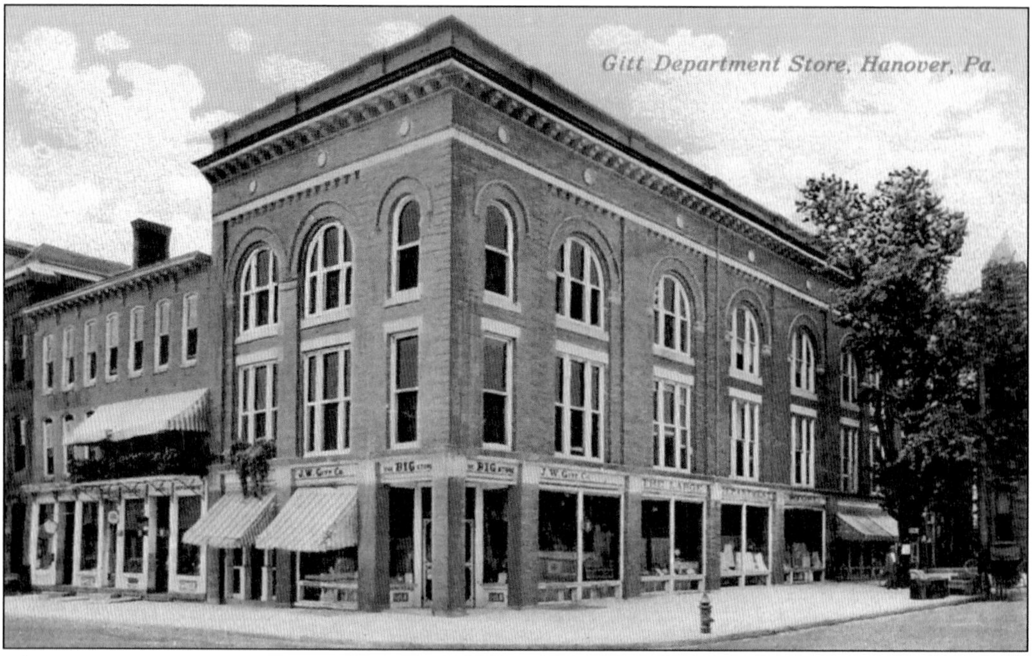

The Gitt Department Store was located at the southwest corner of Center Square and Baltimore Street. The store slogan was the "Big Store."

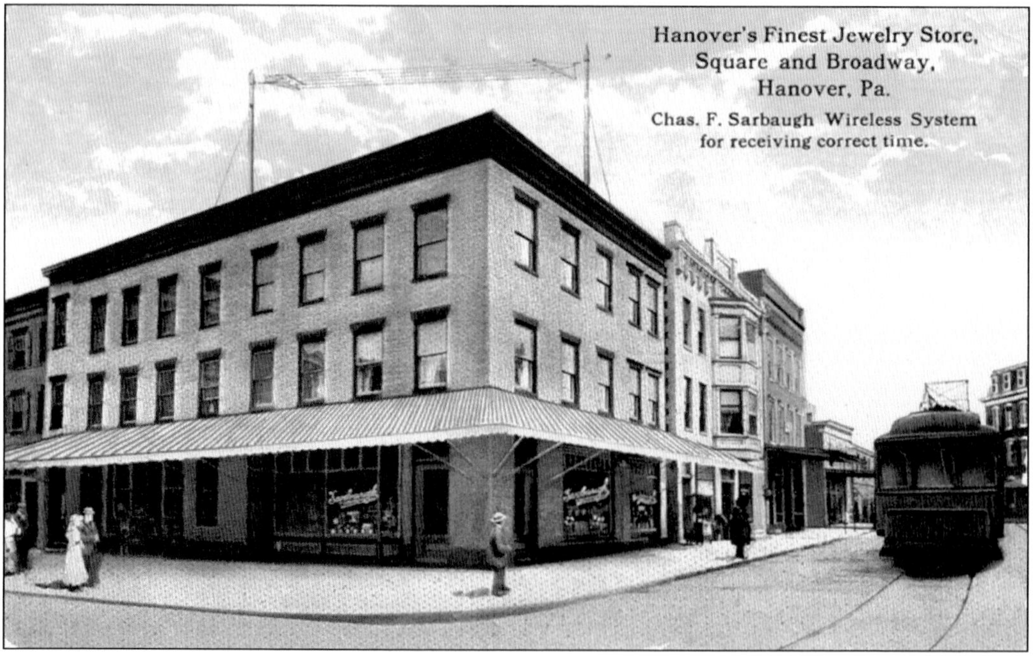

"Hanover's Finest Jewelry Store," located at the southeast corner of Center Square and Broadway, was owned and operated by Charles F. Sarbaugh. Note the large antenna on the roof for receiving the correct time from the Naval Observatory. This card was published by Leo Meyer of Easton, Pennsylvania.

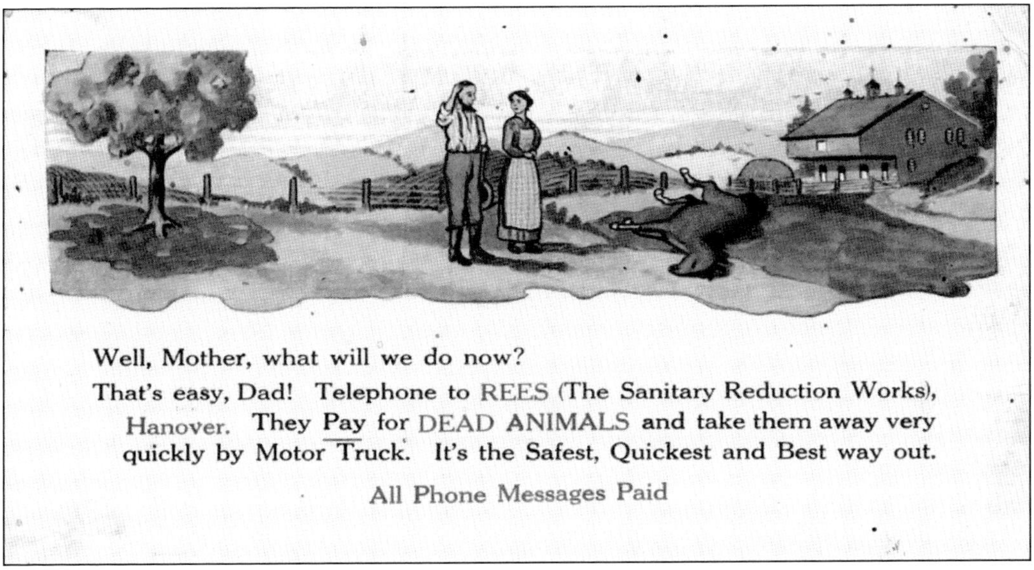

The Albert F. Rees rendering plant was located on Center Street at the Western Maryland Railroad from the 1920s into the 1950s. By-products included hides and tallow. Hanover citizens from that era remember the terrible stench the plant produced.

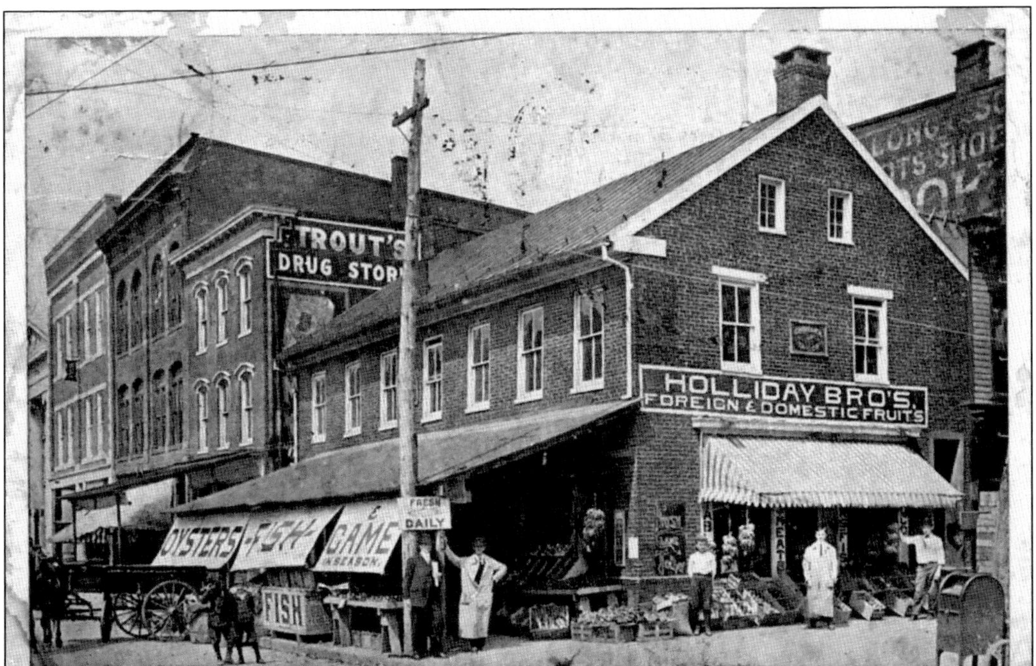

The Holliday Brothers fruit stand was located at the northeast corner of Center Square and Carlisle Street. This postcard, with Stan Holiday, the man in the center wearing a white duster, was mailed June 2, 1910, to grocer E. E. Hamm of Porters Sideling. It offered produce including fancy lemons, 300 size, for $3.25 and bananas, seven to nine hands, for 65¢ to $1.25 per bunch. Edward E. Hamm later opened a furniture store at 408 Baltimore Street.

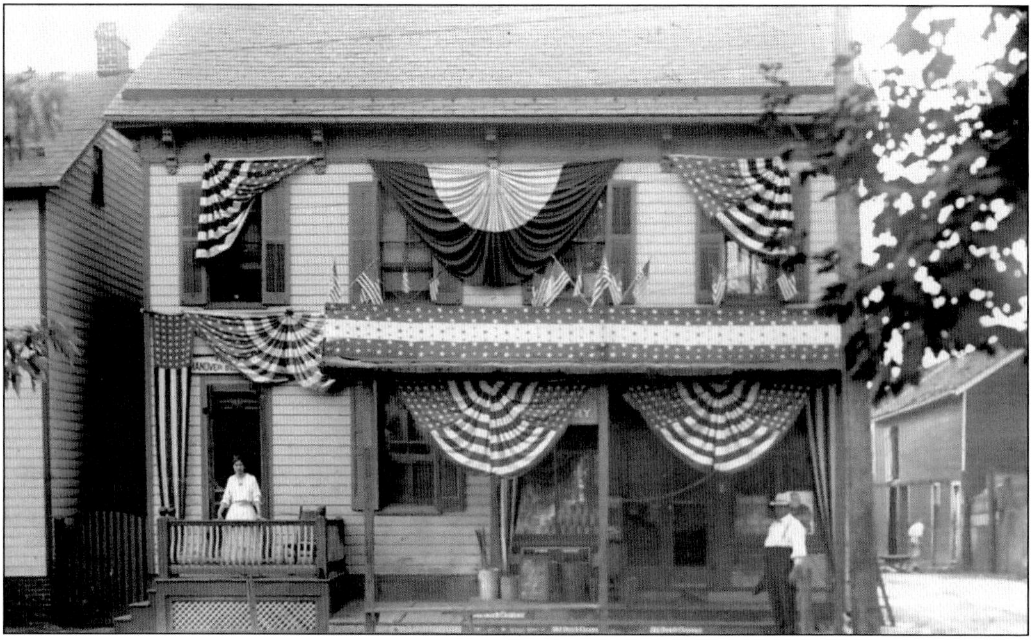

Obles and A. M. Houck Hanover Steam Bakery and Grocery, located at 126 High Street, is decorated for the 1915 centennial celebration. Obles and Anise M. Houck, who lived at 124 High Street, are in the photograph.

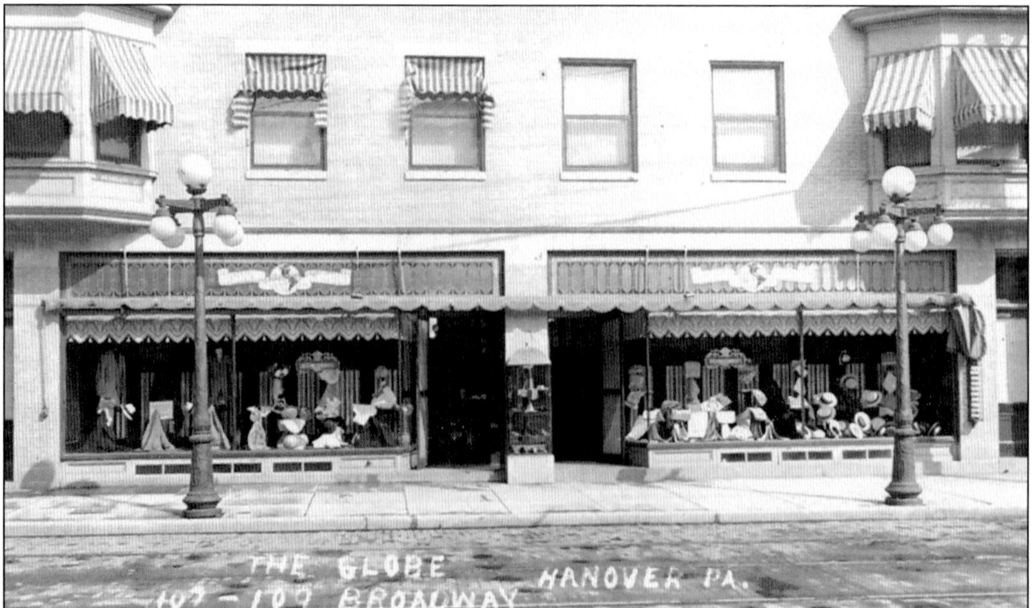

This picture of the Globe Clothing Store at 107–109 Broadway was probably taken in the 1930s.

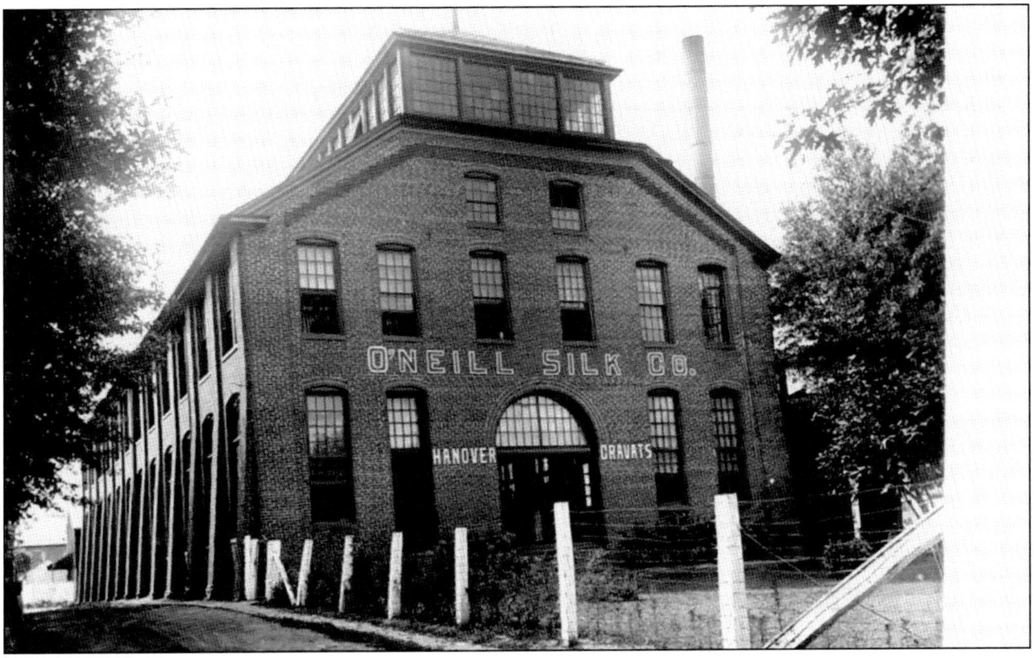

The O'Neill Silk Company was located at 534 East Walnut Street and the corner of Silk Mill Alley in 1917. At the time, another silk company, the Ernest and Herman Levy Silk Ribbon Mill, was located on Ridge Avenue near East Middle Street. O'Neill Silk manufactured tubular neckties. The building has since been converted to apartments.

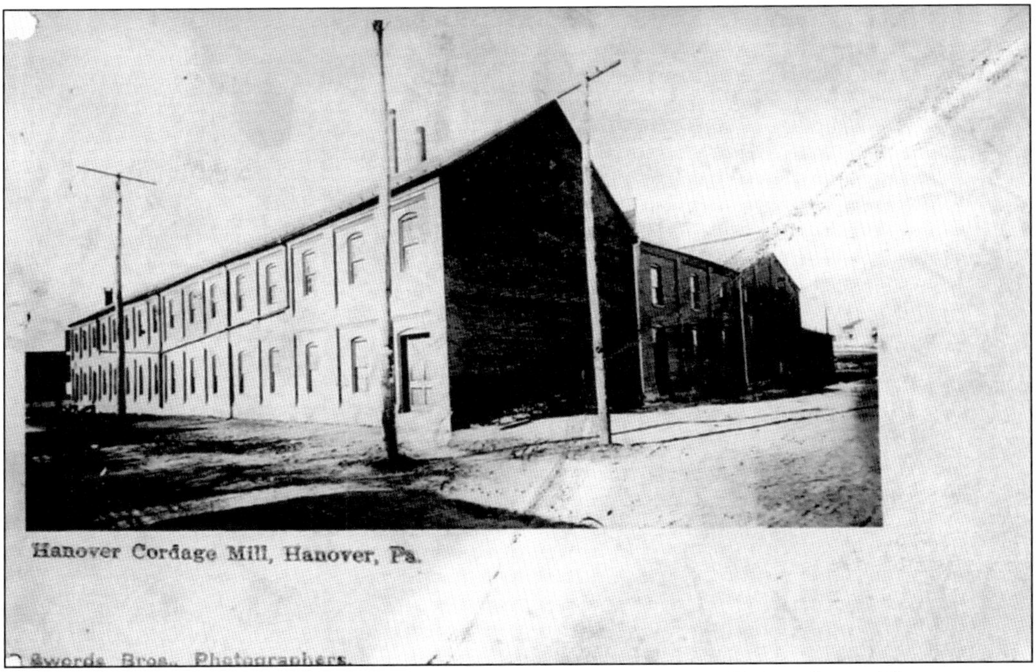

The Hanover Cordage Mill was on East Chestnut Street, just off Broadway. The company manufactured rope and twine and had many nicknames: "The Ropey," "The Fuzz Mill," and the "String Factory."

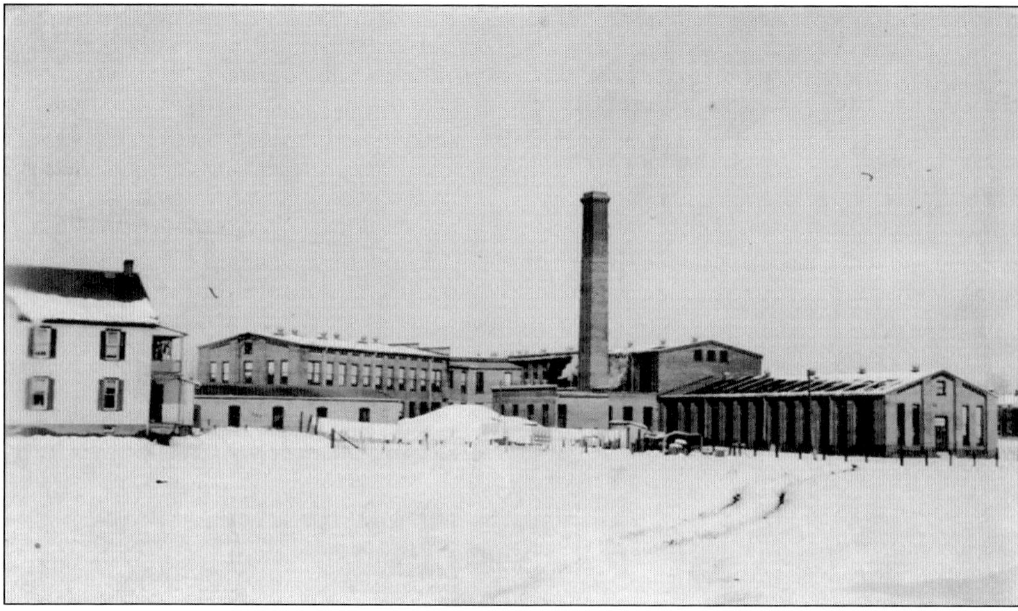

The silk mill of Ernest and Herman Levy was located at Ridge Avenue. The stamp box indicates the card was printed between 1904 and 1918.

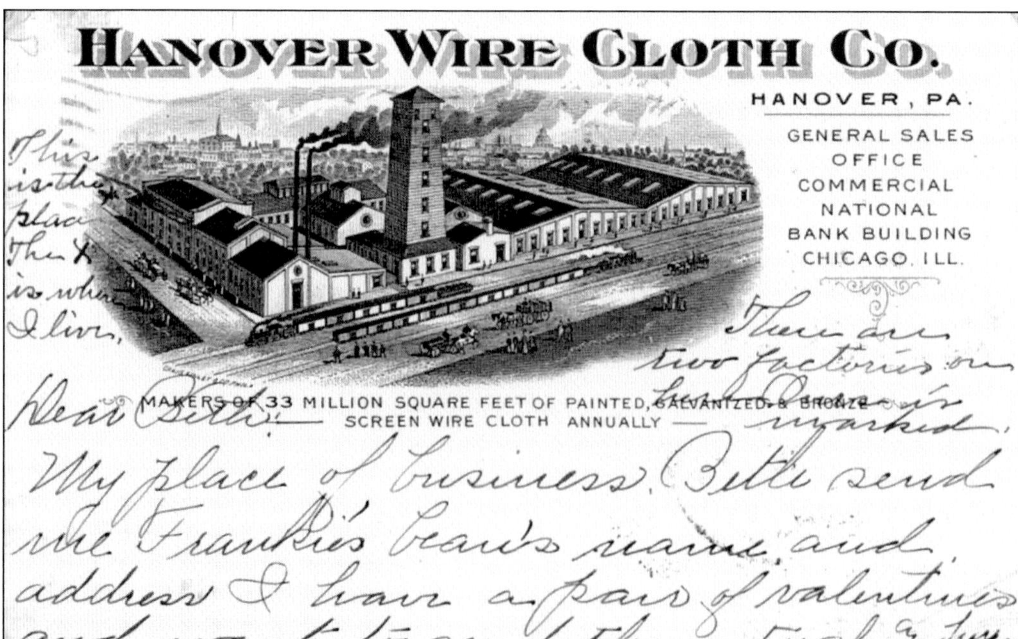

The Hanover Wire Cloth Company was located on East Middle Street. This card is a form of business card and was mailed January 26, 1908.

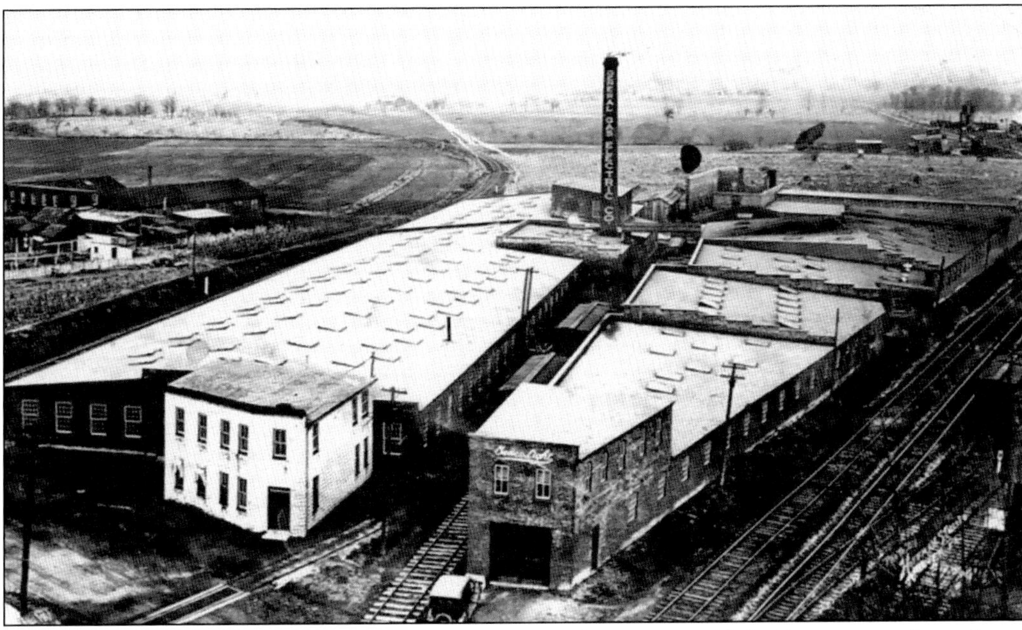

The General Gas and Electric Company was located on East Middle Street near the railroad tracks. GENCO manufactured gasoline-powered electricity-generating plants for rural use. This site later became the home of the Hanover Motor Car Company. The railroad tracks on the left were those of the Pennsylvania Railroad, and the tracks on the right were those of the Western Maryland. Many years later, the building became the Revonah factory.

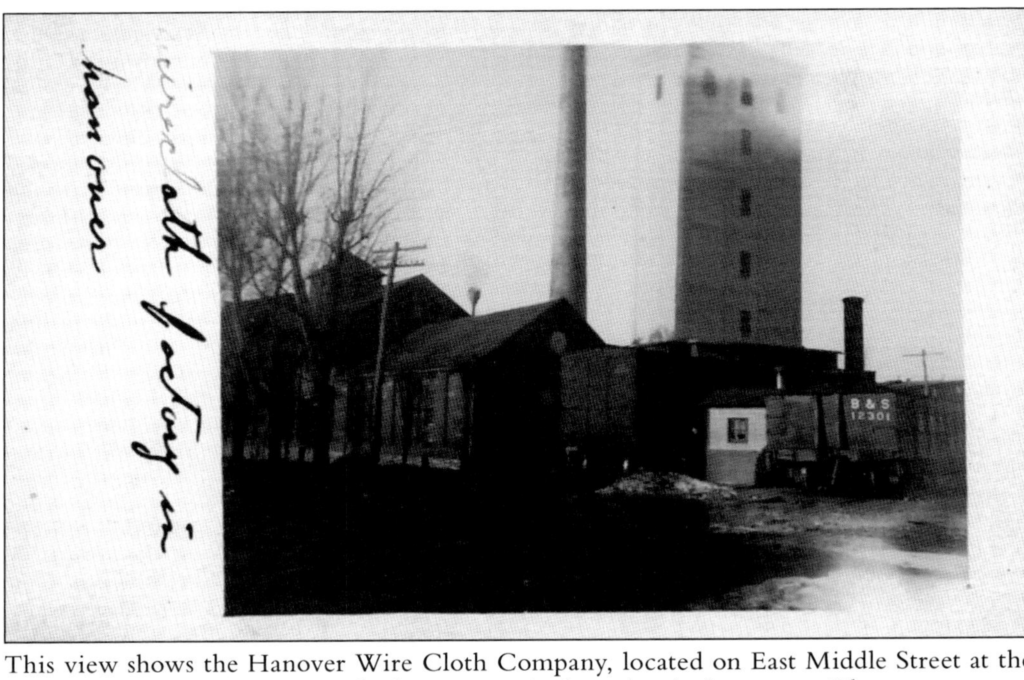

This view shows the Hanover Wire Cloth Company, located on East Middle Street at the Western Maryland Railroad. The large tower is the paint drying tower. The company was incorporated in 1903.

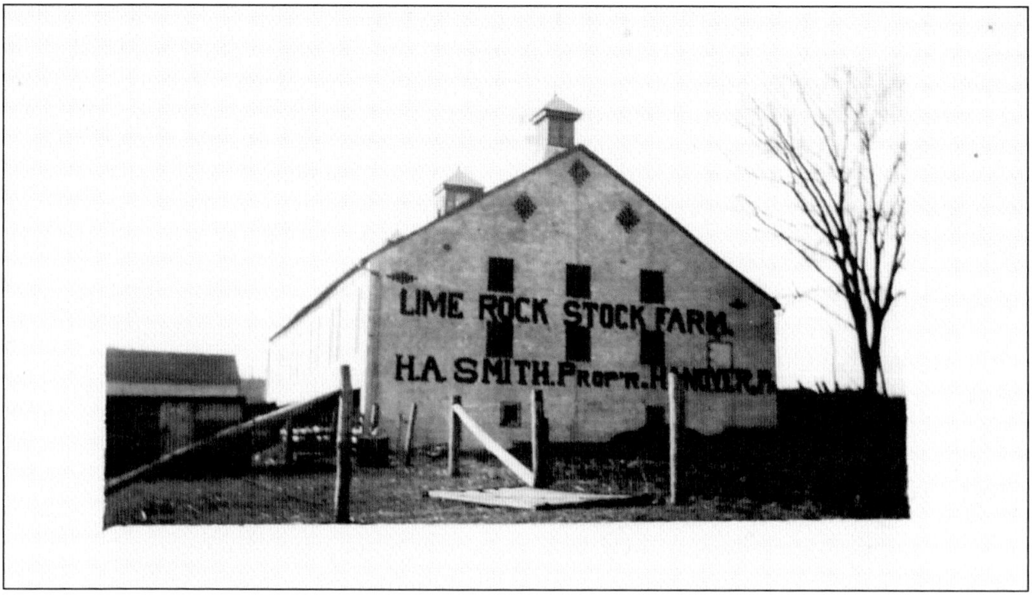

The Lime Rock Stock farm, H. A. Smith, proprietor, supposedly was located on Carlisle Street extended.

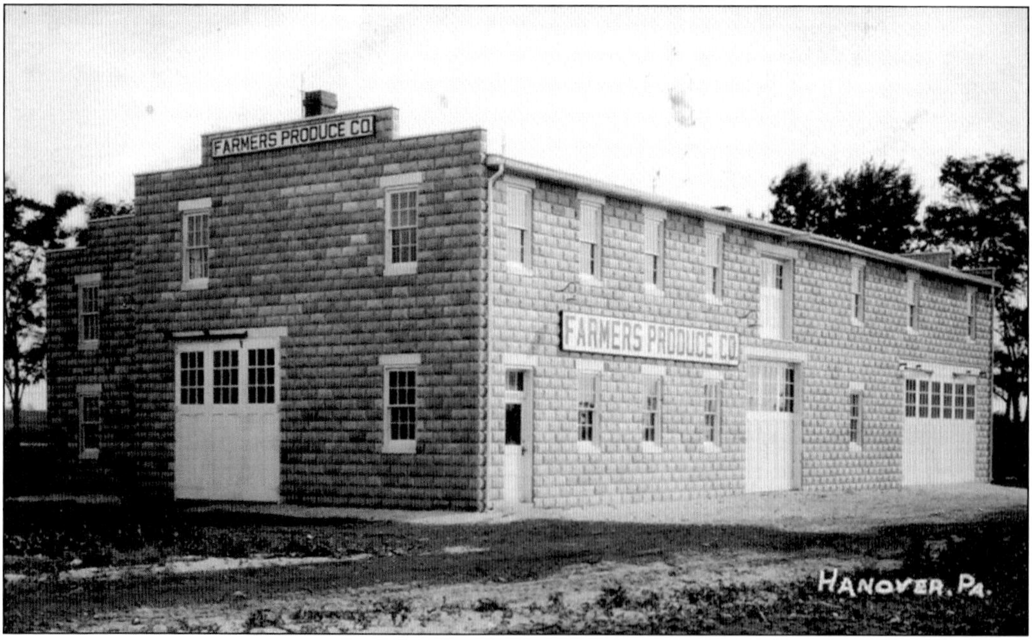

The Farmers Produce Company, owned by Annie and J. Walter Brendle, was located at 316 West Walnut Street. In the 1940s, it became Brendles Poultry. It is now an apartment building at 316–324 West Walnut Street.

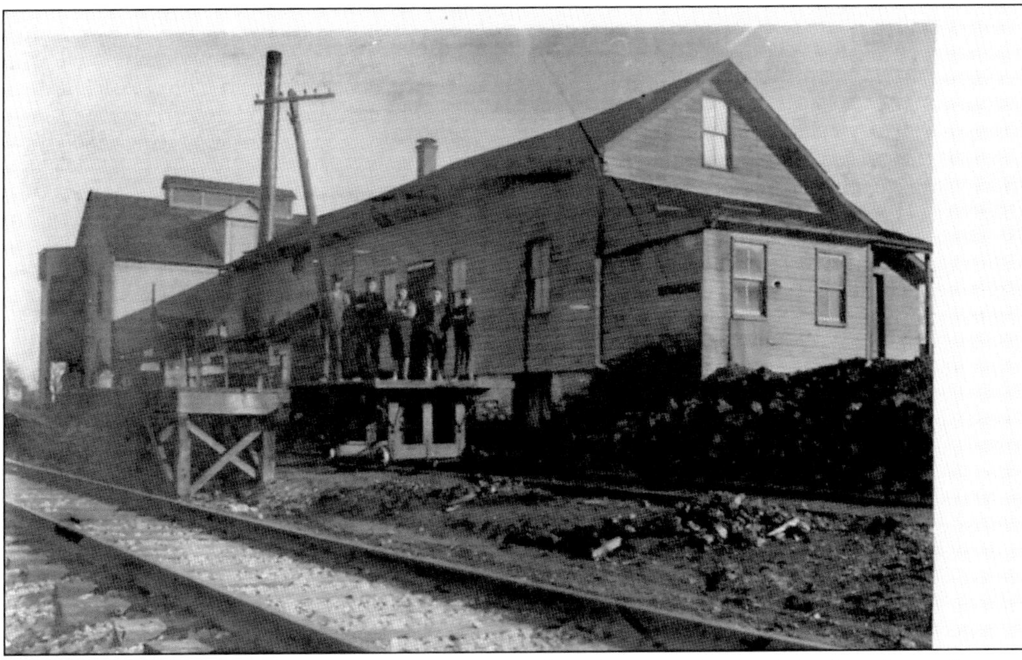

This photograph of the York Road Creamery at the Western Maryland Railroad crossing was taken in 1907. One of the men on the rolling platform is J. W. Haugh.

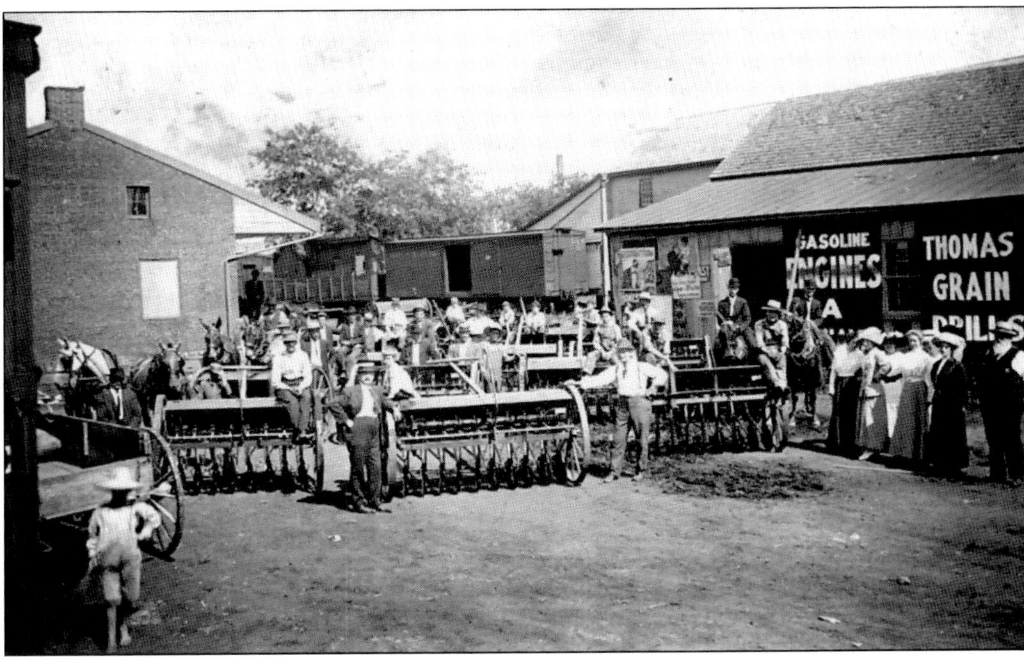

A farm equipment business located in Littlestown featured Thomas grain drills. This postcard was mailed in 1914.

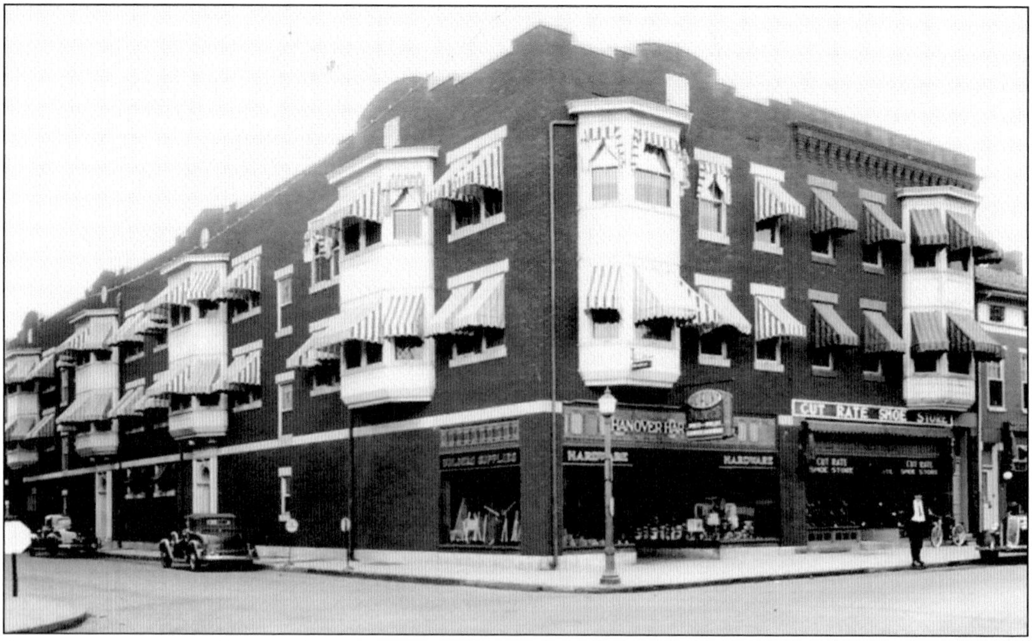

A *c.* 1940s view of the southeast corner of Carlisle Street and Chestnut Street shows Hanover Hardware, the Cut Rate Shoe Store, and the Jordan apartments on the upper floors.

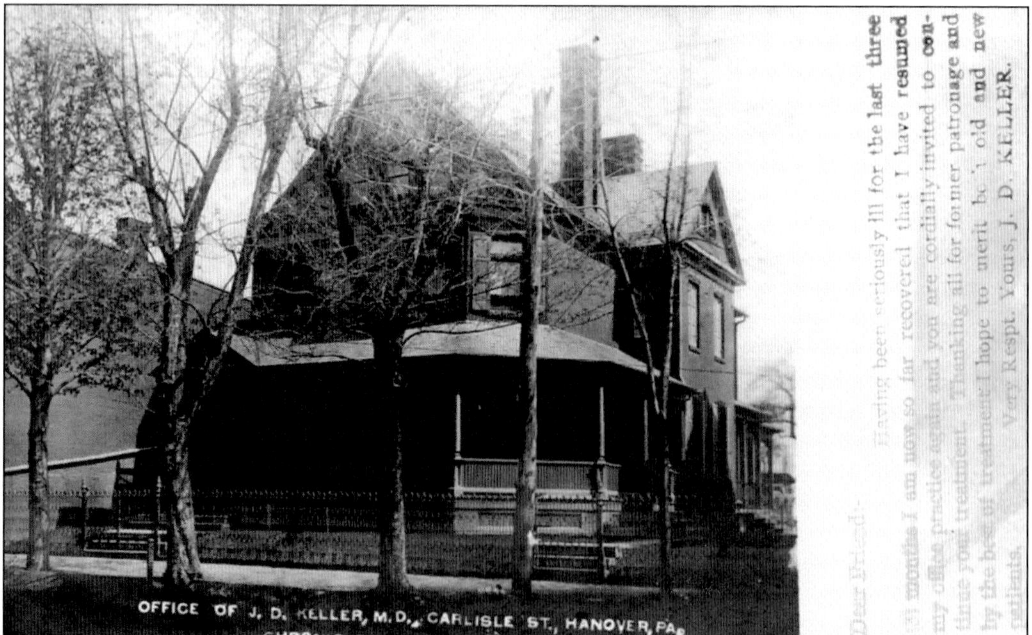

The office of John D. Keller, M.D., at 139 Carlisle Street advertises treatment for chronic diseases. The card was mailed in 1907.

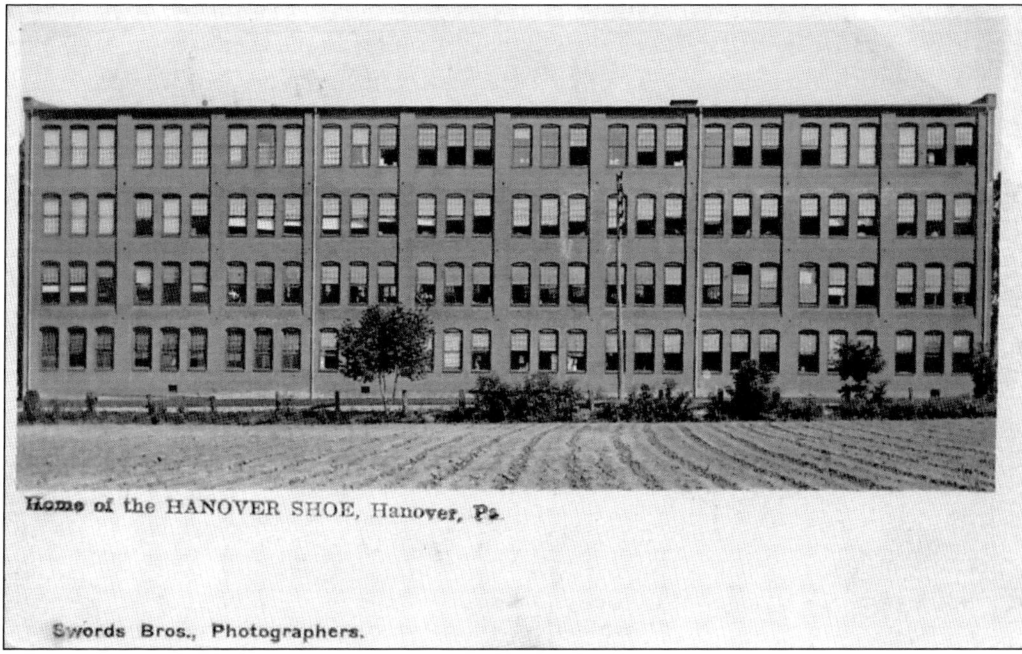

This picture of Hanover Shoe was photographed by Swords Brothers from the north, across the Pennsylvania Railroad. The stamp box indicates the card was printed between 1904 and 1920.

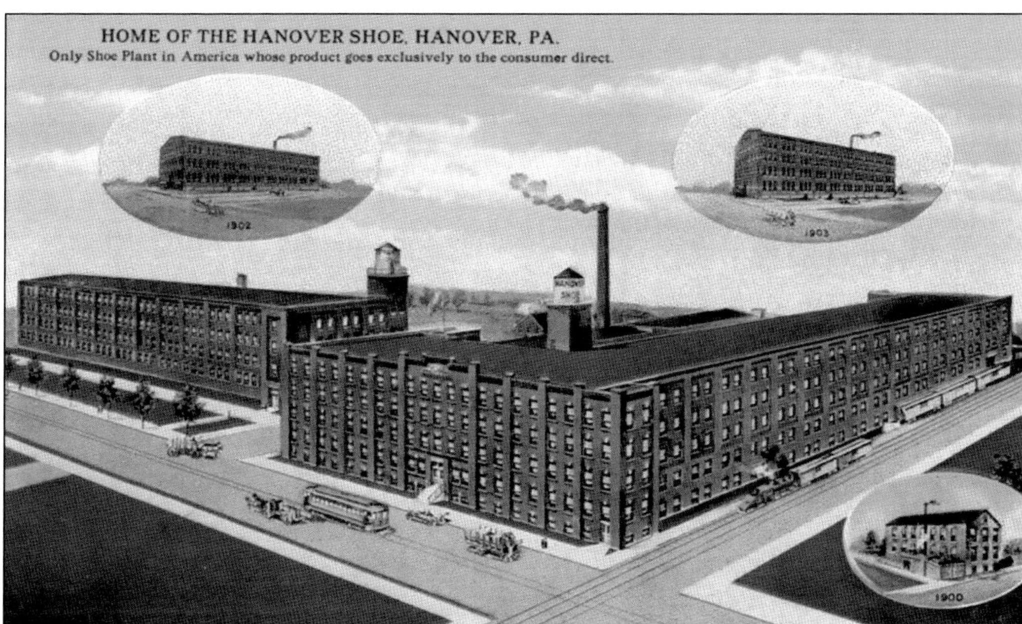

This postcard by C. T. Photochrome offers another picture of Hanover Shoe.

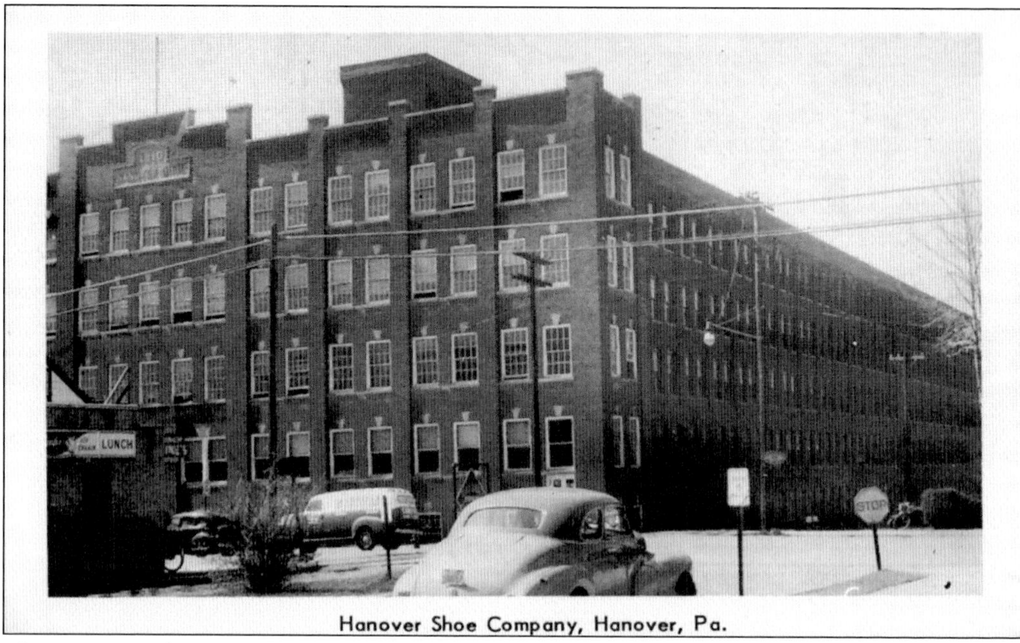

The Hanover Shoe Company was on Carlisle Street at Library Place. Cline's Lunch Room is on the bottom left. This postcard was published by C. Seeman of Philadelphia and is ink-stamped, "From the collection of W. E. Croom, Memphis, TN."

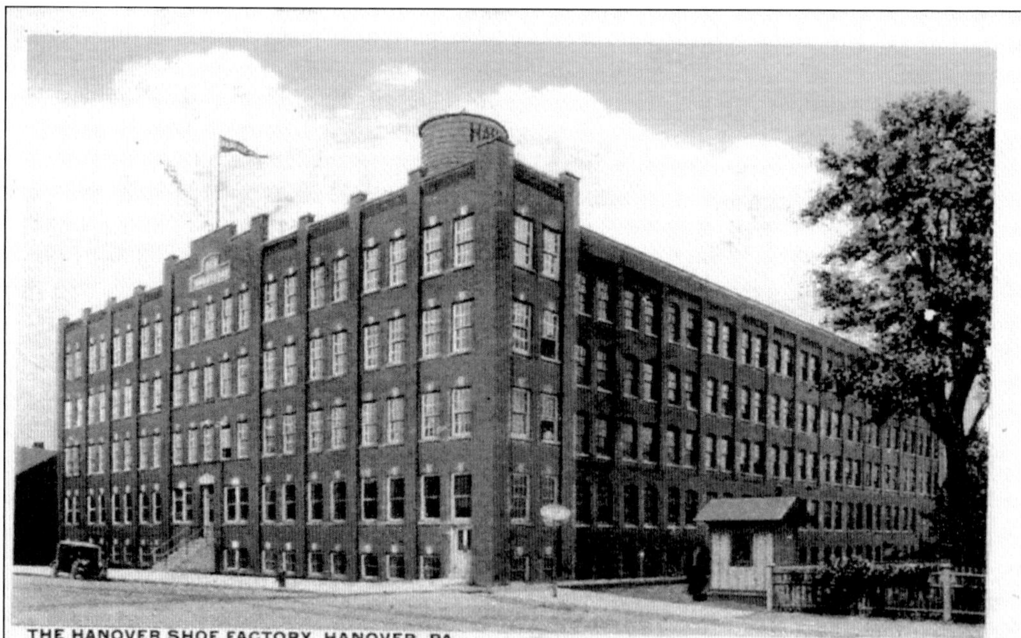

The Hanover Shoe Factory was on Carlisle Street and Library Place at the Pennsylvania Railroad crossing. The railroad flagman's shanty is evident. The card was published by David Kauffman of Baltimore and was mailed in 1922.

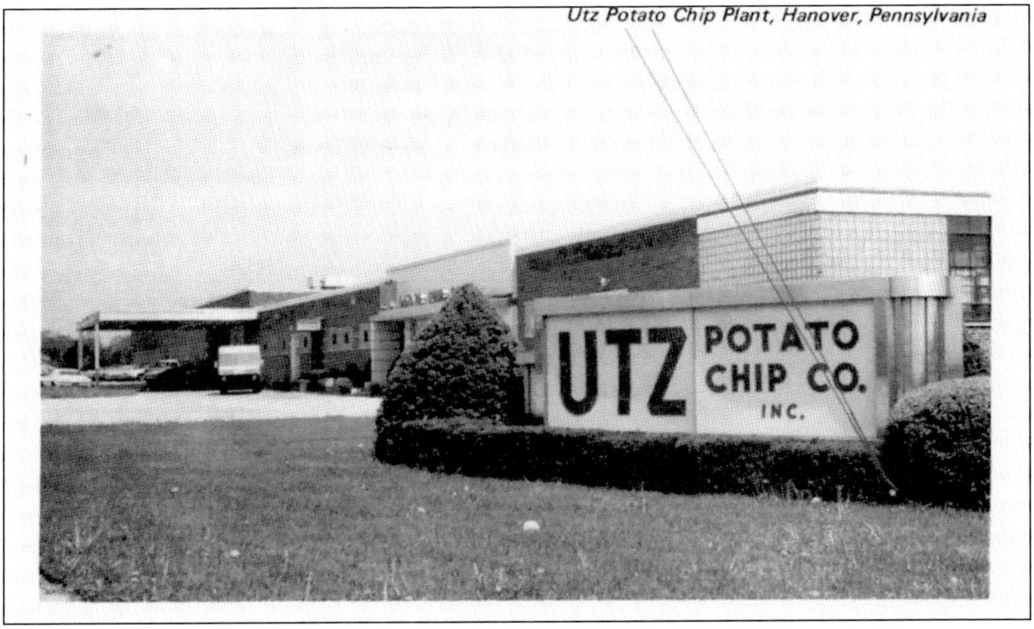

The Utz Potato Chip Company plant is shown at the southeast corner of Clearview Road and Carlisle Street.

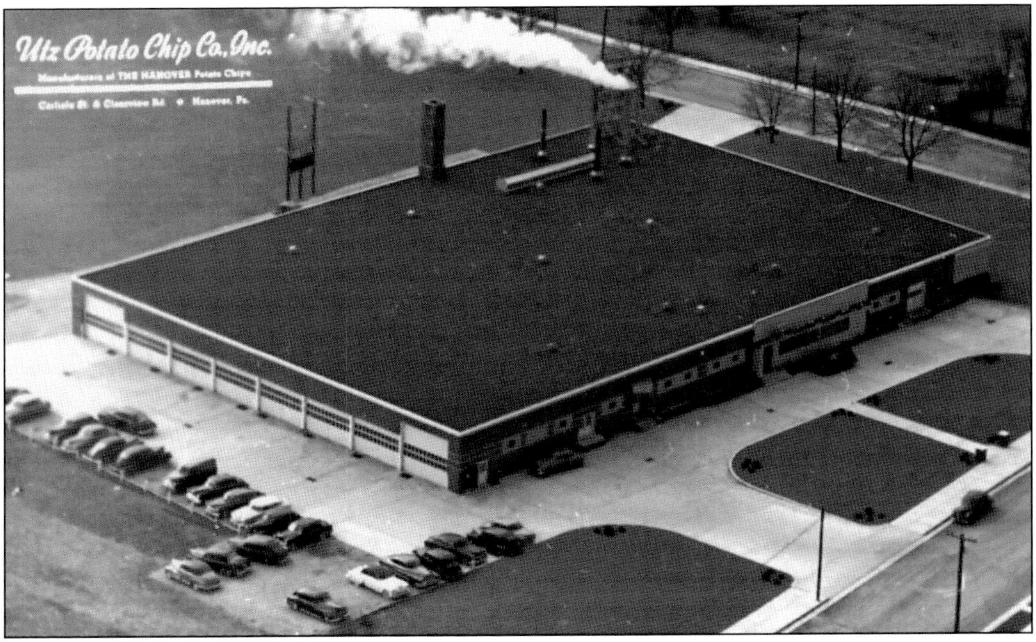

An aerial view shows the Carlisle Street Utz Potato Chip Company plant.

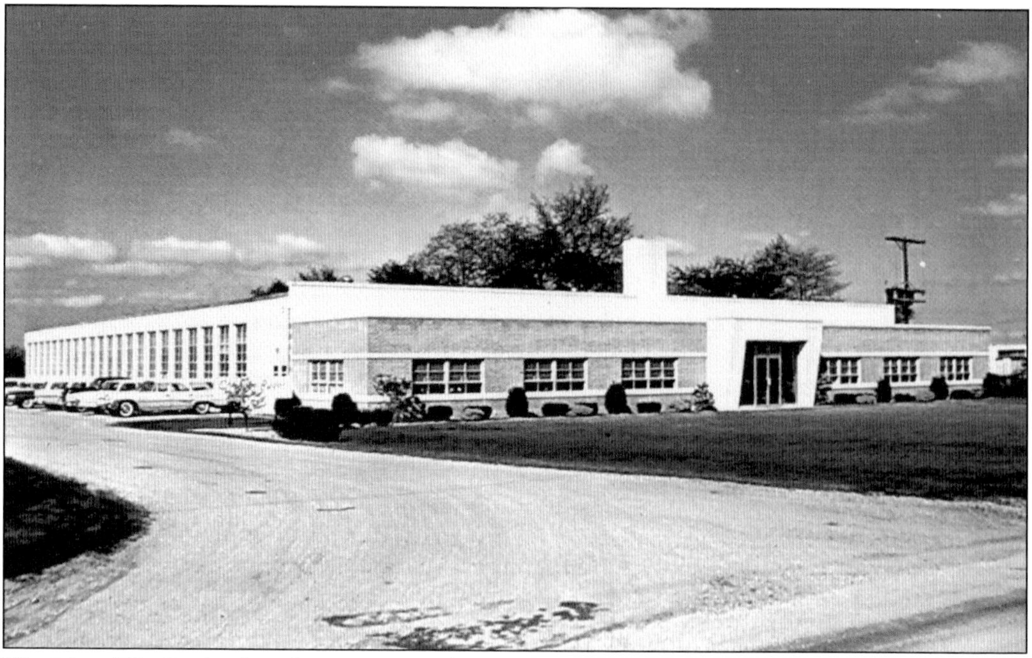

The New Way Packaging Company on Blettner Avenue manufactured packaging machines for industry. This postcard was printed by Dexter Press of West Nyack, New York, and published by Poist's Studio at 20–22 East Middle Street in Hanover.

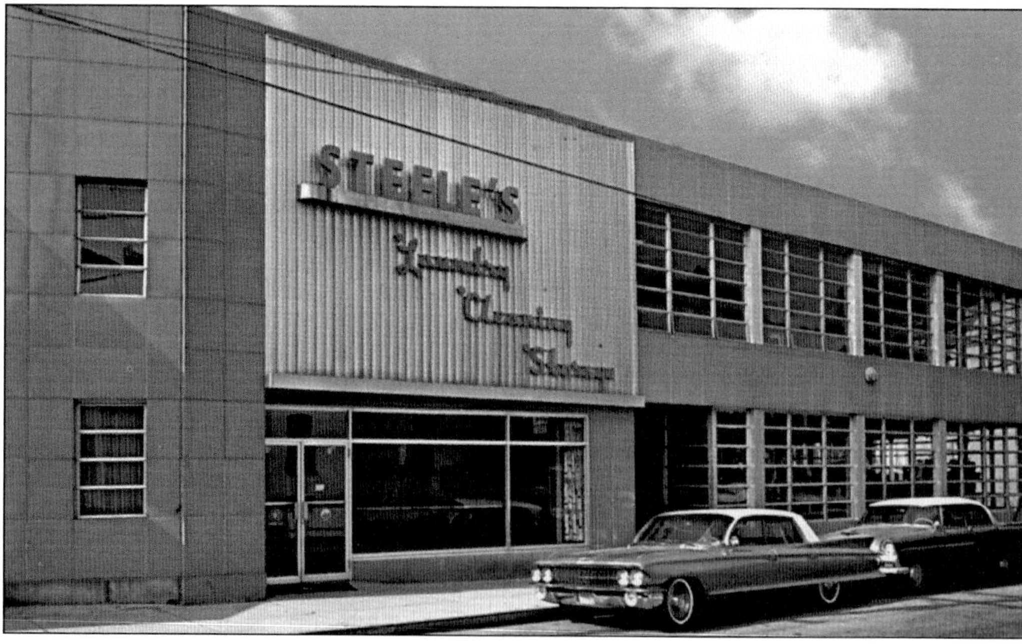

Steele's Laundry was located at 110 High Street.

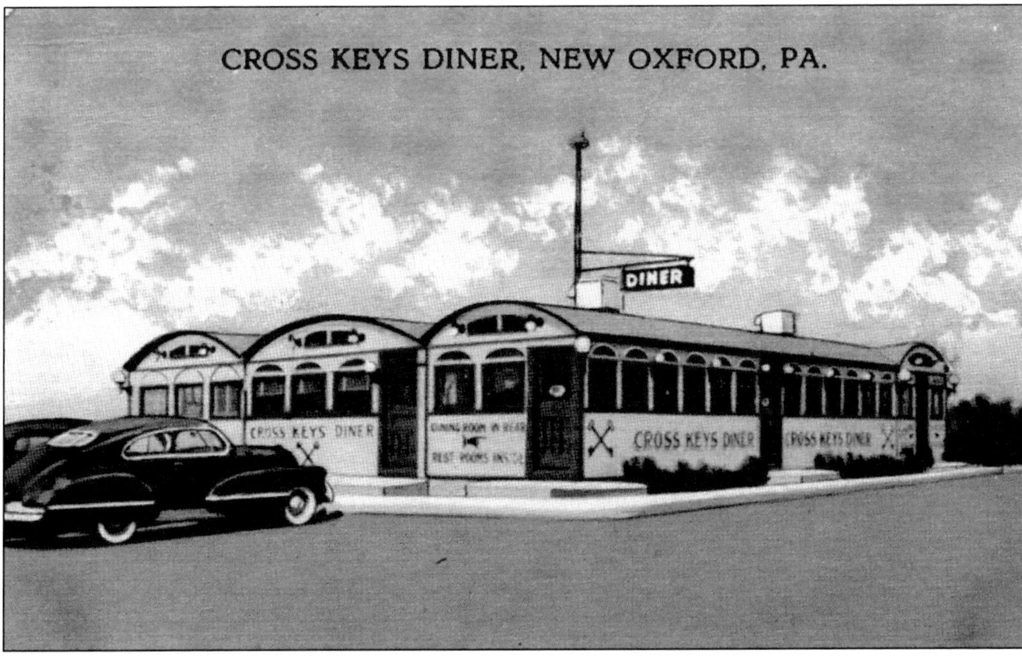

The Cross Keys Diner in New Oxford, Pennsylvania, is at the northeast intersection of Routes 94 and 30. The diner was established in 1937. This card was printed by Seals of Des Moines, Iowa, for John E. George, proprietor of the Cross Keys Diner.

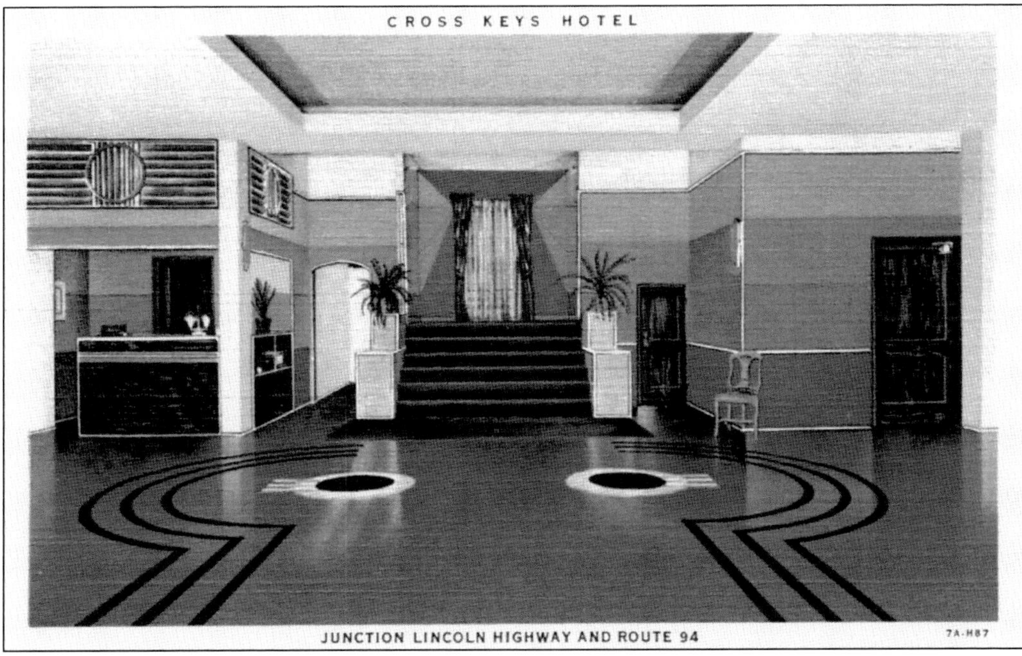

The Cross Keys Hotel, with its art deco interior, was at the junction of Routes 30 and 94 north of Hanover. The building is now part of the Brethren Home Retirement Community.

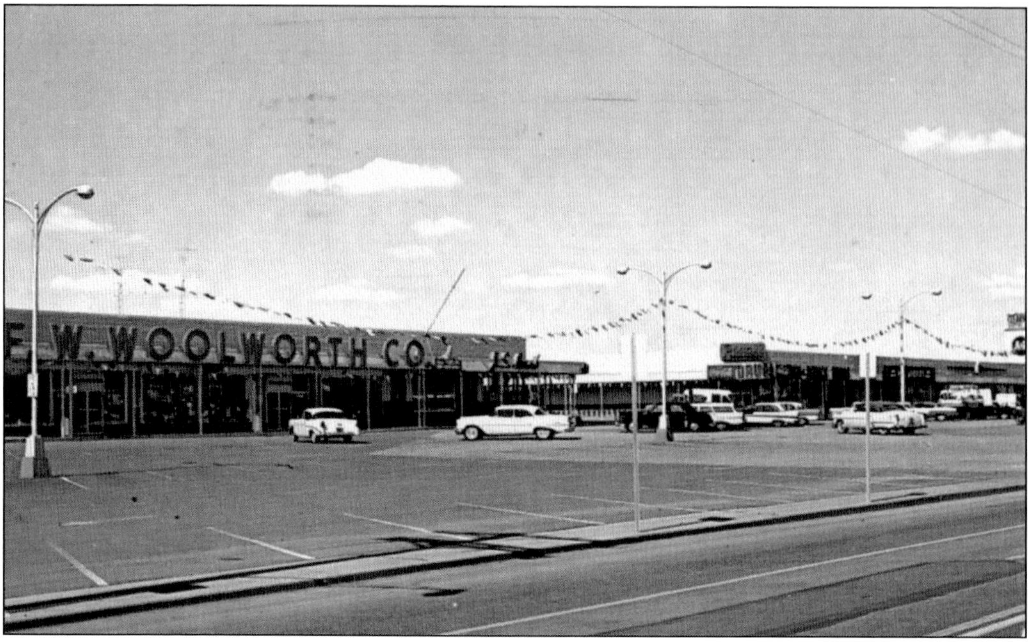

This view of the Clearview Shopping Center on Carlisle Street extended was printed by Colourpicture Publishers of Boston for Mebane Card Company of Wilkes-Barre, Pennsylvania. AAA of southern Pennsylvania now occupies the Woolworth site.

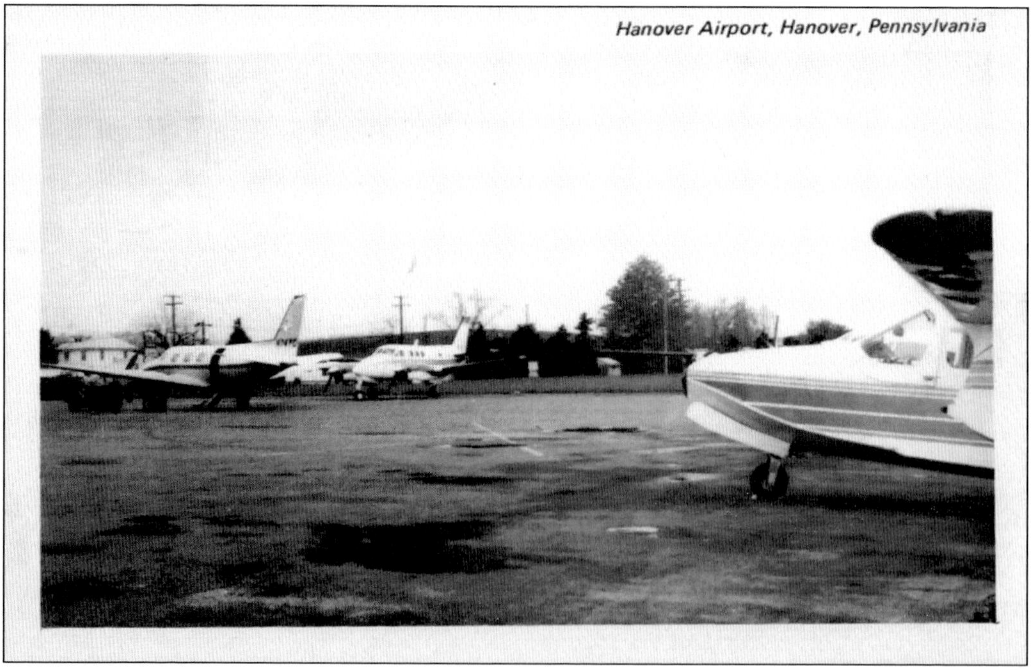

The Hanover Airport was on the northeast edge of Hanover and was owned and operated by Ray Devner. It is no longer in operation.

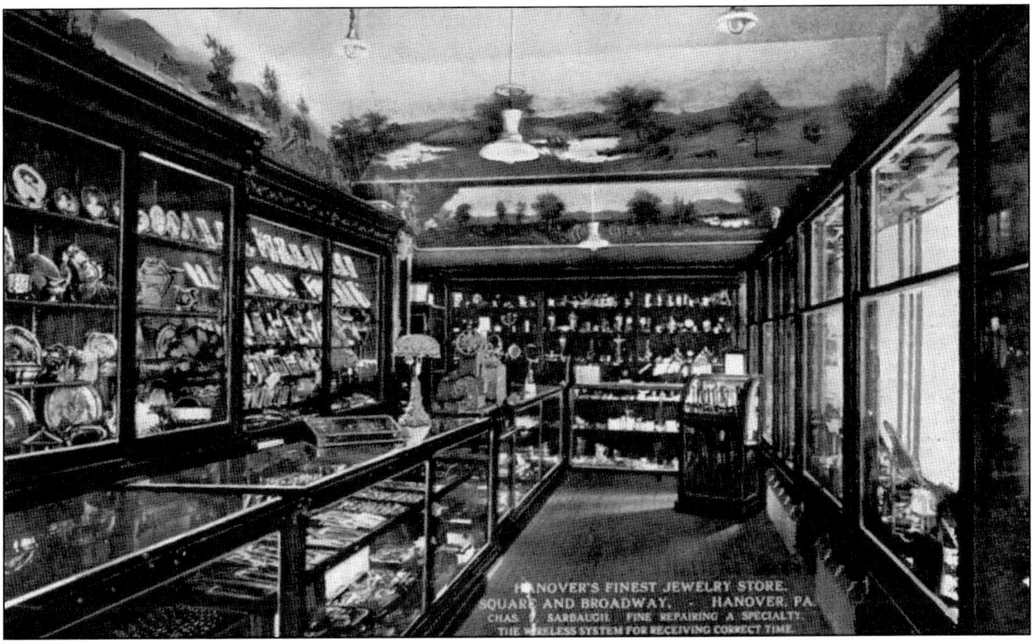

"Hanover's Finest Jewelry Store" on Center Square and Broadway advertised "the wireless system for receiving the correct time." This postcard was published by Leo Meyer of Easton, Pennsylvania and was mailed April 1923.

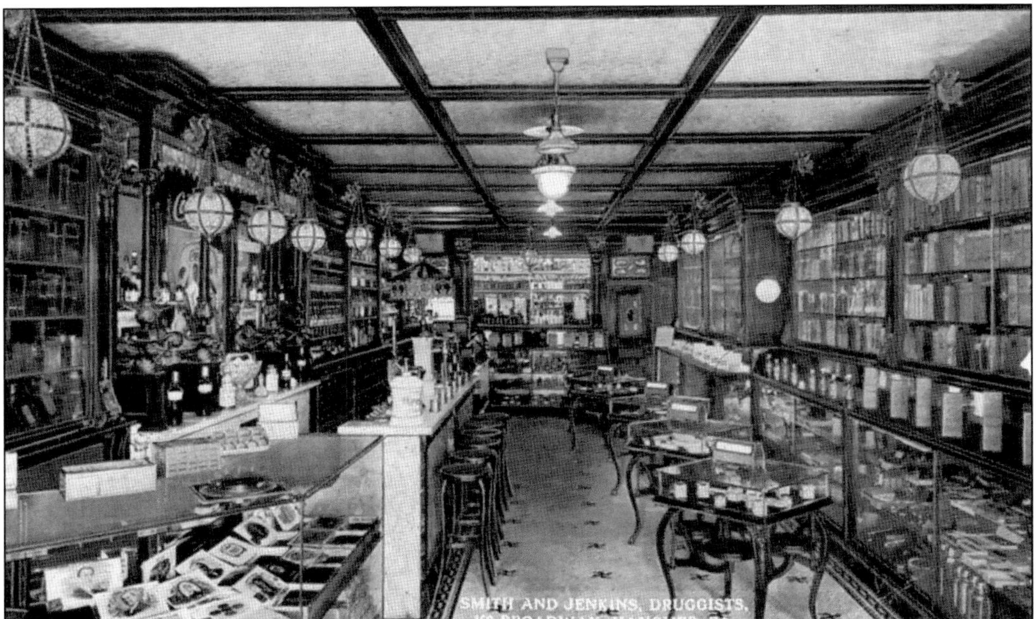

Smith and Jenkins Druggists did business at 100 Broadway, the intersection of Broadway and Railroad Street.

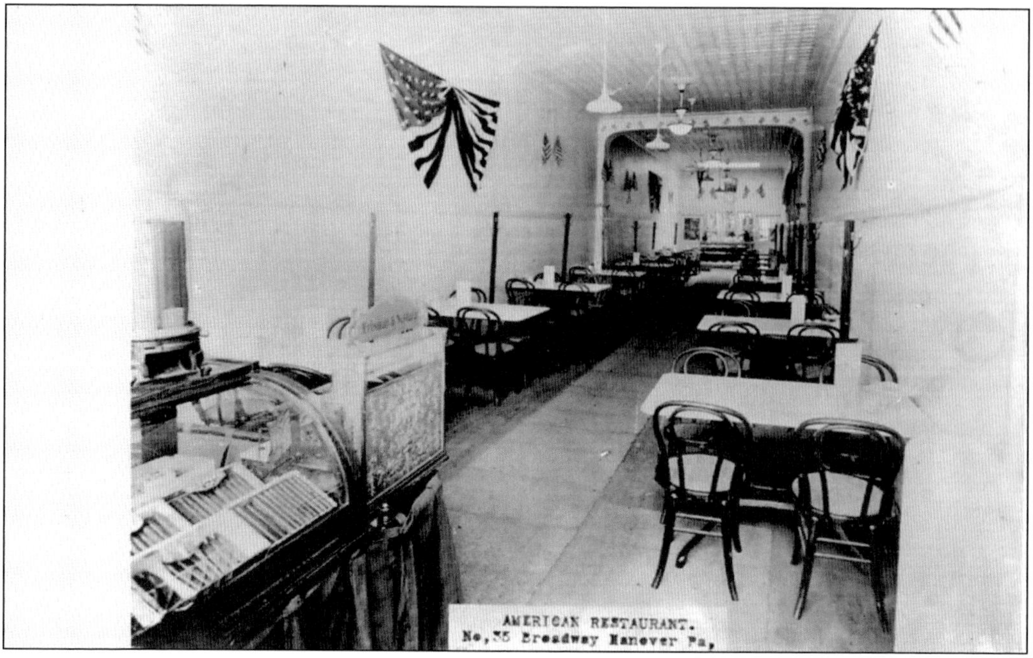

This is the interior of the American Restaurant at 35 Broadway. From the 1920s through the 1940s, the Hanover Quick Lunch operated from this location.

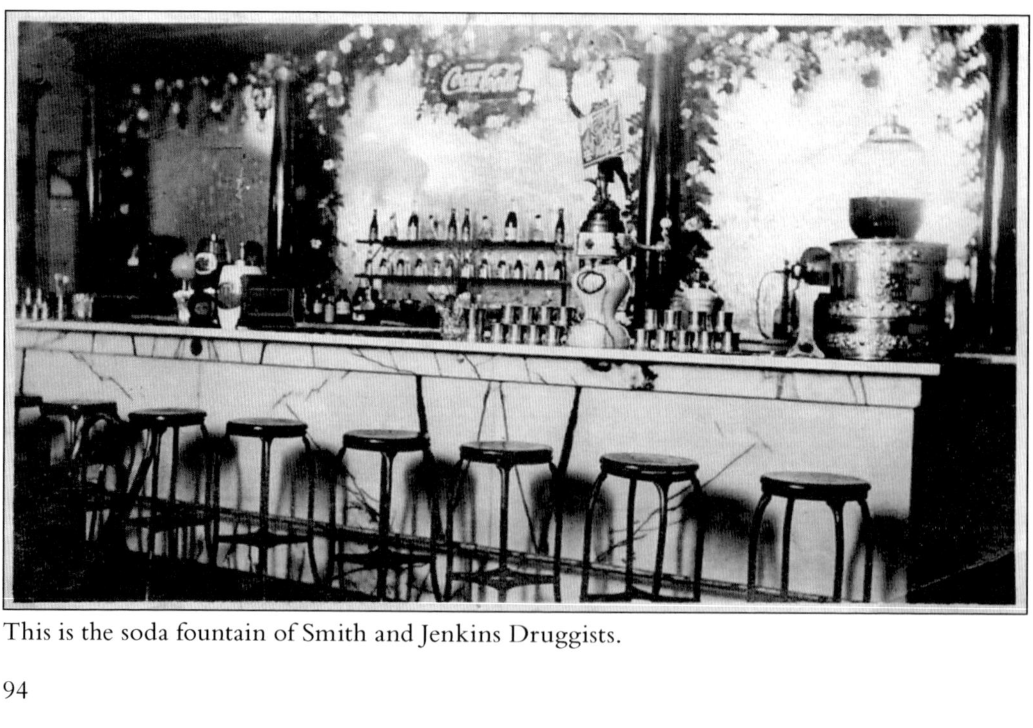

This is the soda fountain of Smith and Jenkins Druggists.

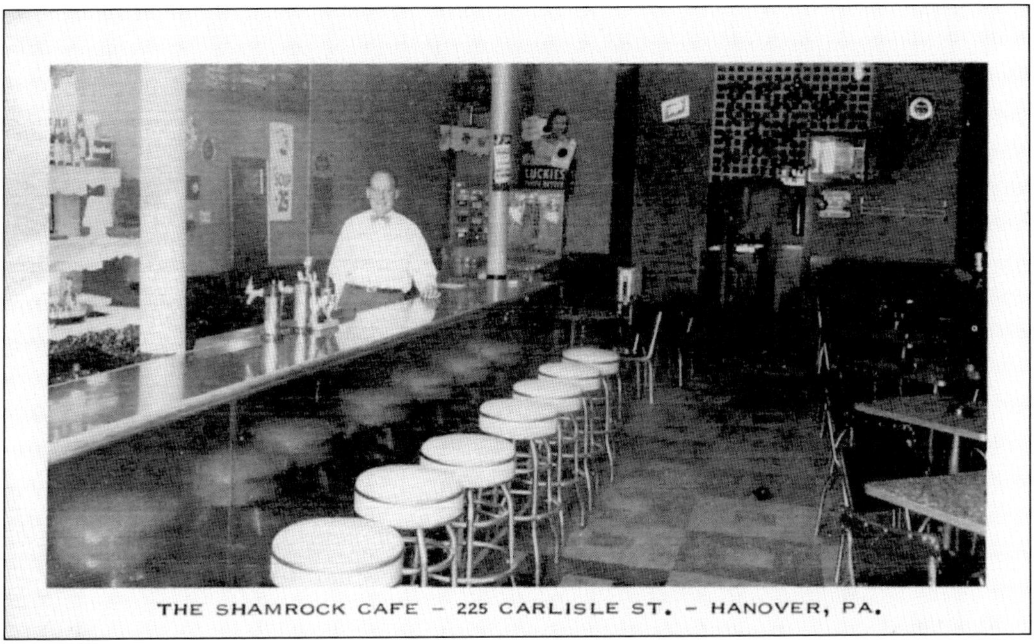

The Shamrock Cafe at 225 Carlisle Street had a number of owners, including Earl Maugans, Paul Koontz, and Alvin Henry. It was located at Carlisle Street and Library Place.

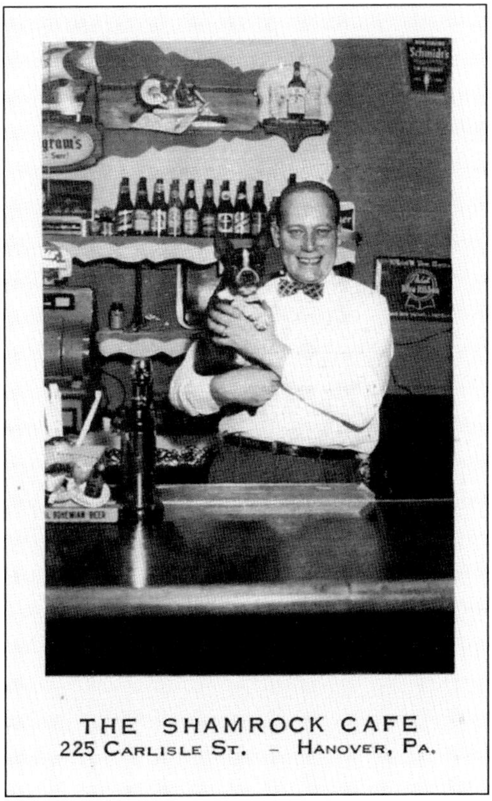

This is another picture of the Shamrock Cafe.

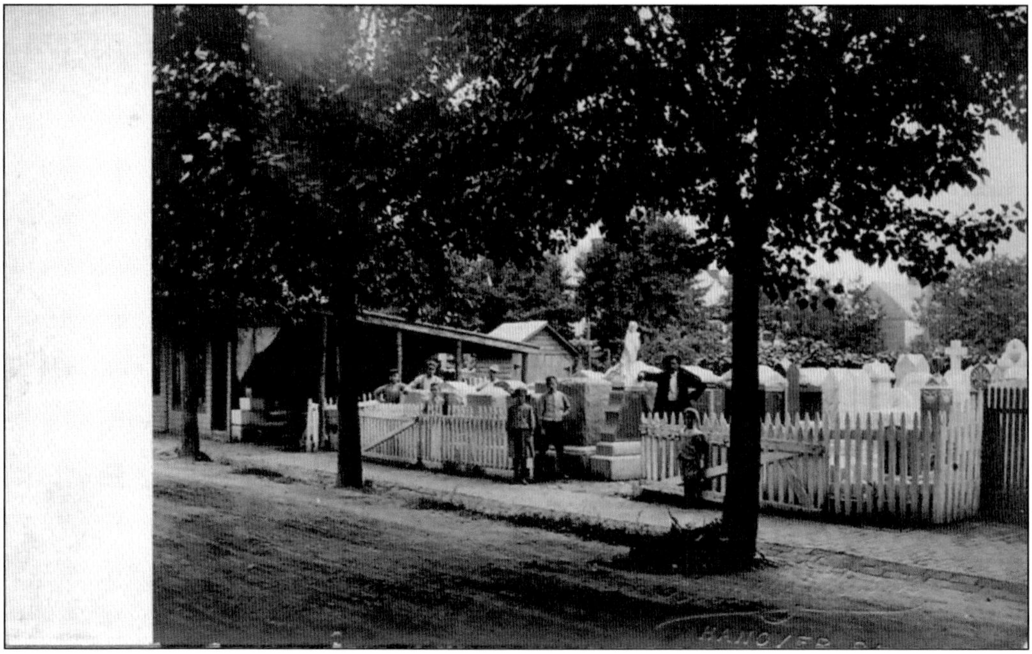

The Charles Redding marble yard is on East Middle Street. Redding is in the dark coat in the center. The *c.* 1915 photograph is by Feeser's Studio of East Middle Street.

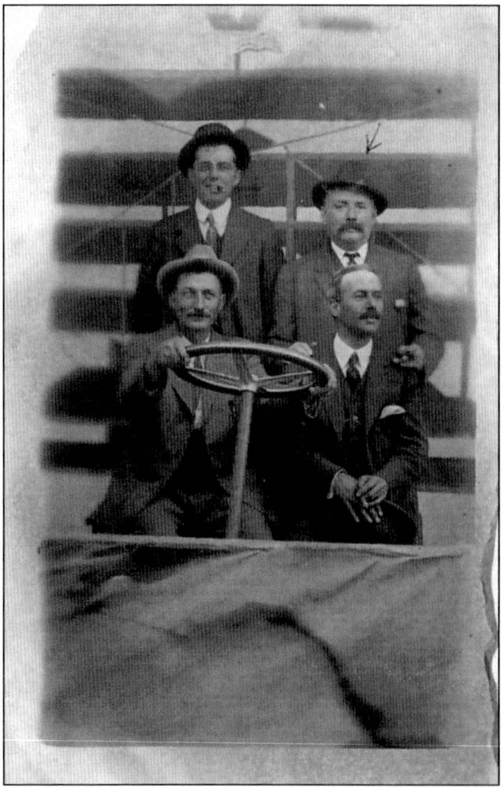

The four men in the picture are, from left to right, as follows: (first row) Charles Redding, owner of the Garford solid tire truck, and an unidentified man; (second row) Ian Mathias and J. C. Sprenkle. Redding used the truck in his tombstone business.

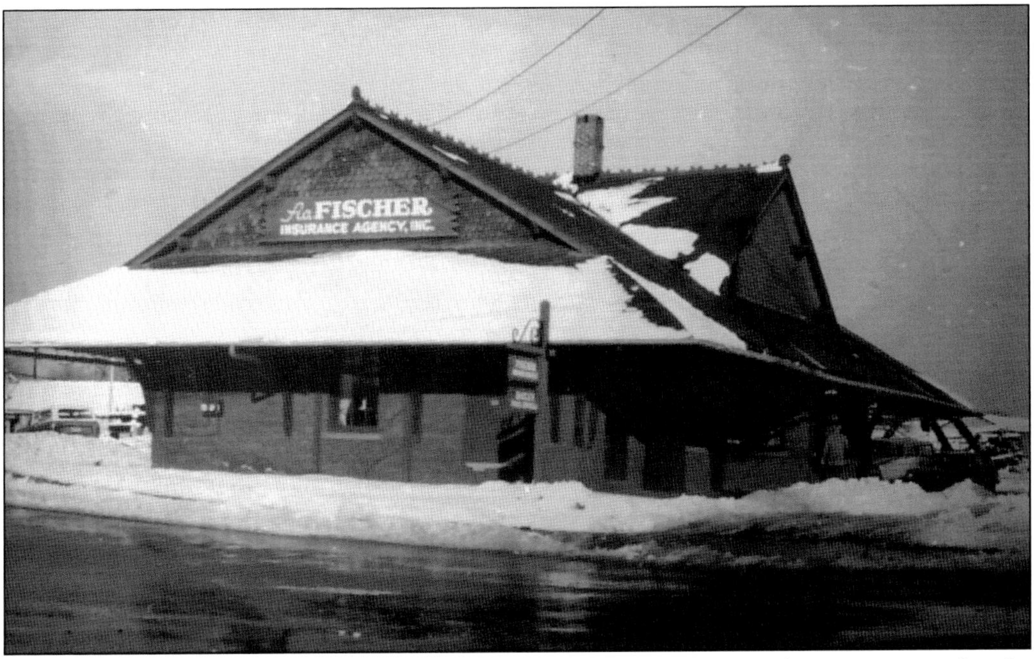

The former Union Station is now the Fischer's Insurance office. It was the passenger station for the former Western Maryland Railroad on the left and the former Pennsylvania Railroad on the right.

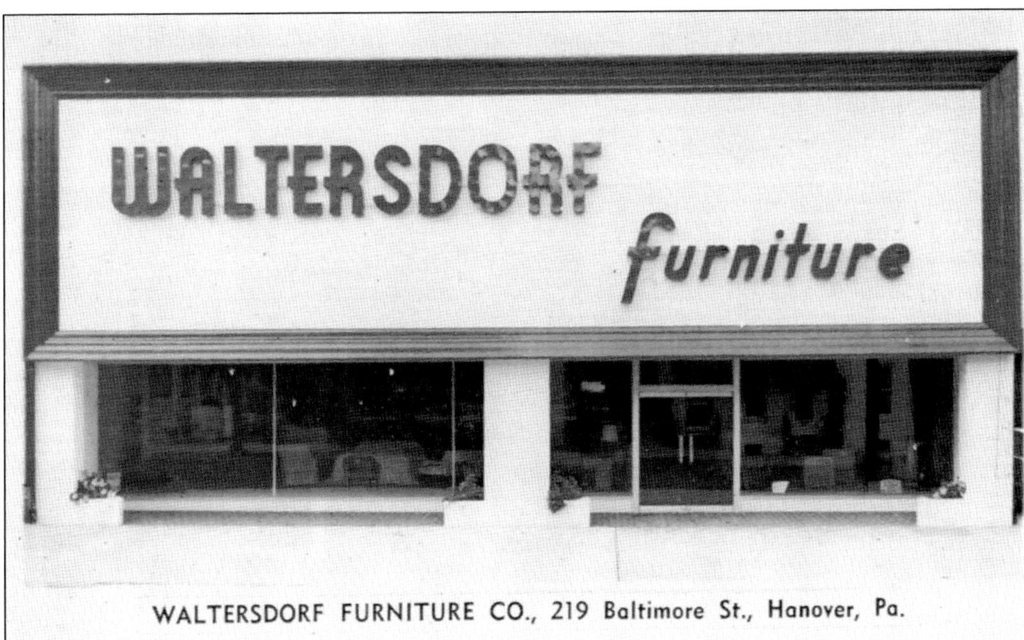

This picture of the Waltersdorf Furniture Company, located at 219 Baltimore Street, was published by Poist's Studio at 20–22 East Middle Street.

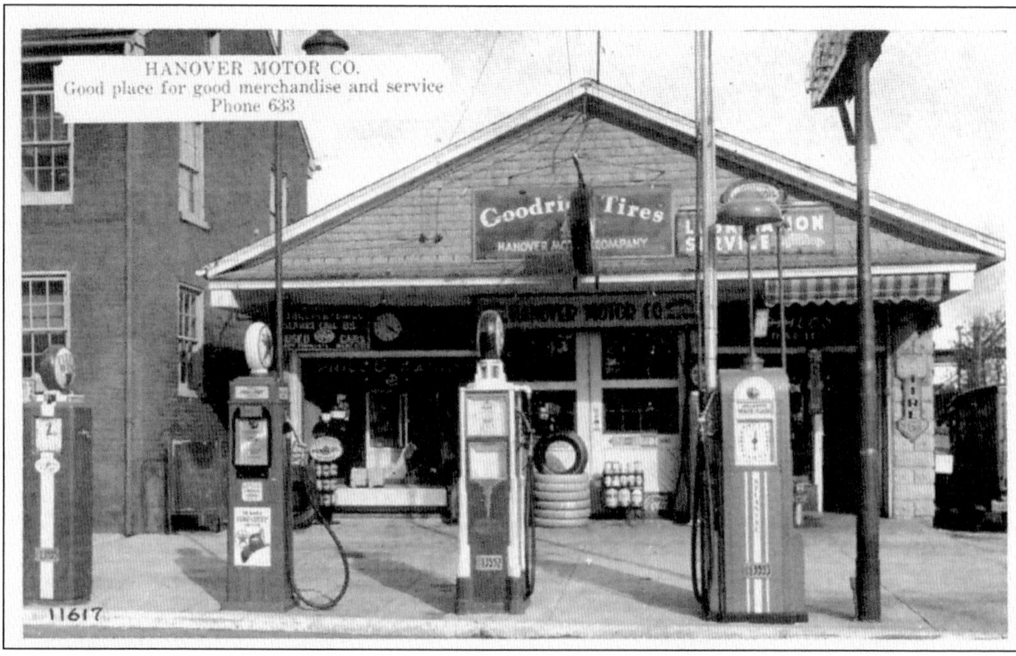

The Hanover Motor Company, owned and operated by Charles E. Huff, was located at Broadway and Stock Street. This postcard was mailed November 29, 1939.

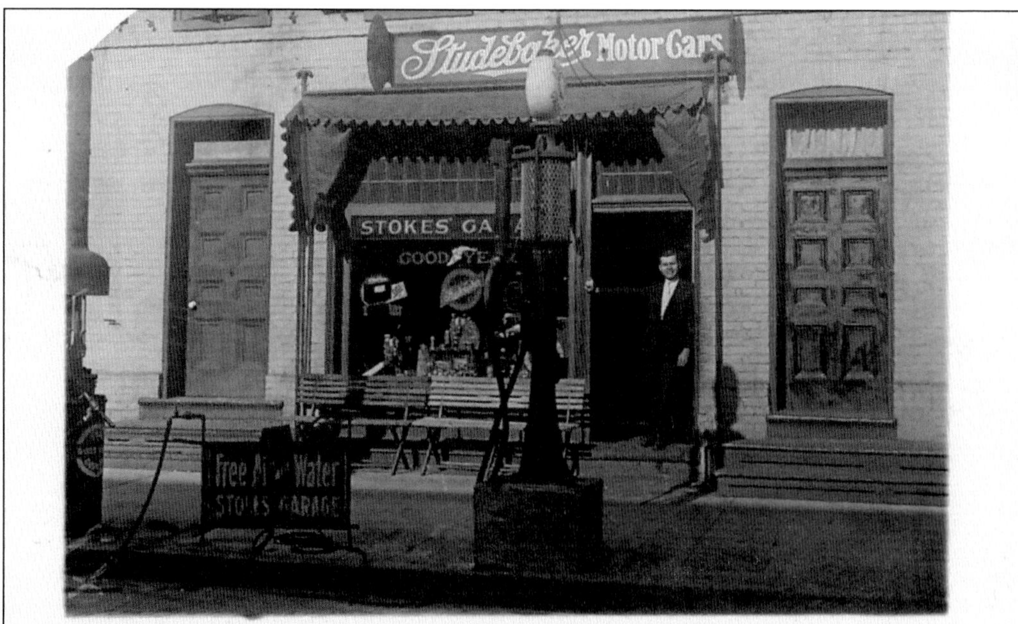

The Stokes garage, owned by Leroy B. Stokes, at 30–34 Baltimore Street, sold Studebaker, Overland, and Willy's-Knight touring cars, as well as Goodyear tires. John L. Kaltreider, the bookkeeper, is standing in the doorway in 1917. Kleffel's Clothing Store subsequently occupied this building until an April 3, 1990, fire destroyed the structure. It is now the site of Rite-Aid. Note the vintage gas pumps at the street.

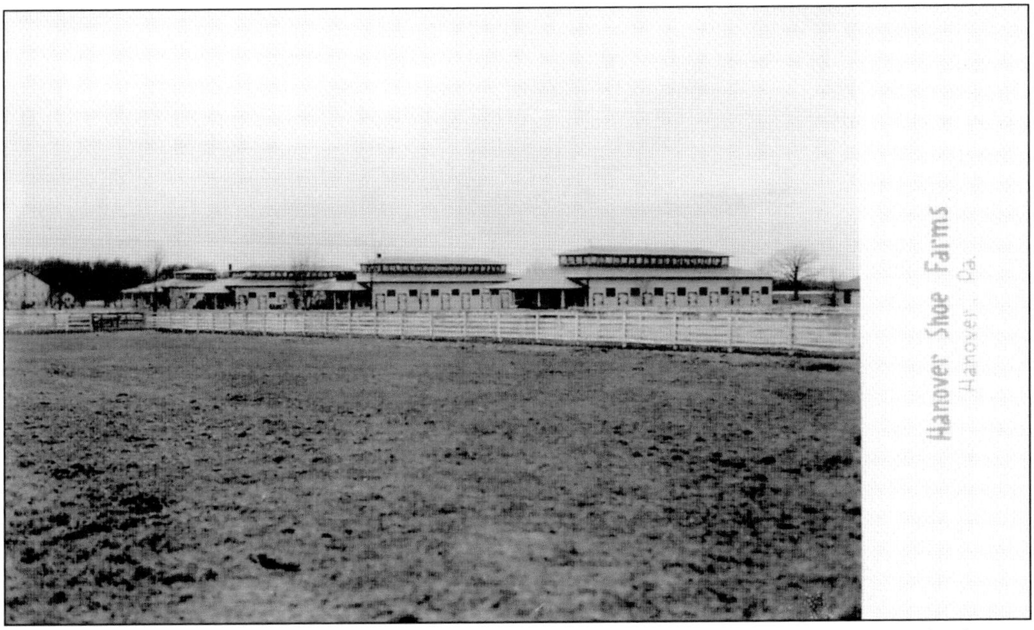

Hanover Shoe Farms, located on Route 194 between Littlestown and Hanover, is the largest Standardbred nursery in the world. The stamp box indicates this postcard was made between 1927 and the 1940s.

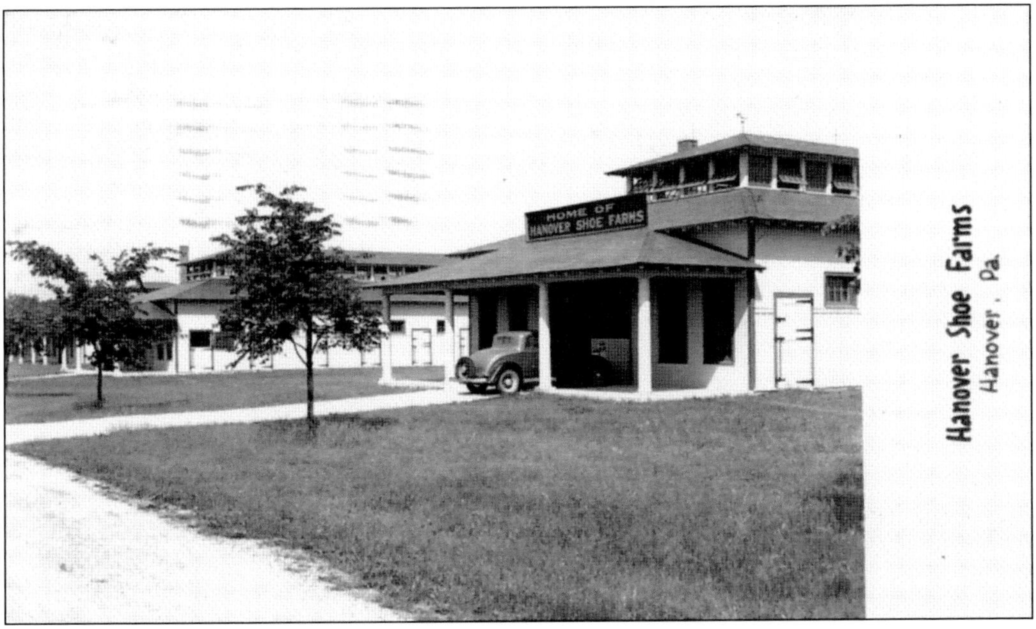

Hanover Shoe Farms on the Littlestown Pike, just outside Hanover, is the world's largest Standardbred horse farm. These buildings were erected in 1926. The farm now encompasses 3,000 acres. This postcard was sent on November 6, 1937, by Alma Sheppard, daughter of one of the founders, Lawrence B. Sheppard. Alma was born in 1926, the same year the breeding business started. At the age of 11, Alma drove horse Dean Hanover at Lexington and broke a trotting record for three-year-olds at 1 minute, 58 and a half seconds. The young trees were elm trees which have since succumbed to Dutch Elm disease and have been replaced by pin oak trees.

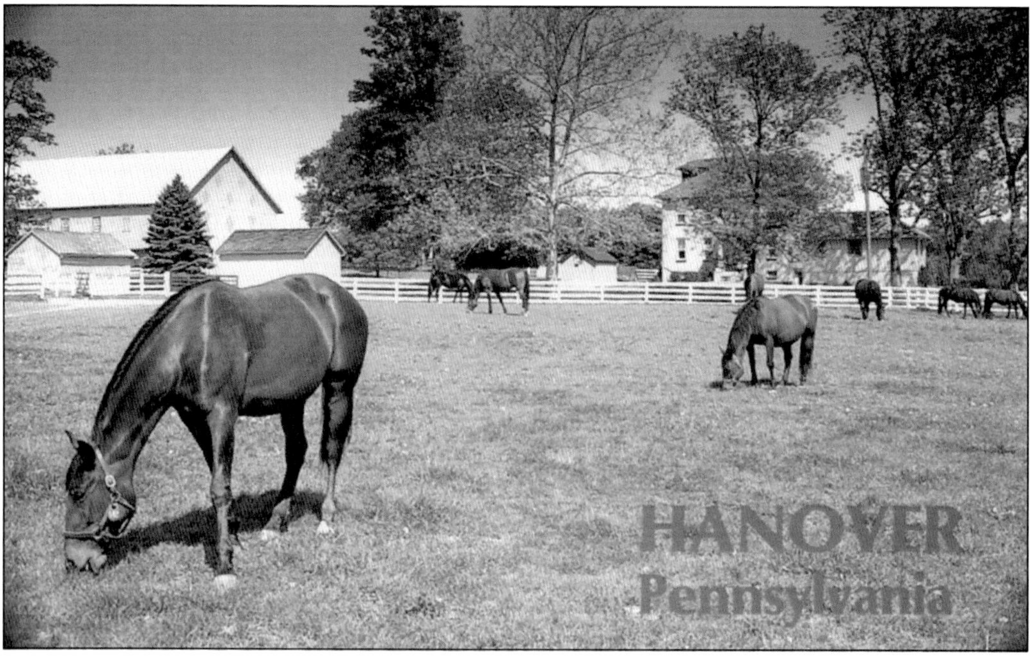

Horses graze at Hanover Shoe Farms. This color postcard was distributed by the Hanover Chamber of Commerce.

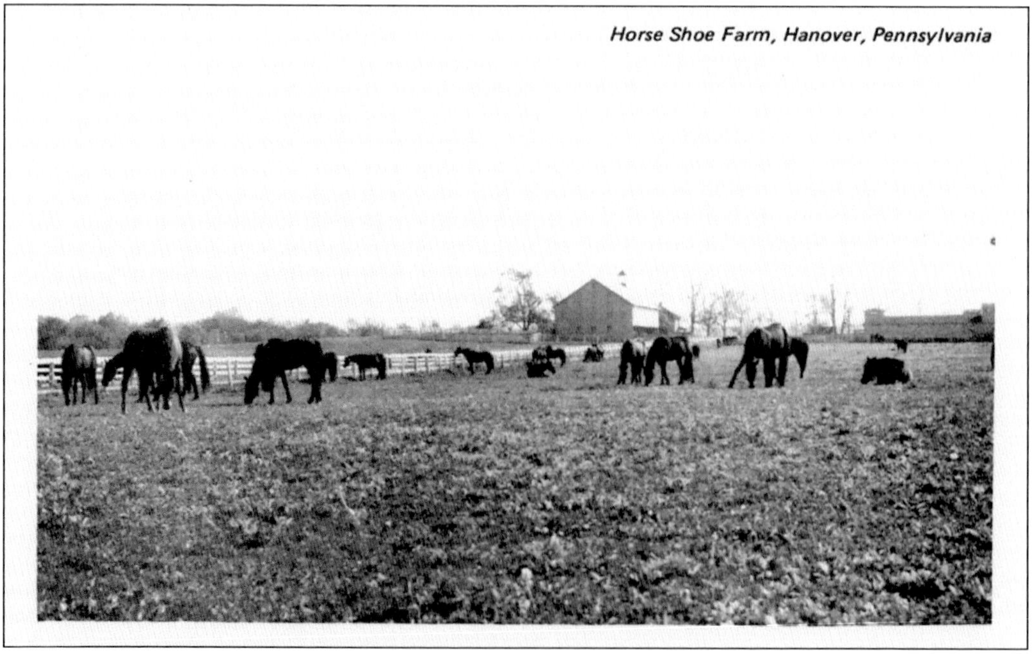

This is another image of Hanover Shoe Farms.

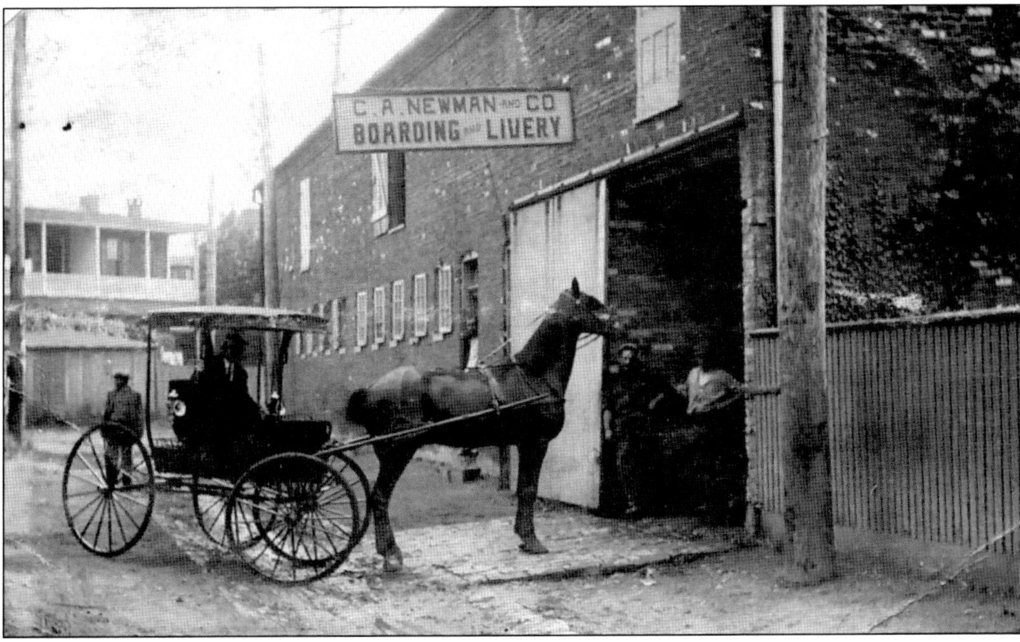

In 1911, the livery stable of Calvin A. Newman was located at 601 Frederick Street.

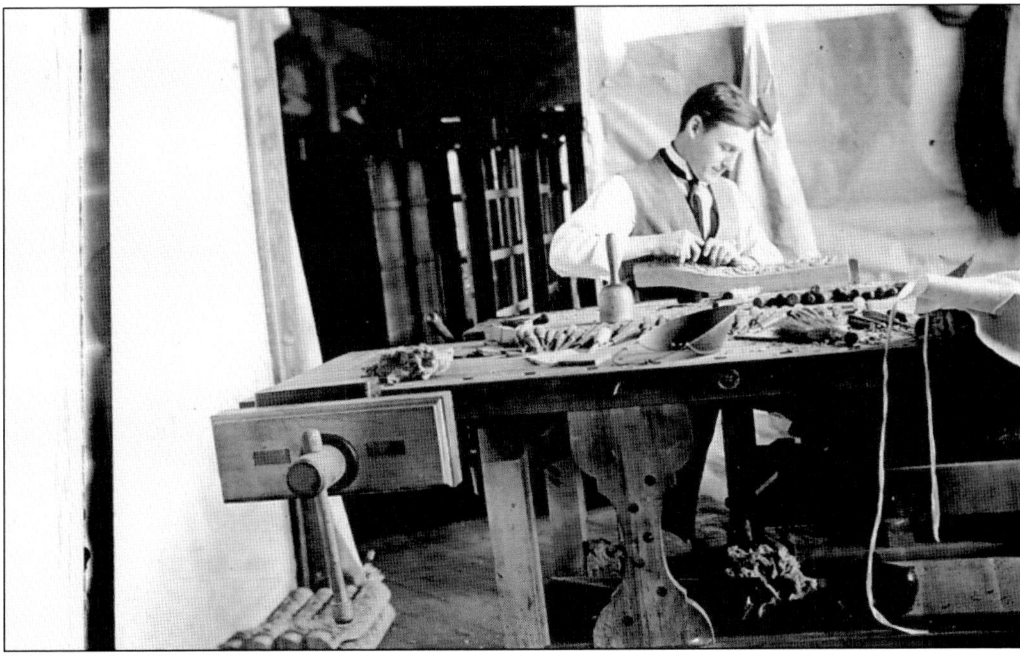

The George A. Long Cabinet Company was located at High Street and Maple Avenue and started operations on March 16, 1902. They advertised in the 1925 Polk's Directory as "manufacturers of complete dining room suites, player piano roll cabinets and record cabinets for use with portable talking machines." China cabinets can be seen in the background.

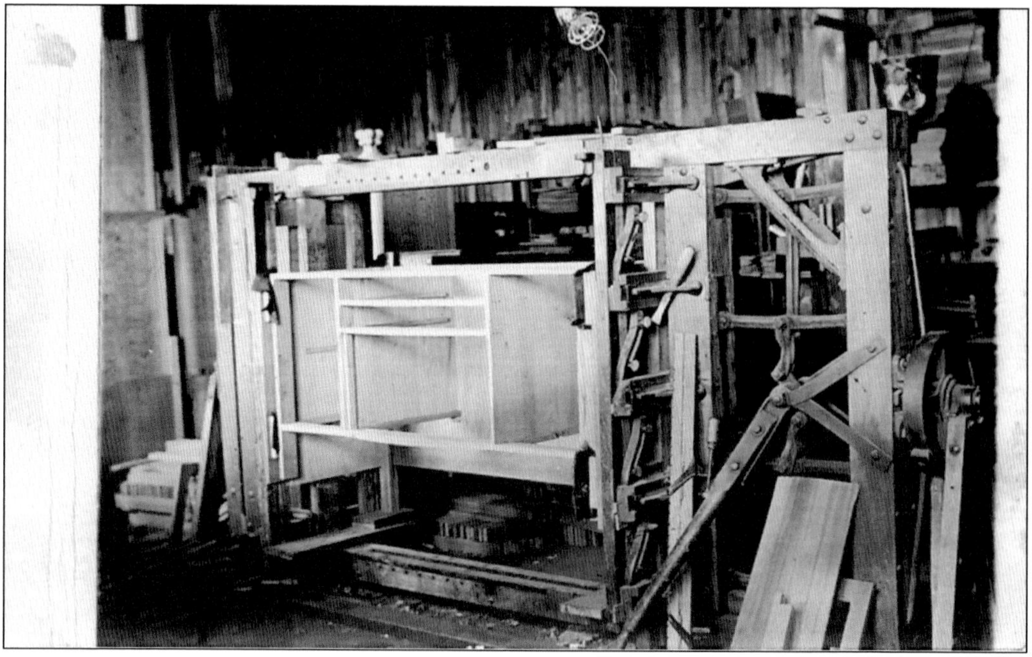

This postcard of the George A. Long Cabinet Company shows a press used to assemble dressers. The stamp box indicates the card was printed between 1904 and 1918.

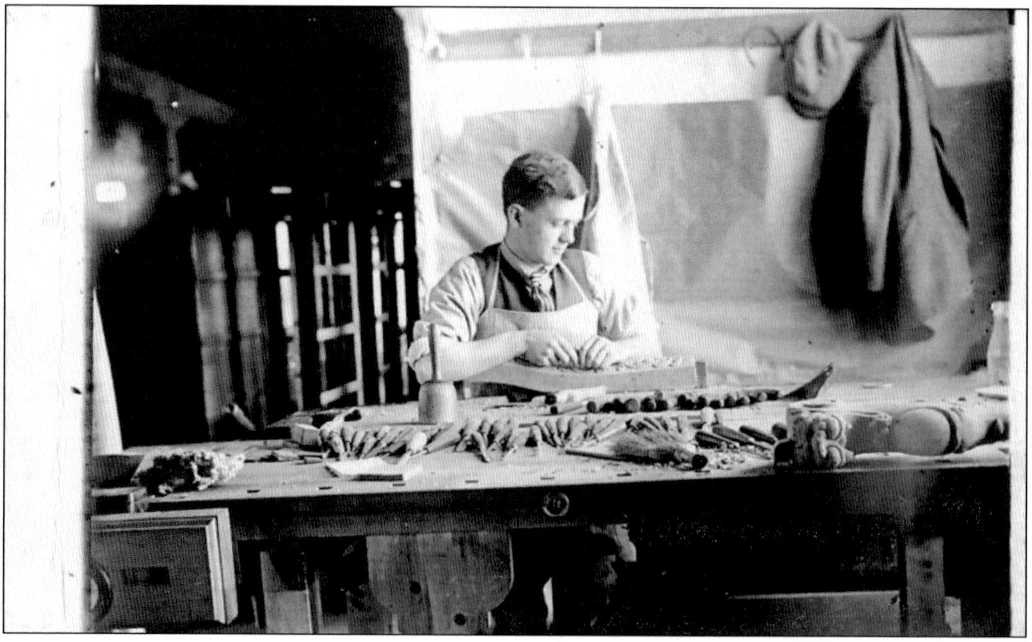

This craftsman carves legs for bow front china cabinets at the George A. Long Cabinet Company. The stamp box indicates the card was printed between 1904 and 1918.

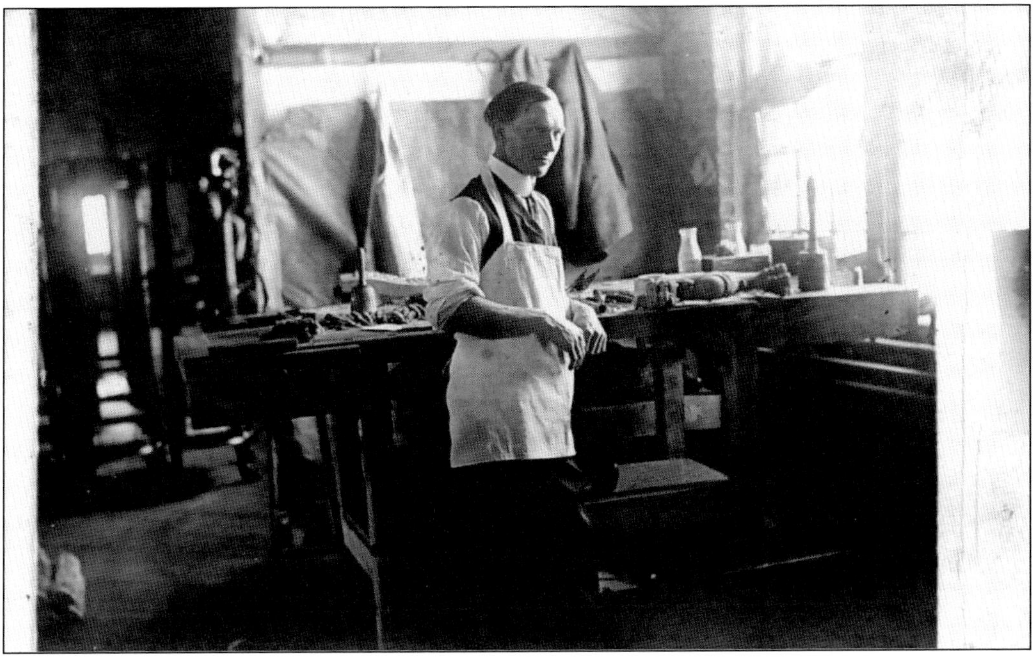

This craftsman carves lions' feet for the legs of a bow front china cabinet at the George A. Long Cabinet Company. The stamp box indicates the card was made between 1904 and 1918.

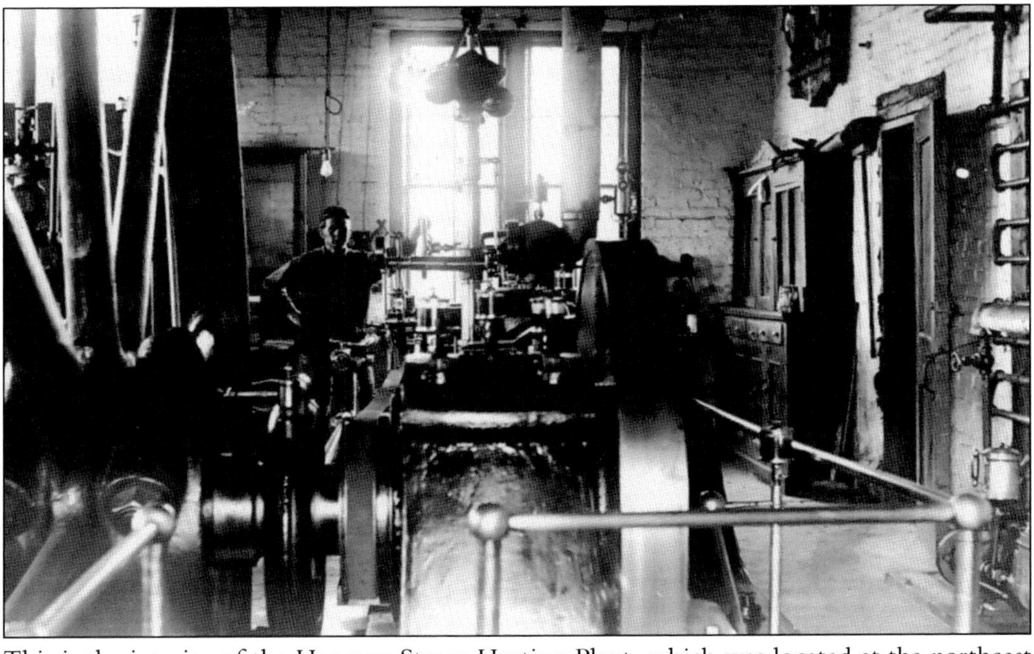

This is the interior of the Hanover Steam Heating Plant, which was located at the northeast corner of South Franklin and West Walnut Streets.

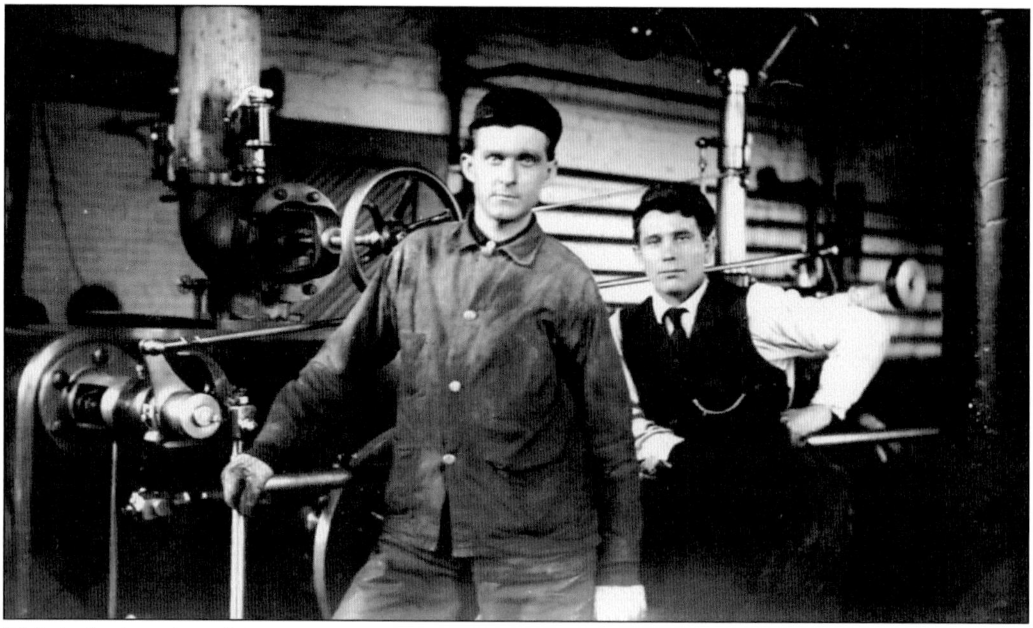

This is the interior of the Hanover Heating Plant. The stamp box indicates the card was printed between 1904 and 1920.

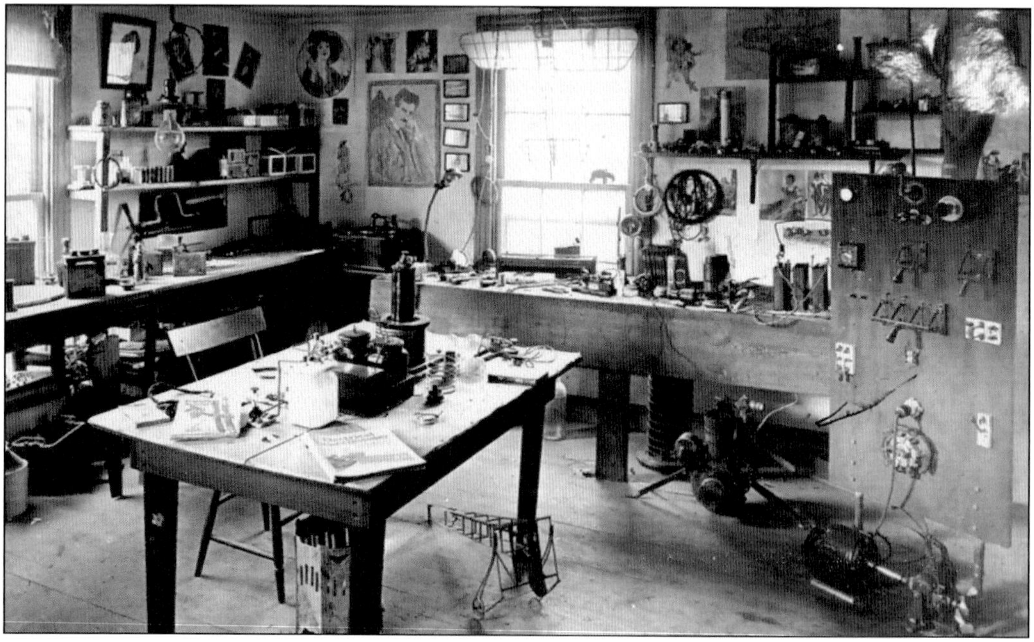

The laboratory is in the back bedroom of E. J. J. Gobrecht at 122 East Chestnut Street.

Seven

INSTITUTIONS

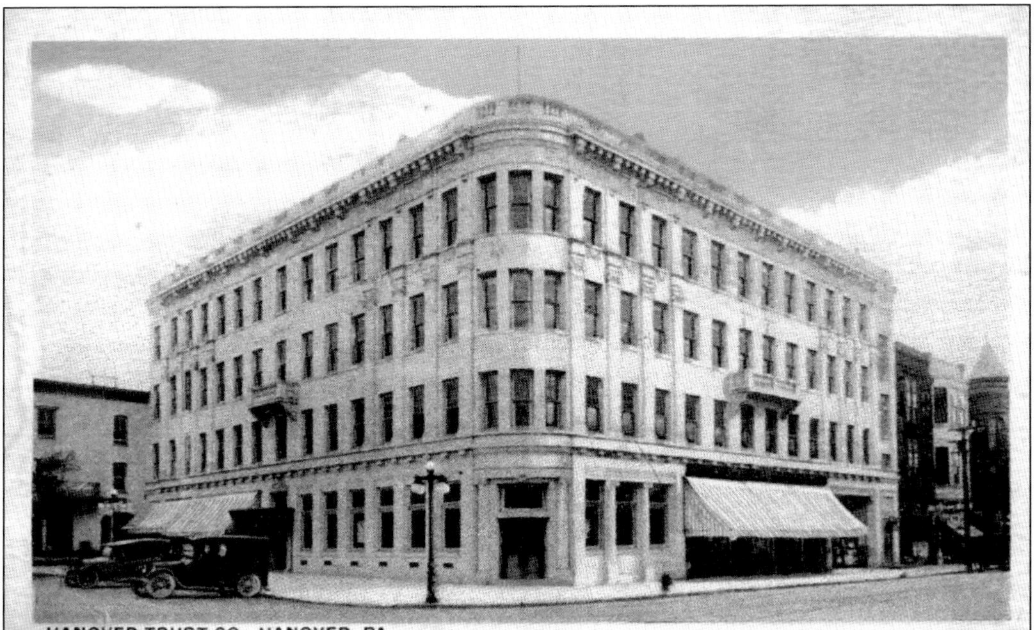

This photograph of the Hanover Trust Company Bank at Carlisle Street and Center Square dates from the 1920s.

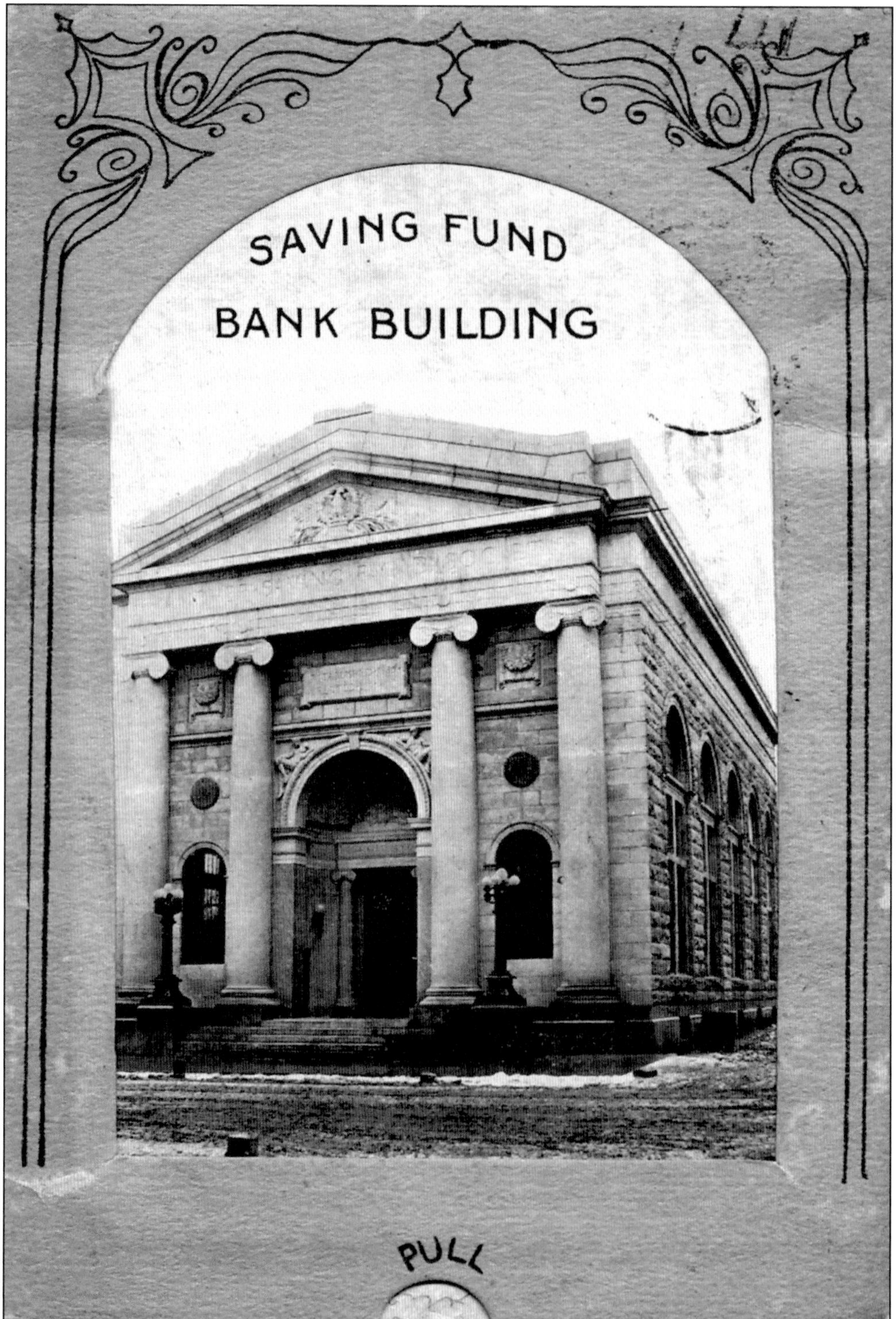

The Hanover Saving Fund Society Bank building was on Carlisle Street. The card has a pull-out tab at the bottom that exposes 12 small Hanover scenes. It is titled "Multiple View Card."

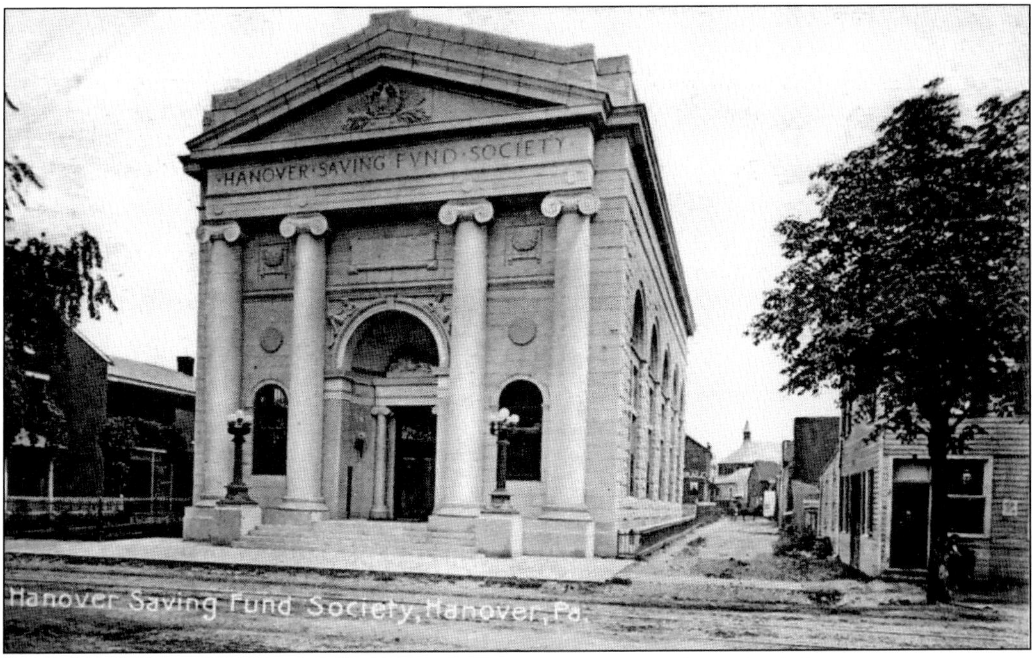

This is another view of the Hanover Saving Fund Society Bank on Carlisle Street.

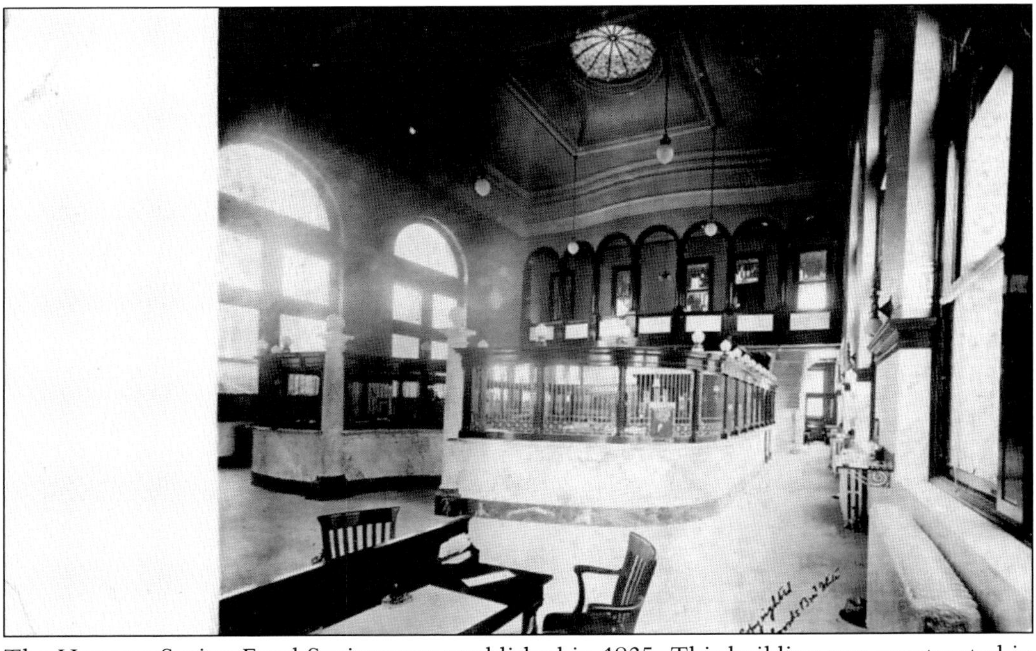

The Hanover Saving Fund Society was established in 1835. This building was constructed in 1906, and eventually became the Bank of Hanover and then Sterling Financial. The interior structure is much the same today, though the teller cage area was moved from the center to the right side. This postcard, copyrighted by Sword's and White, was mailed from Centennial, Pennsylvania, to San Francisco, California, and delivered to a person on the battleship U.S.S. Pennsylvania on March 20, 1908.

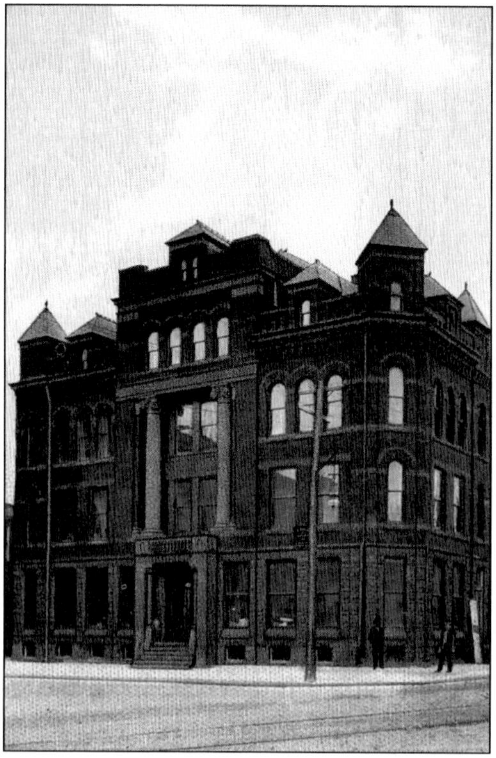

People's Bank was located at the southwest corner of Frederick Street and Center Square.

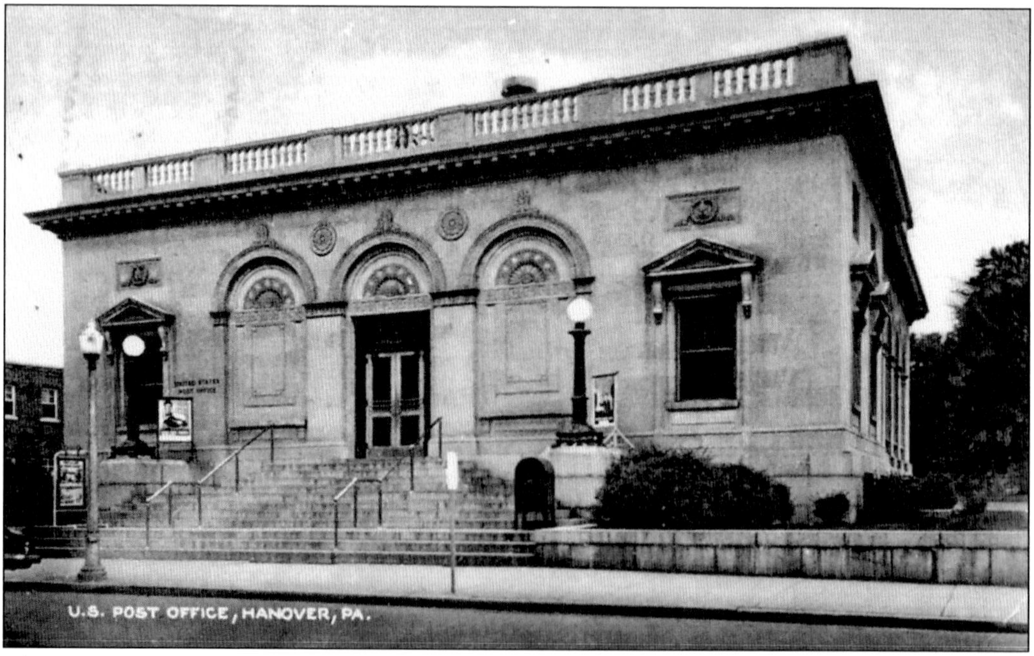

The post office was on the southwest corner of Broadway and Locust Street.

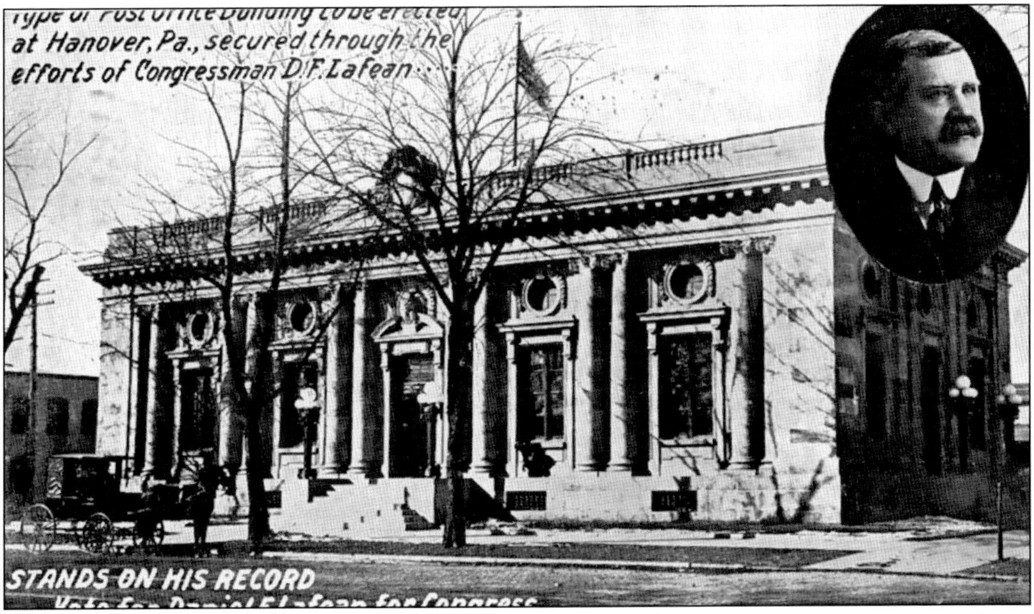

This is a political campaign card put out by Dan Lafean when he ran for U.S. Congress to indicate the style of post office Hanover would have if he were elected. The card was mailed on September 23, 1910. Construction of the Hanover post office began on December 15, 1913.

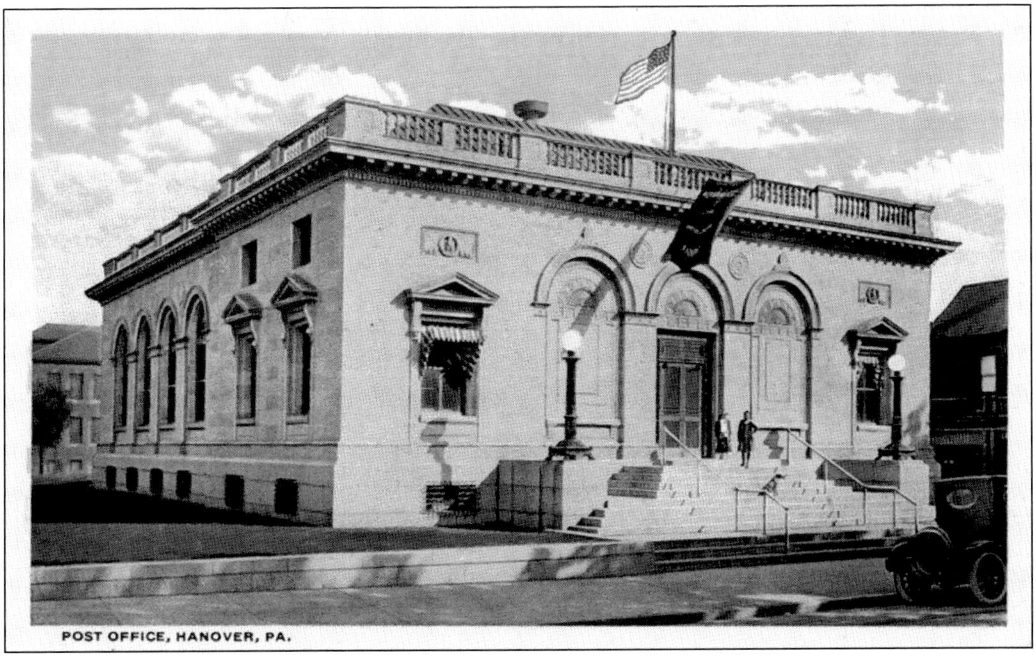

This was a view of the post office when it was located at 141 Broadway.

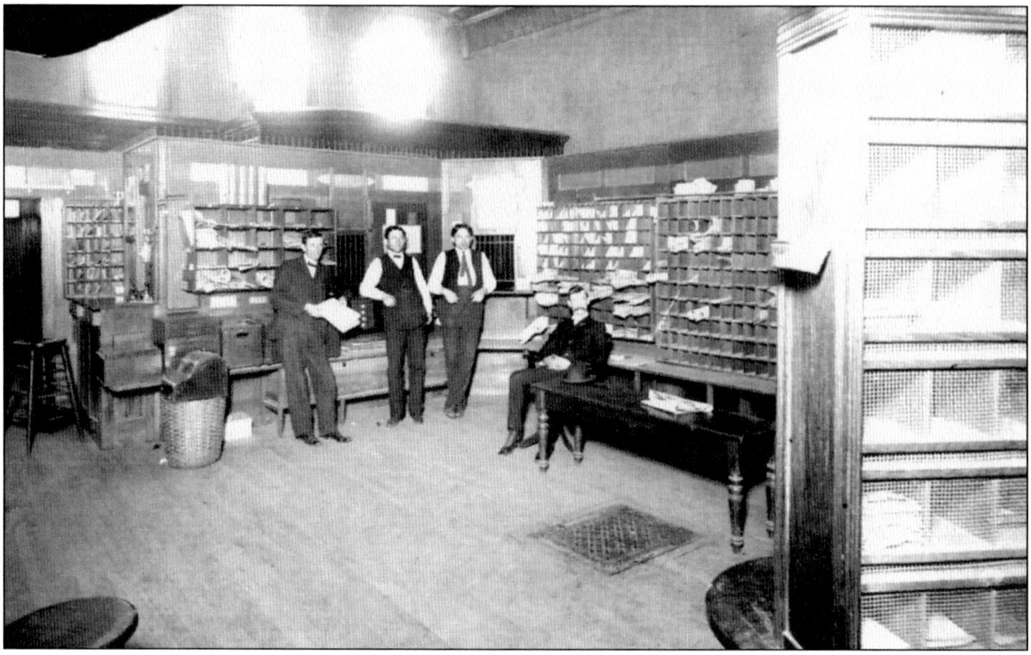

In 1904, the post office was located at 25 Baltimore Street. This postcard is a copy of an original photograph used in the 1994 Hanover Post Office Archives postcard set.

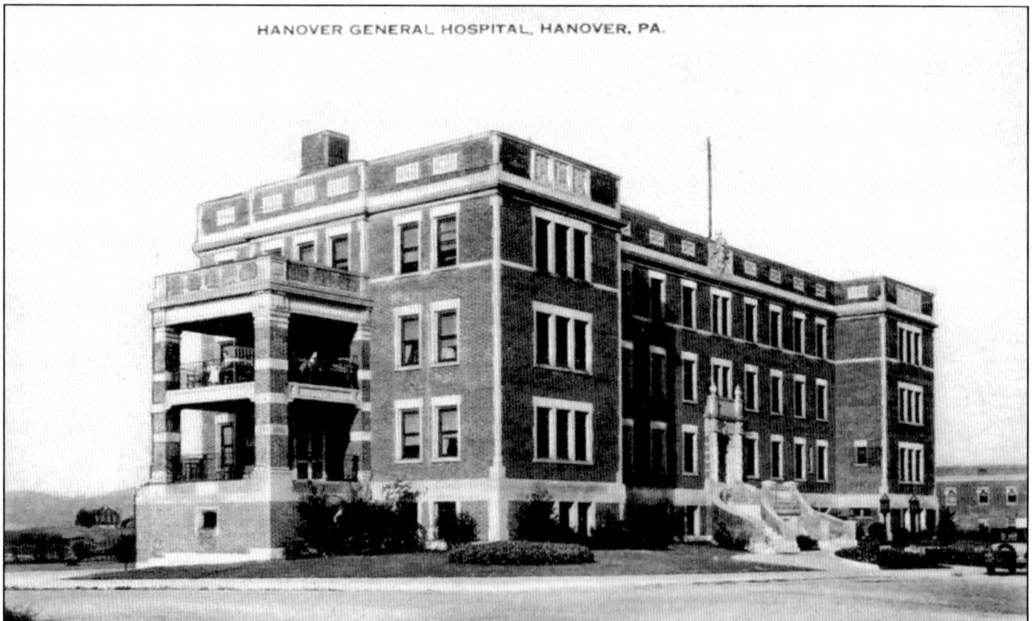

This photograph of the Hanover General Hospital at the northeast corner of Highland Avenue and Charles Street was taken just after its completion. Note the barn in the lower left and the nurses' home in the lower right. The card is stamped February 1, 1935.

The first Hanover ambulance, reported to be on a Packard chassis, was purchased in the 1920s. The photograph is by Hoffman Studio at 113 Broadway.

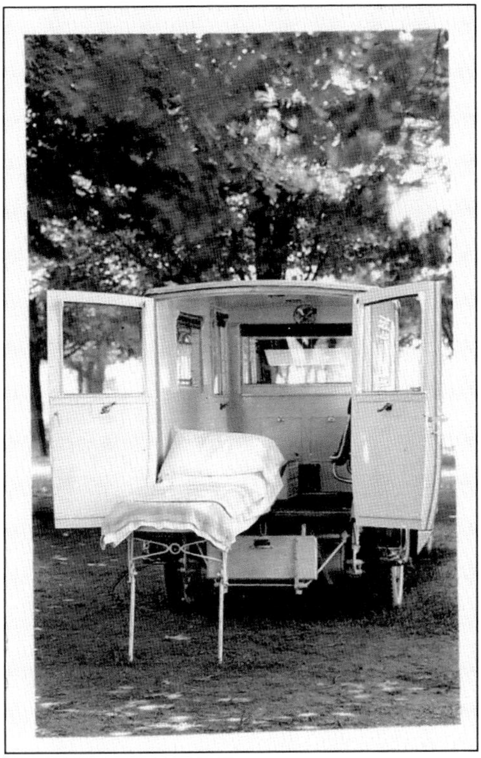

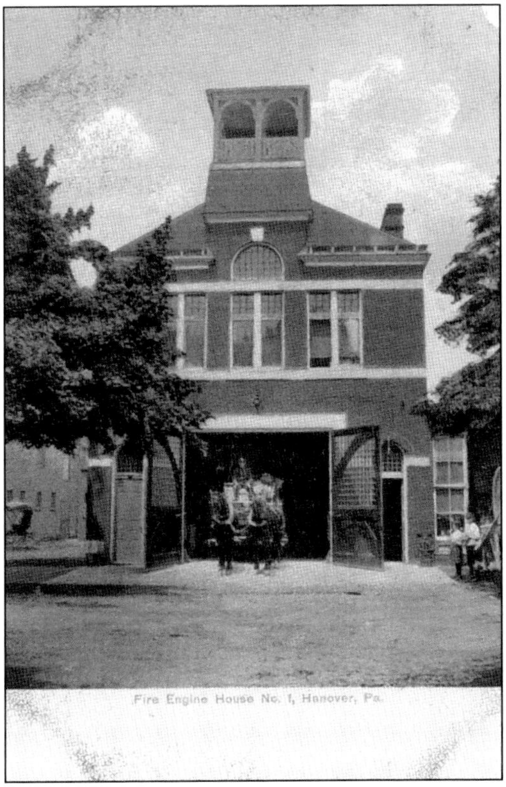

This is Fire Engine House No. 1 at East Chestnut Street. The town lock-up was in the rear of the firehouse.

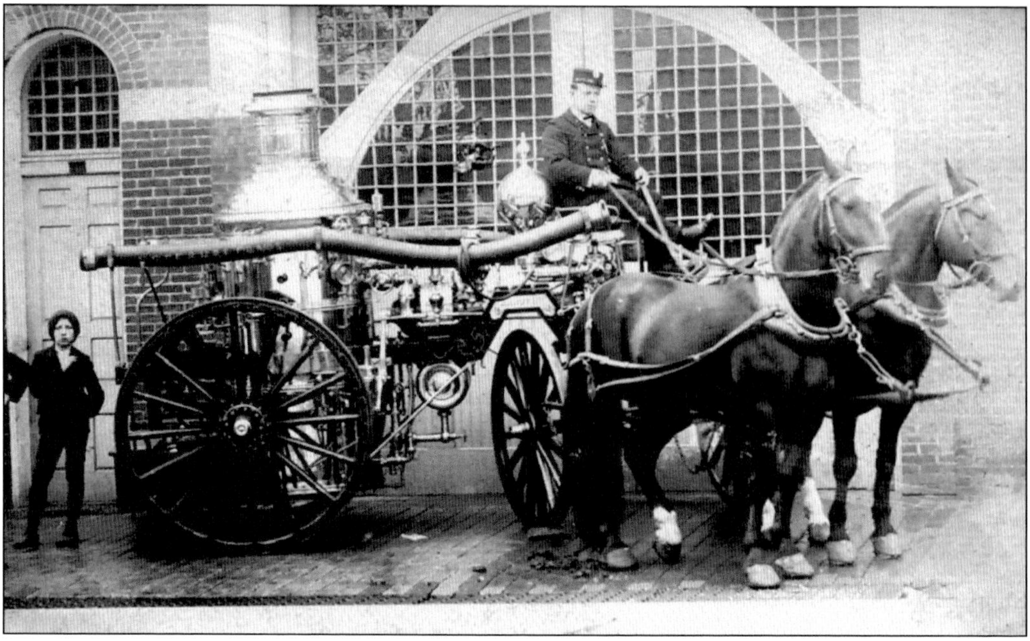

Here is another picture of the firehouse on East Chestnut Street. In case of fire, the horses were secured from Smith's Livery Stable, which was next door to the firehouse.

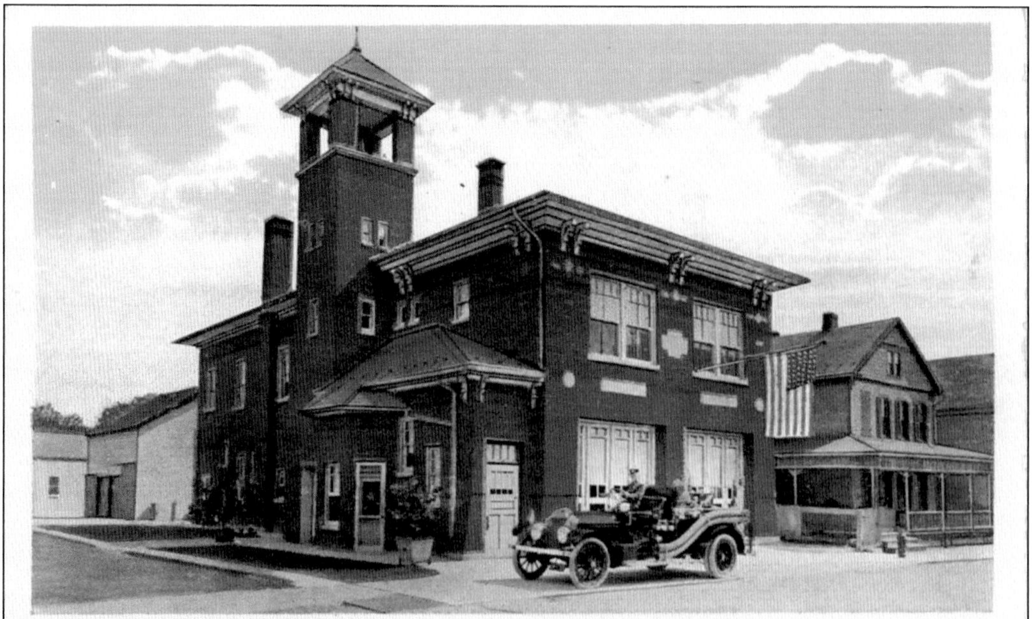

EAGLE FIRE CO., NO. 2, HANOVER, PA.

The Eagle Fire Company No. 2 was located on East Hanover Street.

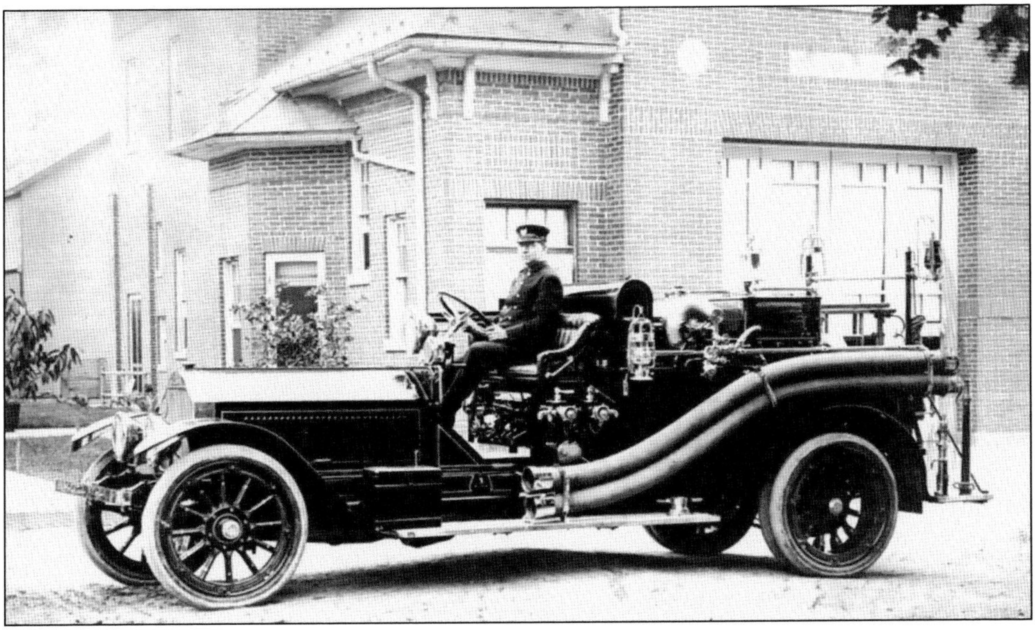

A 1917 six-cylinder American Lafrance fire truck sits in front of the Eagle Fire Company No. 2. This was the borough's first motorized fire engine.

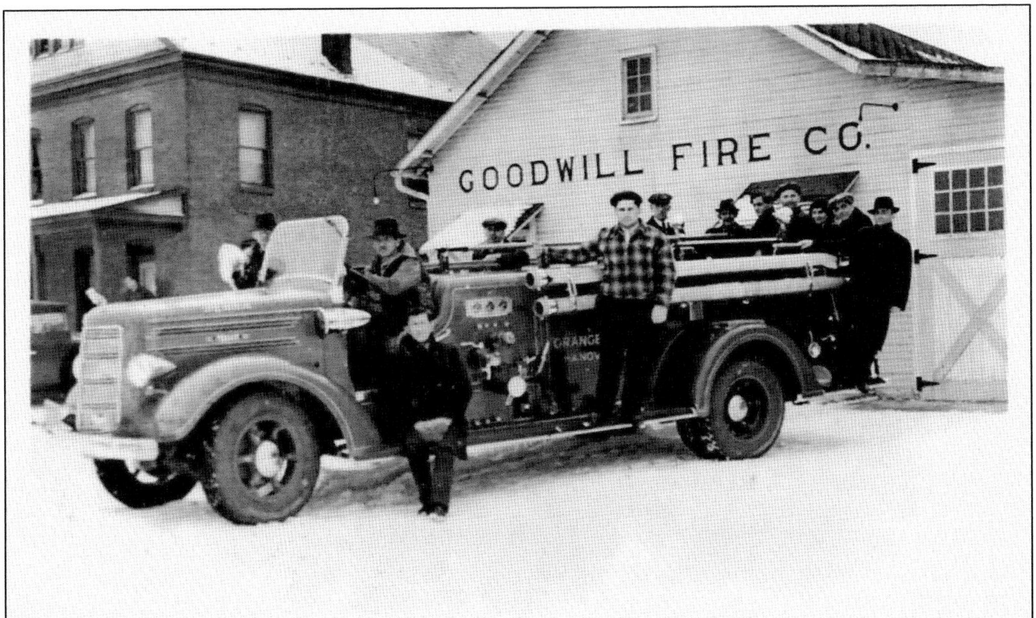

The Goodwill Fire Company, also known as Grangeville Fire Company, was located on McAllister Street in the south section of town, one block off Baltimore Street.

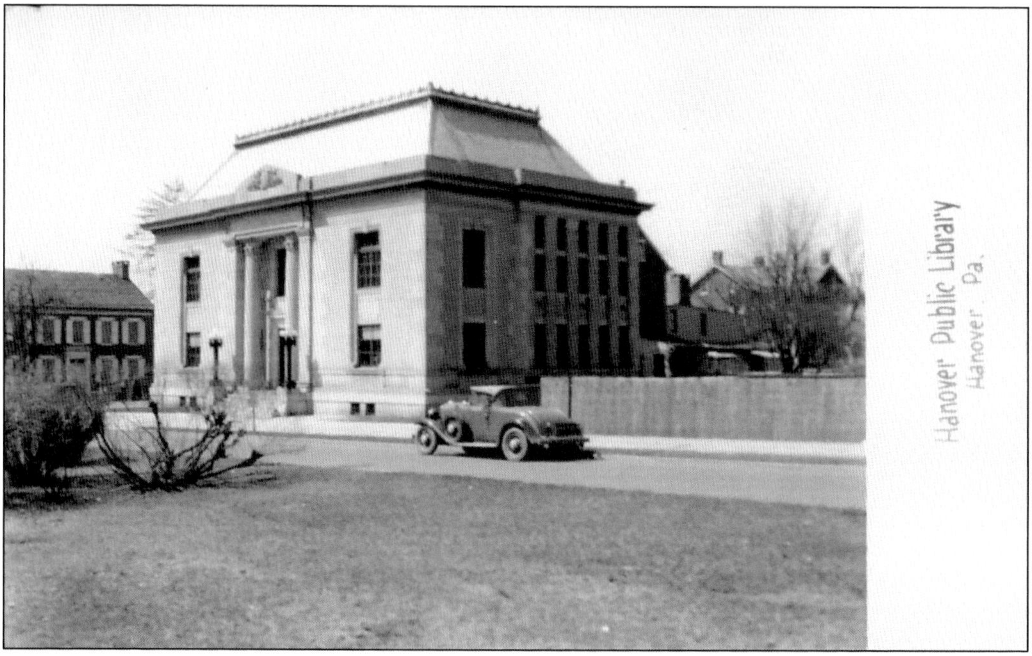

This is a view of the Hanover Public Library from Library Place, looking toward Carlisle Street. The George Young residence at 306 Carlisle Street is evident at the left of the card. The stamp box indicates the card was printed between 1927 and 1940.

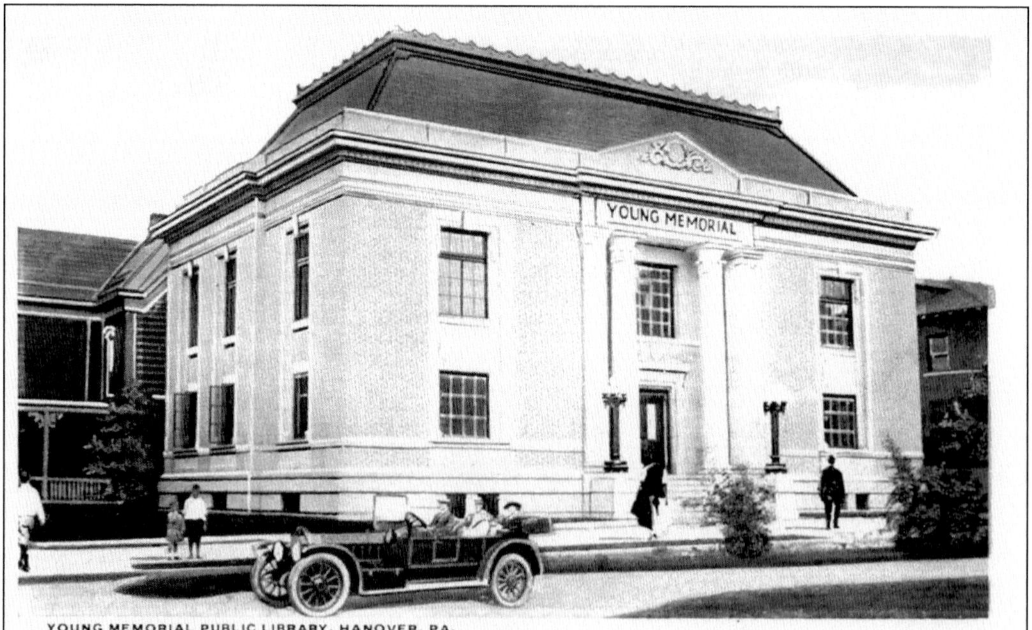

The Young Memorial Public Library, at the corner of Carlisle Street and Library Place at the Pennsylvania Railroad crossing, was bestowed by Howard and Martha Young as a memorial to their son Edward, who died at an early age.

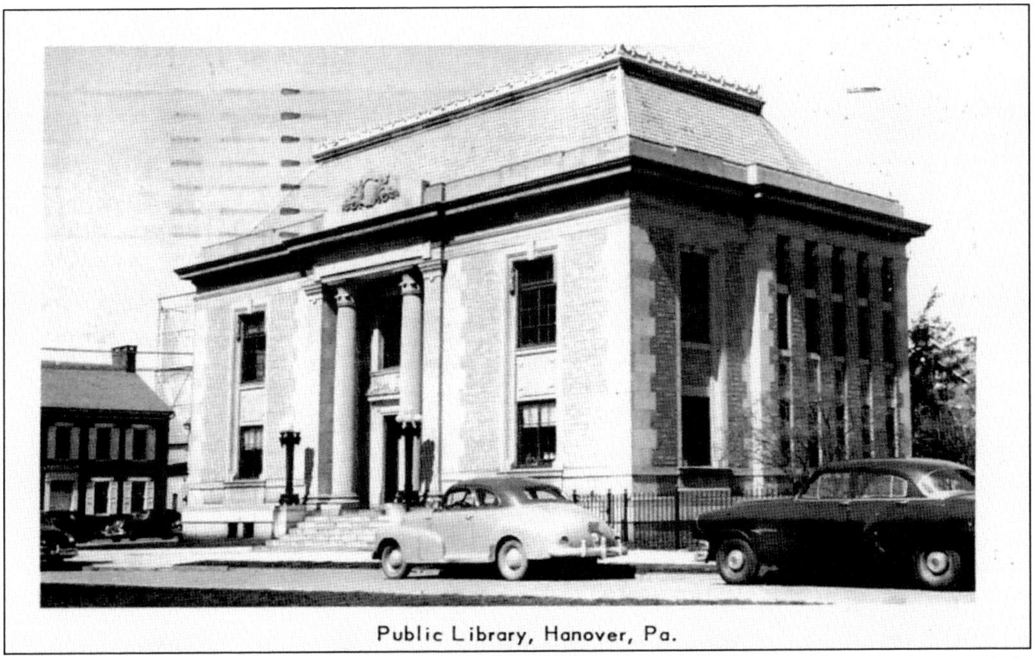

The Hanover Public Library faces Library Place, with the Emily Young residence on Carlisle Street to the left. This postcard was mailed July 1958.

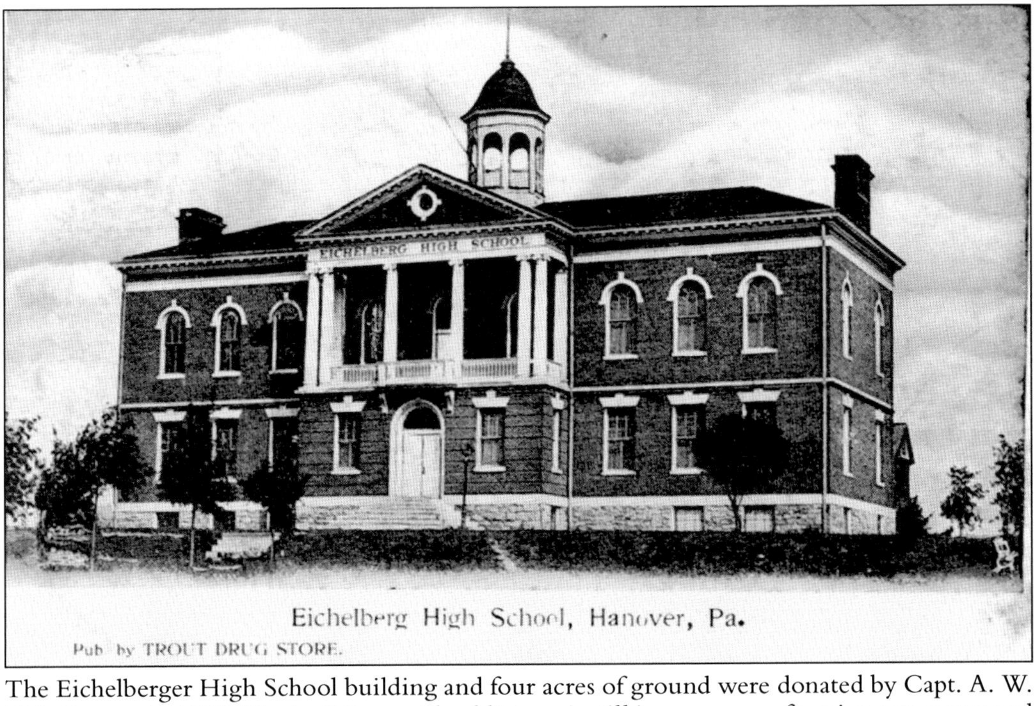

The Eichelberger High School building and four acres of ground were donated by Capt. A. W. Eichelberger in 1900. The building, with additions, is still in use as a performing arts center and professional offices. It is located on Stock Street, east of Carlisle Street. Notice the dropped "er" on the name above the balcony on the picture. For a time, the school was known as Eichelberger Academy. This postcard was published by Trout Drug Store of Hanover.

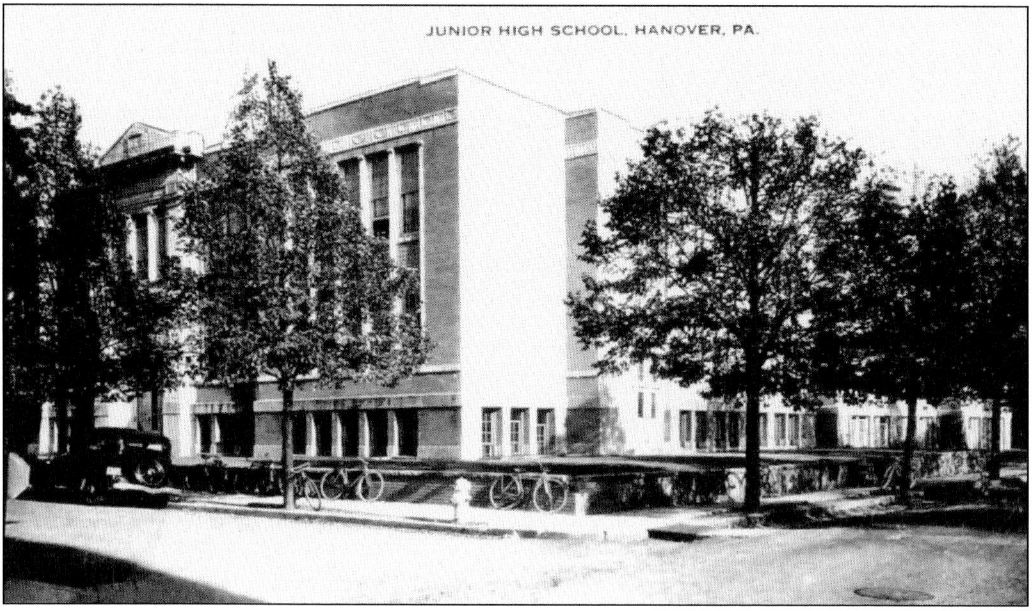

This Walnut Street School building was used as a senior high school while the Eichelberger building was being remodeled. When the high school was moved back to the Eichelberger building, this building was used as a junior high school. The building is constructed of yellow brick and is located at the southeast corner of Centennial Avenue and West Walnut Street. It is now an apartment complex.

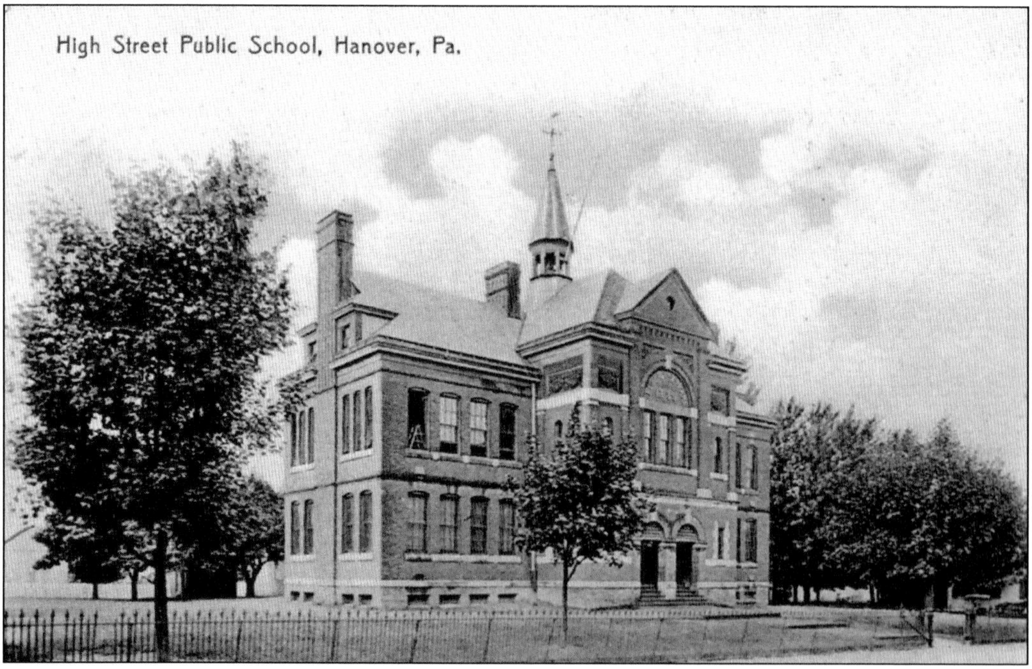

This is the High Street School, located at the southwest corner of West Chestnut and High Streets. The school building was demolished in 1968, and the space is now the site of the Hanover post office.

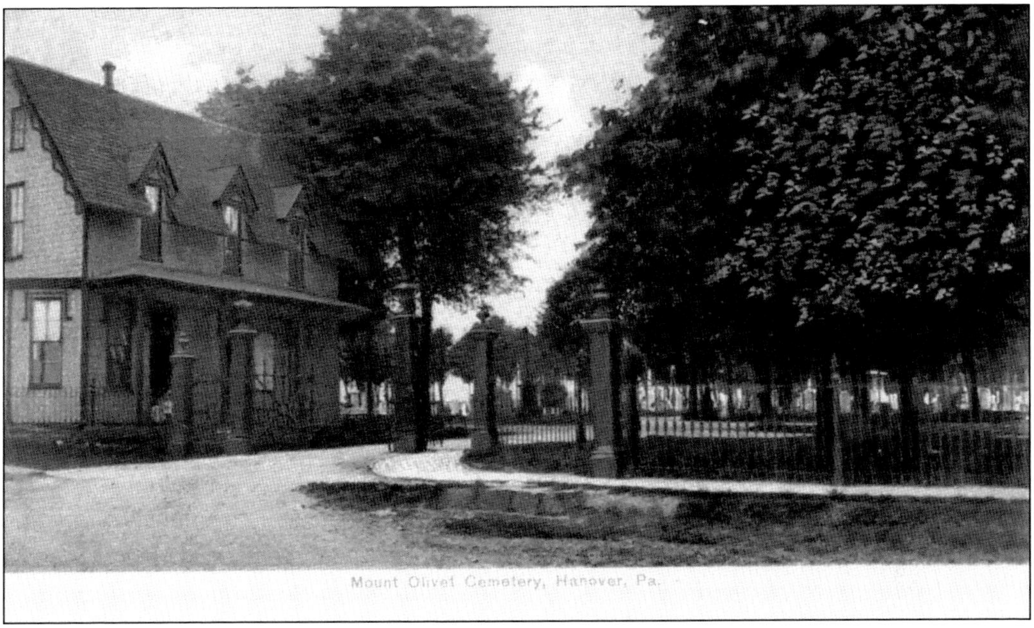

This picture shows the entrance to Mt. Olivet Cemetery at 725 Baltimore Street.

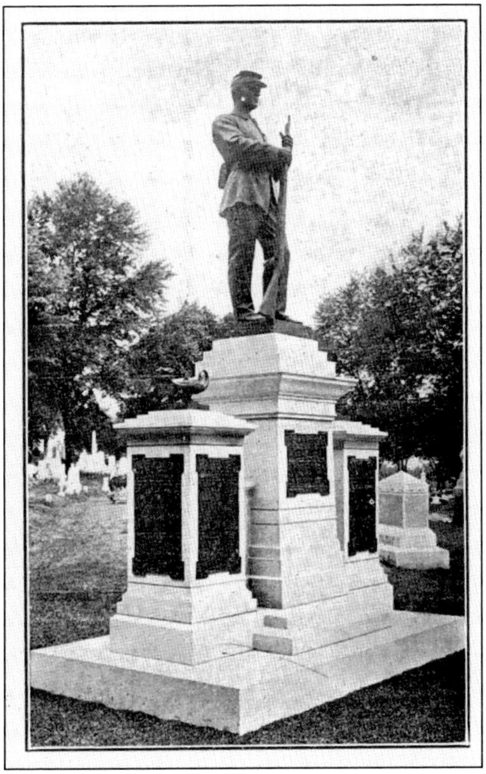
The Soldiers' Monument at Mt. Olivet Cemetery on Baltimore Street was erected in 1913 to honor all of Hanover's Civil War soldiers.

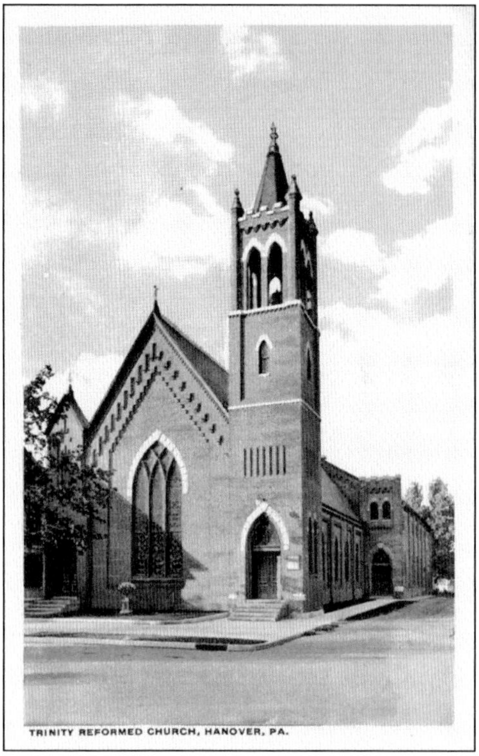

This is a picture of the Trinity Reformed Church at 116 York Street.

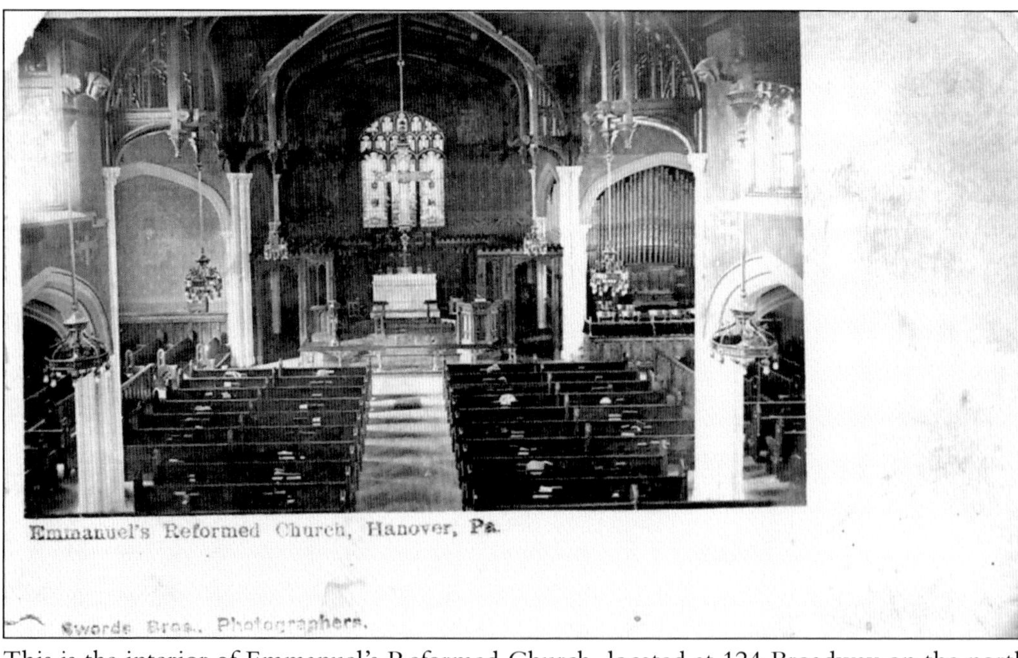

This is the interior of Emmanuel's Reformed Church, located at 124 Broadway on the north side. The stamp box indicates the card was printed between 1904 and 1920. The photograph is by Swords Brothers.

St. Mark's Lutheran Church was located at 107 Carlisle Street. It was built in 1865 and demolished in 1958. Note the tower with the four-face clock, which is now in the archives of St. Mark's.

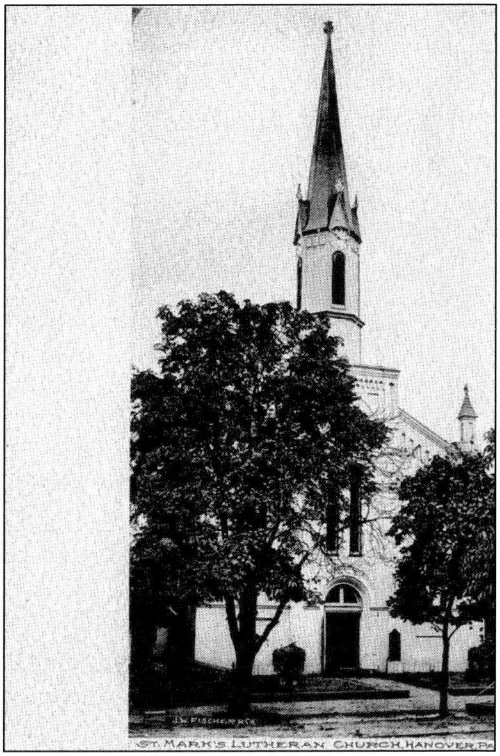

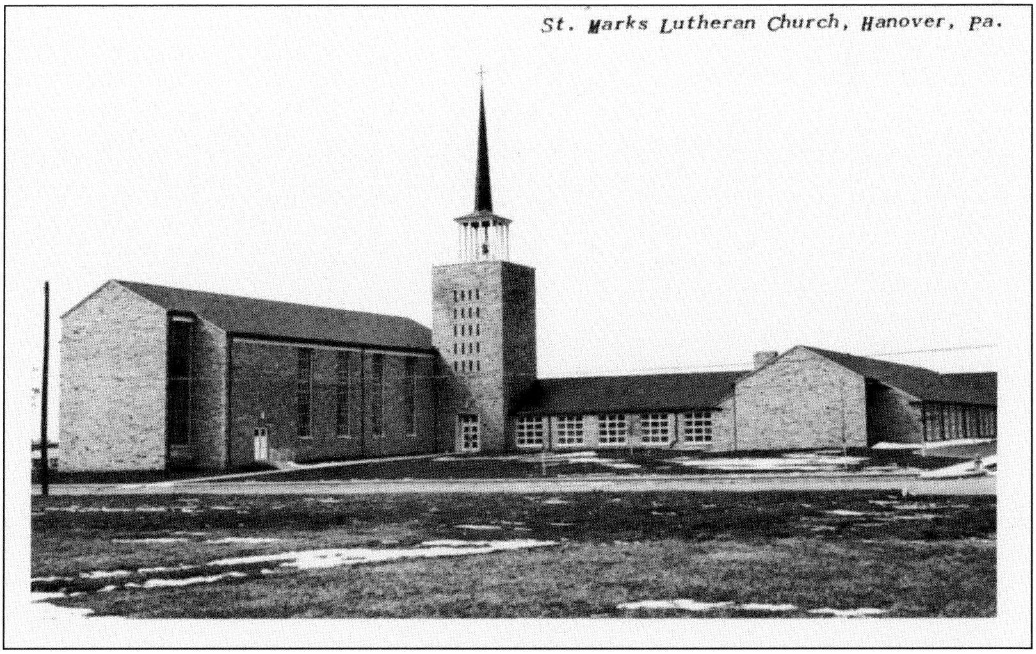

St. Mark's Evangelical Lutheran Church at 127 Charles Street was constructed in the mid-1950s. This postcard was printed by Merrimack Post Card Company of Haverhill, Massachusetts.

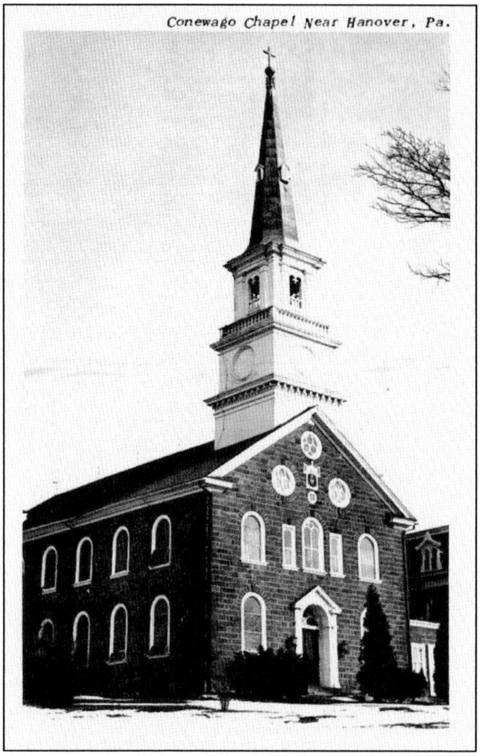

The Conewago Chapel near Hanover was built in 1787. It is the oldest parish church in the world dedicated to the Sacred Heart and, next to the Spanish missions of the west, the oldest Catholic church in the United States.

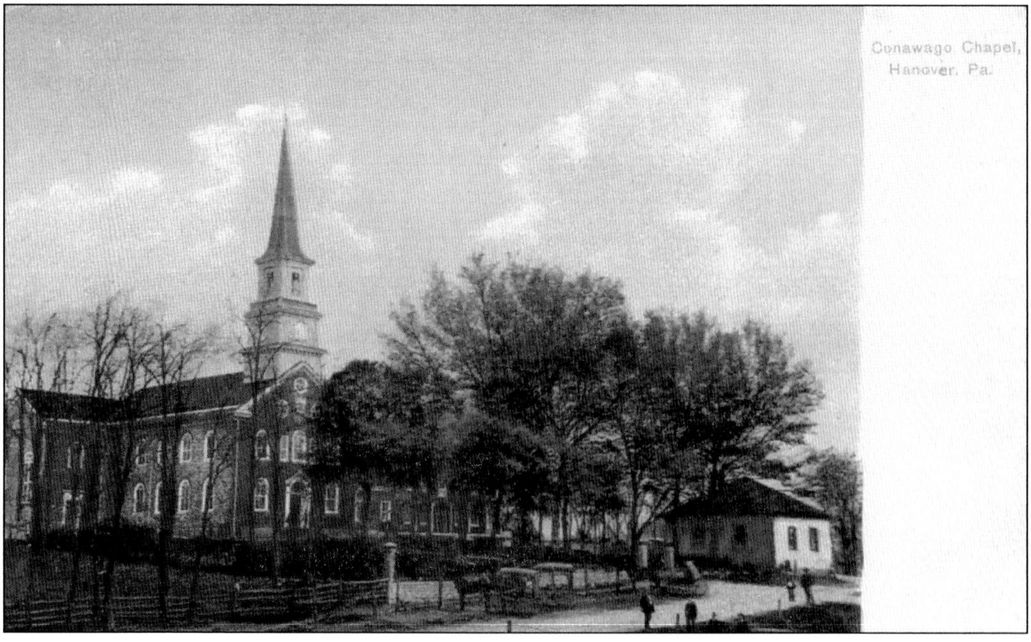

This is the Conewago Chapel on the outskirts of McSherrystown.

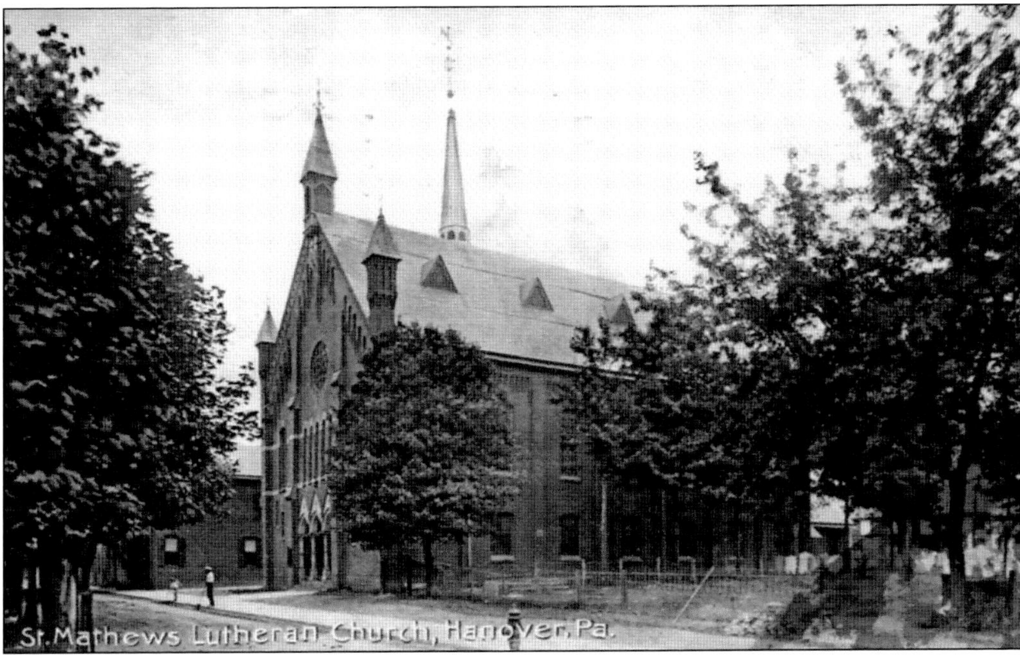

St. Matthew's Lutheran Church stood at 30 West Chestnut Street and has been demolished to make way for the new church. This postcard was mailed August 1923. Note the Christopher Wren-type spire.

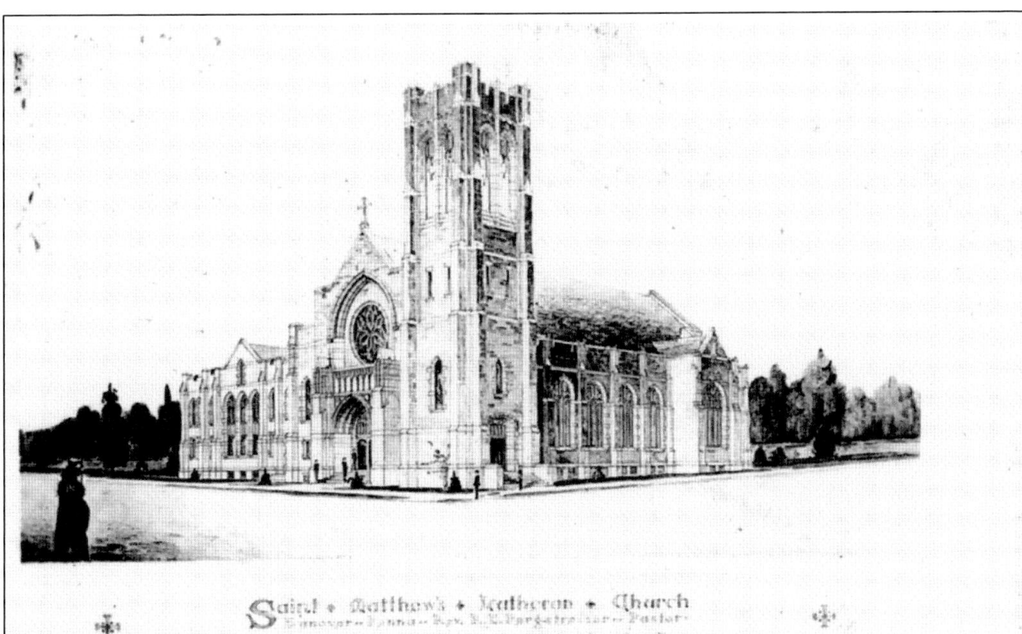

A rendering by a Reading architect shows the proposed new St. Matthews Church on Chestnut Street. The far left portion was not erected as in this plan.

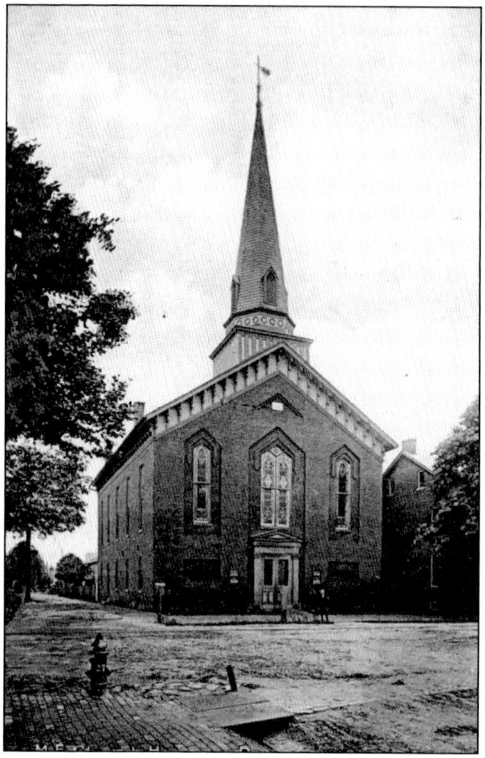

The Methodist Evangelical Church was located at the intersection of Frederick Street and Centennial Avenue. The church faces Frederick Street in the photograph and was later moved to face Centennial Avenue when the new church was built on the corner space.

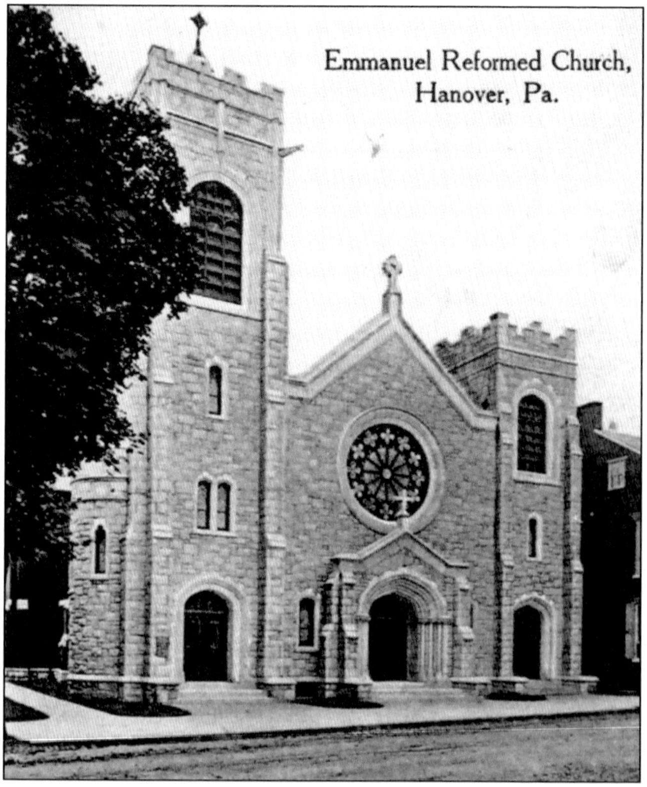

The Emmanuel Reformed Church is located at 124 Broadway. The church was dedicated on September 18, 1904, and is still in use today.

St. Vincent's Catholic Church is located at 220 Third Street near the intersection with High Street. Construction was begun in 1904. The name was derived from Vincent O'Bold, who donated $700,000 toward construction costs. Note the corn field and the rail fence.

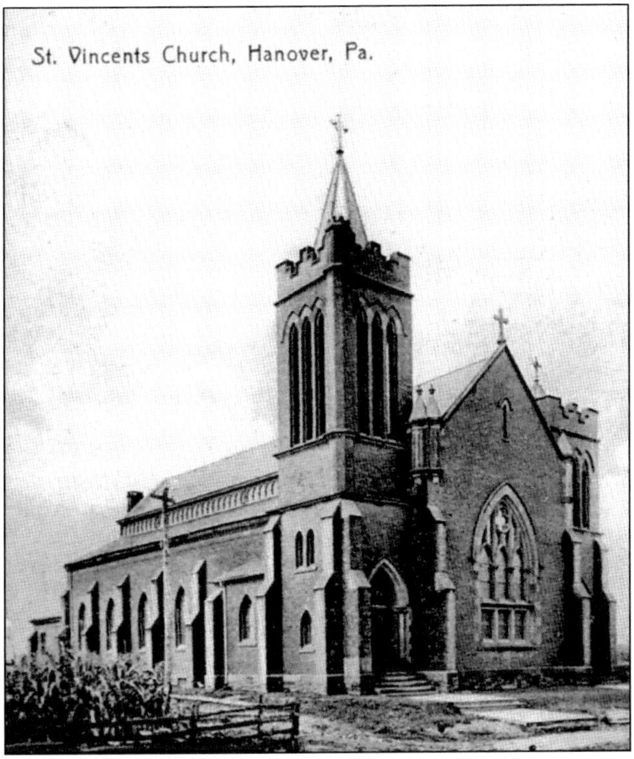

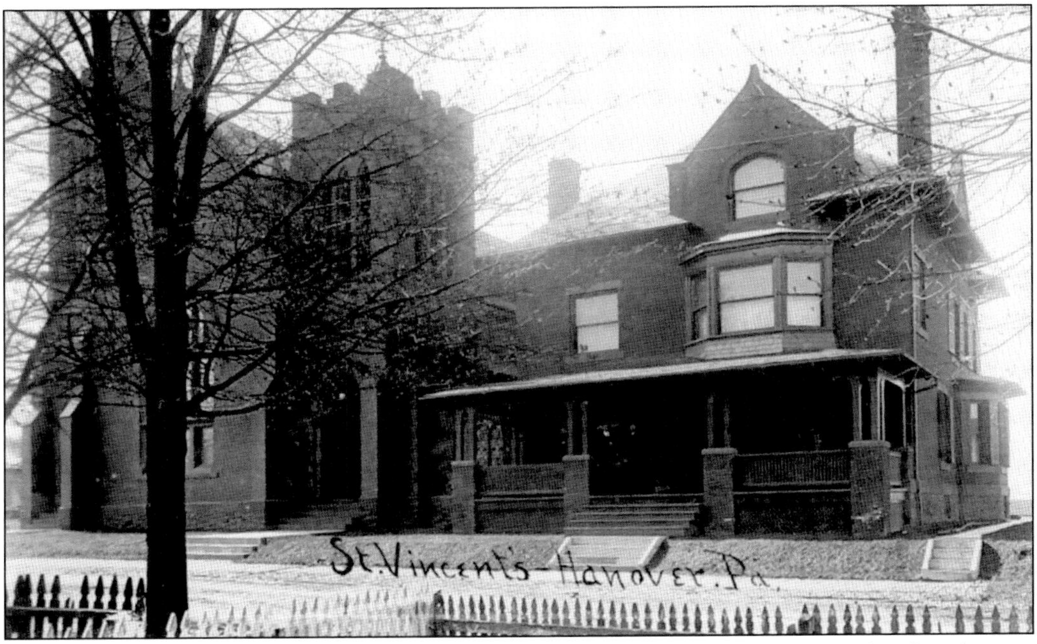

The St. Vincent's Catholic Church facilities are located at 220 Third Street. The church is on the left, and the rectory is on the right.

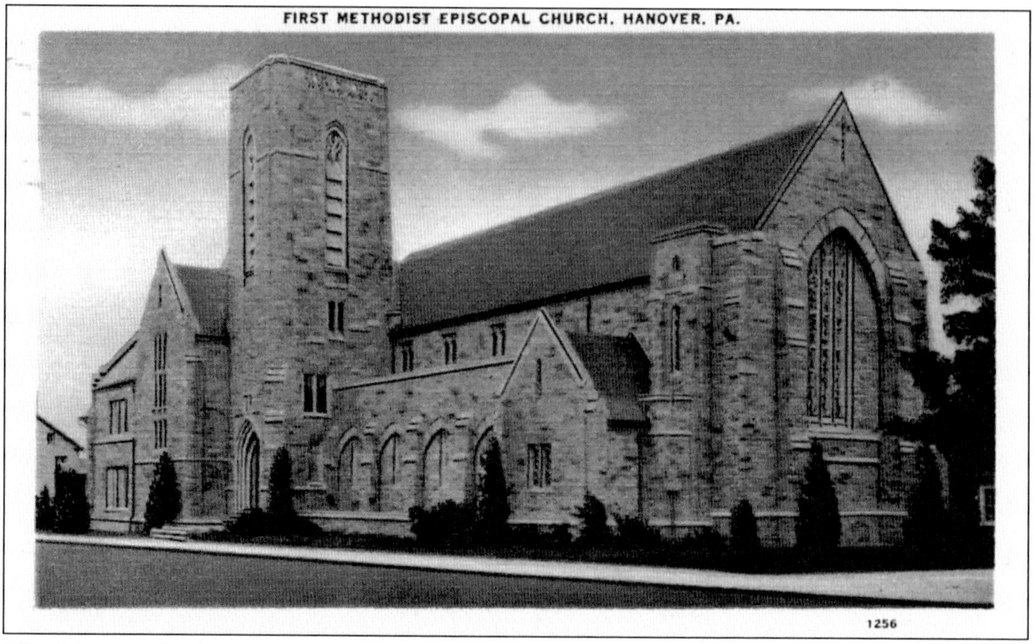

The First Methodist Episcopal Church, facing Centennial Avenue at Frederick Street, was constructed of "butler stone." This postcard is postmarked December 1938.

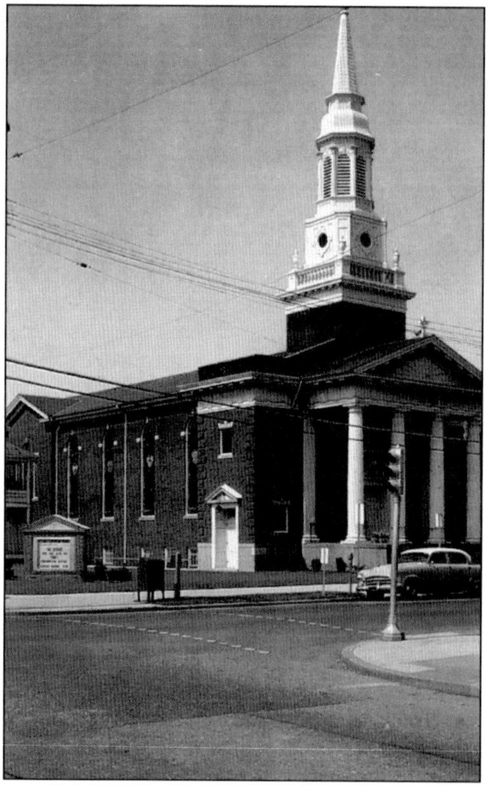

This is a picture of St. Paul's Lutheran Church at 127 York street and the corner of Middle Street. This postcard was printed by Fred W. Rochelle of Philadelphia.

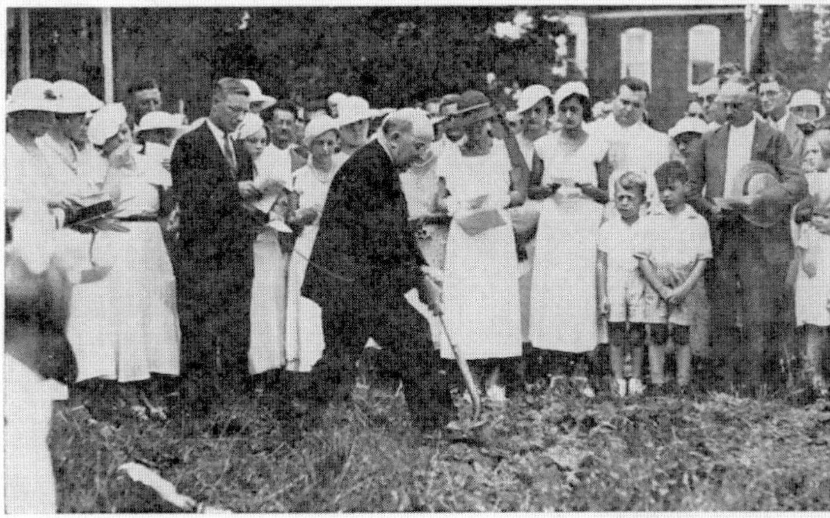

ST. PAUL LUTHERAN CHURCH GROUND BREAKING, JULY 22, 1934

The ground was broken for the construction of St. Paul's Lutheran Church on July 22, 1934. The church was dedicated and occupied in 1935. The gentleman with the shovel is Rev. Oscar Dean. The church is located on the corner of East Middle Street and York Street.

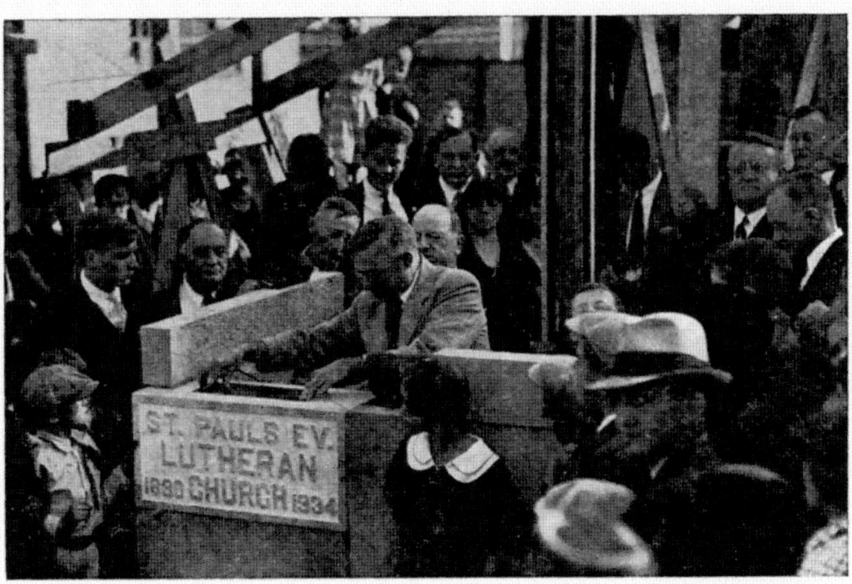

ST. PAUL LUTHERAN CORNERSTONE LAYING OCTOBER 7, 1934

The cornerstone of St. Paul's was laid on October 7, 1934. The man behind the man laying the stone is Rev. Oscar Dean.

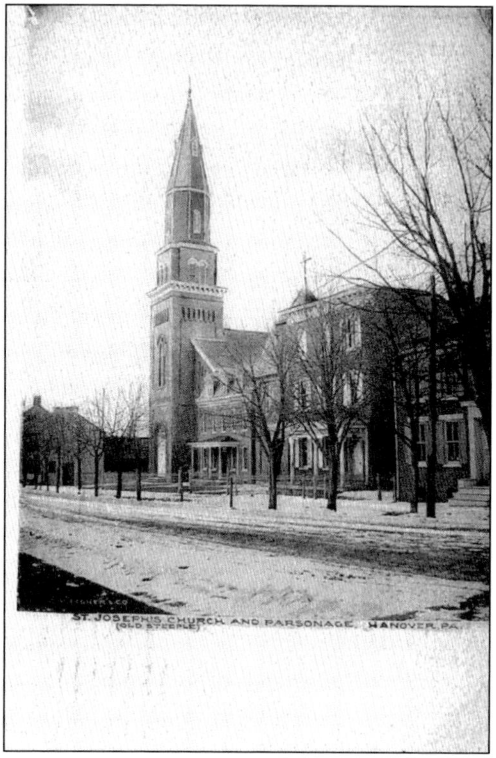

This photograph of St. Joseph's Catholic Church in the 200 block of Baltimore Street includes the church, the rectory, the elementary school, and the sisters' residence. The back of this J. W. Fischer postcard is for address only and is postmarked January 11, 1908. The spire was struck by lightning, and rebuilt as shown on the following card.

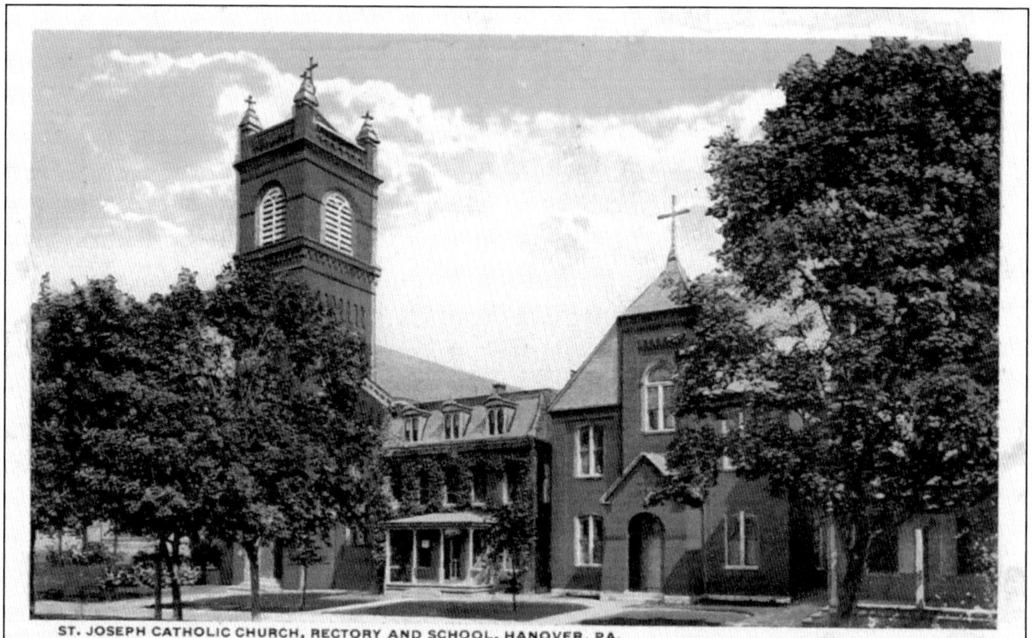

St. Joseph's Catholic Church, as well as the rectory and school, were located in the 200 block of Baltimore Street in the 1930s. This photograph, which shows a low steeple, must have been taken after the higher steeple was struck by lightning.

The Emmanuel Reformed Church was located in the second block of Broadway on the north side of the street. This brick building was built in 1856 and was in use until July of 1900. Note the beautiful old iron fence and gas light. This postcard was mailed in 1907.

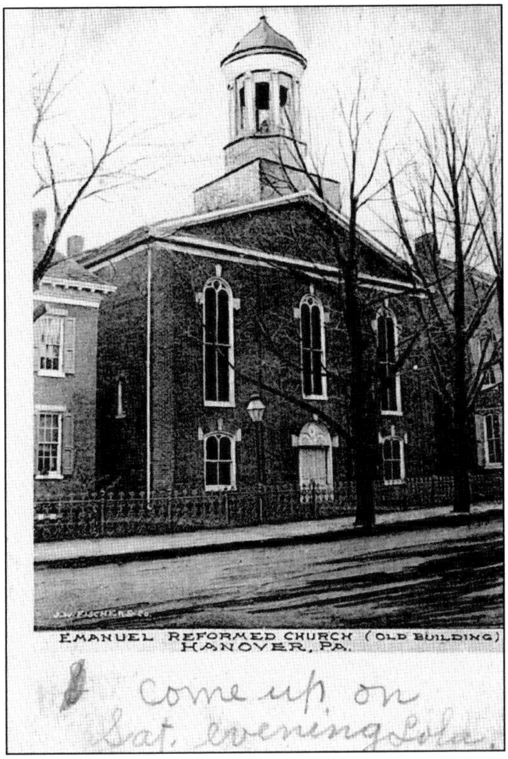

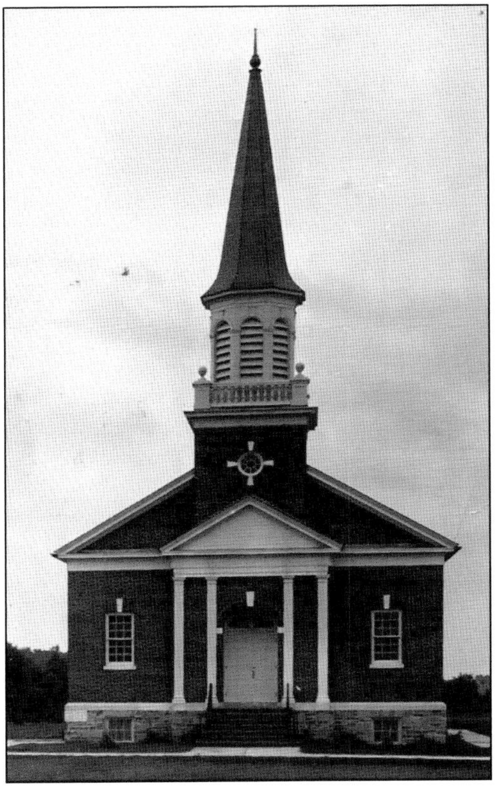

The Brethren in Christ Church was located at 301 Maple Avenue. This photograph is by Hoffman Studio on Broadway. The stamp box indicates the card was printed between 1927 and the 1940s.

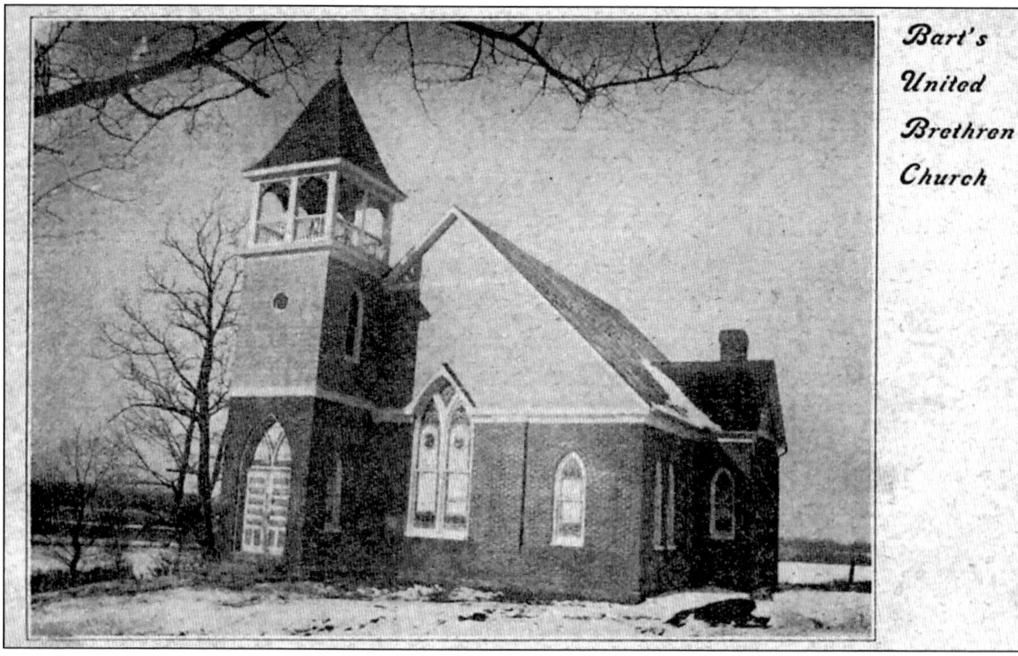

Bart's United Brethren Church was a country church located west of Hanover. The building still stands, but the former congregation has moved into a new church in Littlestown.

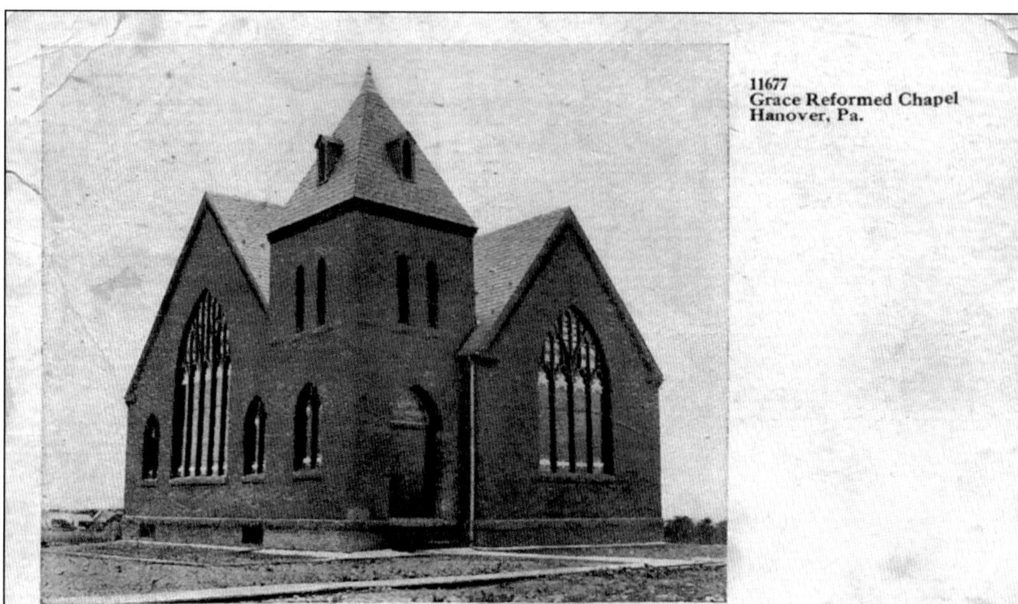

Grace Reformed Chapel is located at Fourth and North Franklin Streets. The chapel was constructed in 1907. This card was mailed on August 8, 1909.